THE COMPLETE BREAD COOKBOOK

THE COMPLETE BREAD COOKBOOK

By Ted and Jean Kaufman

GRAMERCY PUBLISHING COMPANY
NEW YORK

TO MY MOTHER
Who Instilled Within Me
Her Great Love For Cooking And Baking
And Whose Talent In Some Small Measure
Has Rubbed Off On Me.
JEAN SIRIS KAUFMAN

This edition is published by Gramercy Publishing Company,
a division of Crown Publishers, Inc.
by arrangement with Coronet Communications, Inc.
          e f g h
Manufactured in the United States of America.

TABLE OF CONTENTS

INTRODUCTION

Bread! In every language it is written and pronounced as a simple, one syllable word, and yet in every nation no word has been fraught with greater significance in affecting its destiny. Through the lack of bread revolutions sprouted and cruel wars were fought; when it was abundant bread became the prime instrument in settling many a peace. While it is axiomatic to declare that 'man cannot live by bread alone,' an even greater truth is the reality that he cannot live without it. For, to paraphrase the words of one American writer: "All life moves to one measure—Daily Bread."

Of all foods, bread has been the most important discovery in man's search and struggle for basic sustenance. And when he finally found it—at what specific date no one knows—his status on earth underwent a drastic change. From being a hunter, he became a planter and the long march toward creating a civilization had its start. From that Stone Age day until the early Pharaonic period in Egypt, bread was made by a most elemental method: The wheat (or other grain) was pounded into a crude flour by rubbing it between stones, and the crushed grain mixed with water to form a dough which was baked by covering it with hot ashes.

During succeeding centuries other slight refinements were undoubtedly added to baking methods, but it was not until sometime during the heyday of Egyptian civilization that the greatest advance was made: the discovery of leavening as an ingredient for bread. Although the Egyptians had already discovered yeast, they were using it only to manufacture beer.

History does not record just how its most important wedding —the mating of yeast with dough—took place. But legend, ever bolder than fact, recounts the tale that an Egyptian baker's batch of dough somehow absorbed some of the brewer's yeast, and as he left the dough out in the air and warm sun it fermented, forming the miraculous leavening gases. It is not diffi-

7

cut to visualize what must then have taken place. In order to save the dough—and probably his head, too!—he must have punched the risen dough down and put it to bake, with the result that mankind's first light loaf of bread was born.

` However it may have happened, and although since that time the entire process of grinding grain, making dough, and baking bread has been simplified and refined, it nevertheless was that adventitious combination of flour and yeast which remains, to this day and in all lands, the basis of all bread baking.

Although this basic method of bread manufacture is universal, the types of cereal grains used, and the size and shapes of the loaves, differ from country to country. In some countries rye takes precedence over wheat; in others, such grains as corn, whole wheat, bran, oatmeal, etc., may be favored. As for the variations in sizes and, more especially, in the shapes of the loaves, a single volume could not describe them all. For not only do they differ widely from country to country, but within any single country they further differ from region to region. To illustrate the nature and extent of such regional variations we have compiled a partial list, inserted elsewhere in this book, of some presently available in Great Britain alone. And, incidentally, while our choice of that nation to illustrate our point was made at random, similar lists could be compiled of the many regional breads of Scandinavia, Germany, Italy, France, Spain, etc.

In our own country, as in most others, it is infinitely easier, and often cheaper, to buy a loaf of bread than to make one at home. But what a difference there is between the two loaves! For, once having scented the inimitable and comforting aroma of home-baked loaf, then having tasted it, who can ever forget it? Little wonder that bread recipes are handed down as prize possessions from generation to generation. And in each such generation there are, fortunately, women who have inherited the very special qualities and virtues so uniquely necessary to attaining success in that ultimate of all culinary goals: bread baking.

To begin with, bread baking requires great patience. In using and handling yeast, we are dealing with a living organism whose processes cannot be hastened, substituted, duplicated or camouflaged. Next comes persistence. All bread recipes, however well-defined and detailed, are like sheets of music: they cannot take the place of experimentation and practice. For with that practice comes the eventual "feel" of the dough, and

8

the development of a sense of affinity with it: the "bread thumb."

When with delicate care the dough is set to rise, who can refrain from stealing a casual peek to watch its rising! Then comes the time for kneading—the punching down, pounding, and rolling of the dough. Was ever a better way than this invented for woman to get release from the daily frustrations which plague the busy housewife?

With the dough prepared and set in the oven to bake, a series of doubts—common in all creative activity—assail the mind. Will the bread rise properly? Will the dough bake thoroughly? Will the crust be crisp and evenly browned? It is a dramatic moment when, breathlessly, expectantly, the loaf is removed from the oven. It is a beautiful thing to behold! Anxiety evaporates, to be replaced by a feeling of pride and a sense of accomplishment which more than repays the housewife for her industry. Bread—the sustainer of life—has been born!

Bread baking is not at all difficult. The ohs! and ahs! of the family; the looks on their faces as they sniff the singular aroma of a fresh-baked loaf and the knowledge that her effort has contributed to her family's health should be sufficient inspiration for any housewife to try her hand at it.

Our book starts with a chapter especially created for those who may have never previously baked bread. Besides providing quick and easy instructions for delicious home-baked breads and rolls, the recipes also almost guarantee excellent results. Above all, in starting with these simple recipes, the beginner will quickly develop that unique and essential "feel" of bread dough which, once attained, will instill such confidence and encouragement in the baker as to make her genuinely eager to proceed with the ensuing chapters.

Before you tackle the other bread recipes, it would be advisable to read over the outline we have prepared on the basic steps in baking bread. This will give you a general idea of the sequential steps employed in the process. While no two ovens are alike, and room temperatures, too, are variable, we have made every effort to ensure success with our recipes by carefully experimenting with them before detailing directions. If it is at all possible to venture a basic rule of the thumb in bread baking, it is this: The flour, yeast and all other ingredients used should be gently warmed or kept at room temperature to insure a "well-risen" bread. Bread baking *can* be really fun. But always remember that it is patience and practice which will make the breads perfect!

Once you have learned, and developed, the art of bread baking, do not be fearful of changing or varying the recipes. Try experimenting with all available flours until you create your very own specialty. In this respect the footnotes to many of our recipes, with their suggested variations in taste and flavor, should be of help to you. A number of other baking guides have been included in this book. The information they contain, such as weights and measures, ingredient proportions, oven temperatures, and the requisite pans and utensils, will be found useful as auxiliary aids in preparing the recipes. And the Glossary will acquaint you with the meaning of terms and items used in bread baking.

If you have never before baked bread, you face a most exciting culinary adventure. And, as you share your creative triumph with your family, you will understand the full meaning of the word "Lady," which the ancient Anglo-Saxons originated and used to designate the "Giver of the Loaf."

Happy Baking!

—Ted and Jean Kaufman

AN OUTLINE OF THE BASIC STEPS IN BREAD BAKING

This outline details the usual steps employed in baking an average loaf of bread. No ingredient quantities are given; for more detailed information as to ingredients, methods and the numerous variations possible in bread baking, always refer to the specific recipes.

PREPARING THE DOUGH

1. Warm a large bowl by running hot water around the entire inside; drain off the excess water.
2. Pour specified quantity of warm water into the bowl. (We always boil the water and let it cool to lukewarm.) To test the proper warmth of the water, dribble a few drops on the inside of your wrist. If it feels comfortably warm, it is just right for the yeast.
3. Sprinkle the yeast over the warm water.
4. Add the sugar; stir until well mixed.
5. Cover and set aside until foaming and doubled in volume.
6. Add salt and shortening.
7. Put in the flour as directed and beat well.
8. Add just enough of the remaining flour, as directed, to form a soft, pliable dough.
9. Turn the dough onto a lightly floured breadboard.

KNEADING THE DOUGH

1. Rub a little flour on your hands.
2. Work the soft dough into a ball.
3. Knead hard, always toward the center of the dough. As you knead, turn the dough over and around repeatedly.
4. Keep folding, pushing and turning until the dough is smooth, springy and satiny in texture. The kneading generally

11

takes from 8 to 10 minutes. If the dough gets sticky or tacky during the kneading, sprinkle a *little* additional flour over it—but not too much!

5. Several times during the kneading process you may, French-baker fashion, lift the dough up and bang it down hard on the board. Long and vigorous kneading makes the dough fine and regular.

6. When kneading is completed, shape the dough into a ball and place into a warm, well-greased bowl.

RISING OF THE DOUGH

1. Turn the dough around in the bowl so that the dough becomes greased all over. Cover with a piece of wax paper first and then, over the paper, with a thin, lightweight kitchen towel. Do not cover tightly.

2. Set the lightly covered bowl to rest in a warm place, free from drafts. The bowl may be set near, *but never on,* a warm range.

3. The yeast in the dough will cause it to rise, slowly, and change it from a firm, heavy mass to a large puffy one. Do not touch the dough until it has doubled in bulk (usually from 60 to 90 minutes, but the time may vary due to the type of flour used, room temperature, etc.) There are no prohibitions against peeking!

4. To be sure the dough is properly risen, give it this test: Press two fingers deeply into the dough, and remove them quickly. If the depressions remain, the dough is ready; if the depressions disappear quickly, allow more time for the dough to rise.

5. When the dough is ready, punch it down.

Note: Braided loaves should be allowed to rise a little longer, or until slightly more than doubled in bulk. Repeat the rising process for a second time if directed in the recipe.

SHAPING THE DOUGH

1. Turn out the punched-down dough onto a lightly floured breadboard. Divide it into as many equal ball-shaped parts as the recipe directs.

2. To shape a loaf, flatten a ball of dough with the palms of the hands into a flat oblong. Fold in half, lengthwise, and flatten again.

3. Seal the dough by tucking in the ends.

4. Place the sealed dough, seam-side down, into well-greased and lightly floured loaf pans. Repeat above steps with remaining portions of the dough. These are your loaves.

5. Cover the loaves with a clean cloth and place in a warm place to rise.

6. When the loaves have doubled in bulk, brush the tops with a mixture made from one egg yolk beaten with one teaspoon of milk or water. This will give the loaves a shining glaze.

Note: The recipes will specify the number of loaves which the dough yields and, when indicated, directions for specially-shaped loaves.

BAKING THE LOAVES

1. *Preheat oven* from 400° F. to 425° F. for 15 minutes.

2. Place loaves into the oven and bake for 15 minutes.

3. Reduce heat between 350° F. to 375° F. and continue baking for about 25 minutes, or until nicely browned.

4. To test the loaves for doneness, tap them briskly with the fingers—if they sound hollow, they are done.

5. When done, remove the loaves from the pans and place them on cooling racks, or tilt them on edge, to better procure a free circulation of air around the loaves. This allows the surface to cool first, insuring a crisp crust and proper moisture retention in the loaf. Do not cover the breads while they are warm.

Note: Careful baking is very important, for even perfect dough can be ruined in the oven. As stated in our Introduction, no definite rules can be established for the baking, as no two ovens are alike. There is, however, this general guide: Keep the oven at a steady temperature, just hot enough as the recipes and/or your practice will indicate. The best way to test and maintain oven heat is by using an oven thermometer.

If the oven is too hot, a firm crust will form before the bread has expanded enough and, as a result, the bread will be heavy. If the bread is baked with too hard a crust, it may be saved for use by rubbing it over with butter, wrapping it with a damp towel, and then covering it with a dry towel.

When serving warm bread at the table, heat the knife before using it to cut the loaf.

STORING BREAD

The food freezer or refrigerator freezing compartment provides the best method for storing bread. The bread must be cooled before storing, then wrapped (airtight) in any material that is moisture-proof. This method of storing helps the bread retain its moisture, keeps it free from mold, and enables the bread to retain its freshness for several weeks.

If bread is stored in a breadbox, the box should be well ventilated and the bread wrapped in wax paper. The bread will remain fresh for days, but it will be more subject to mold than if kept in a freezer.

GLOSSARY OF BAKING TERMS

Baking Powder. A compound used as a leavening agent, principally in quick-bread batters, to produce carbon dioxide gas bubbles, and speed the baking.

Batter. A mixture of flour, liquids and other ingredients.

Cream. To blend one or more combinations of ingredients together until they are creamy soft.

Cream of Tartar. A fine-grained baking powder which is sweeter and keeps moist longer than most others.

Cut. To incorporate the shortening with the dry ingredients, usually done with a knife, fork, or a blender.

Dot. To toss or place small pieces (usually butter) atop a surface.

Dough. A mixture of flour (or meal), liquid, and other ingredients, worked into a soft thick mass—stiff enough to manipulate with the hands.

Dust. To sprinkle a surface lightly with sugar, flour or other dry ingredients.

Fold. To combine one mixture *very gently* with another (usually with a rubber spatula) in order to retain the air.

Grease. To rub butter, or other fat, over a cooking utensil before admitting other ingredients. The easiest way to grease a pan (or bowl) is with a brush, or by using a wad of soft paper dipped in the fat.

Knead. The most important step in bread baking. Kneading is the manner in which the dough, taken up with the hands, is punched, stretched, pressed and folded over until the yeast is evenly distributed throughout the dough. The kneading also breaks up the bubbles and circulates the leavening gases. Dough is kneaded until its texture becomes smooth and satiny.

Leavening. Any agent which makes bread light and porous, such as baking powder, yeast, etc.

15

Scald. To heat a liquid almost to, but *always below*, its boiling point.

Score. To make a series of shallow cuts on the surface of the dough.

Sift. To put flour, or other dry ingredients, through a sifter. As most flours sold today are presifted, it is not necessary to put them through a sifter, unless desired.

Sponge. A batter to which yeast or starter has been added.

Spoon. To add to a mixture with a spoon, before stirring.

GUIDE TABLES FOR BAKING

All measures are level and are based on standard measuring spoons and cups. Unless otherwise indicated on containers, flour, powdered sugar and baking soda should be sifted before measuring. The Baking Proportions and Time Tables are general guides only. For specific proportions, baking time and oven temperatures refer to the recipes.

WEIGHTS & MEASURES

General

A pinch	= ⅛ teaspoon
3 teaspoons	= 1 tablespoon
2 tablespoons	= ⅛ cup
4 tablespoons	= ¼ cup
5⅓ tablespoons	= ⅓ cup
8 tablespoons	= ½ cup
12 tablespoons	= ¾ cup
16 tablespoons	= 1 cup or 8 ounces
1 gill	= ½ cup
2 gills	= 1 cup
4 gills	= 2 cups or 1 pint
1 cup	= ½ pint
2 cups	= 1 pint, or 1 lb. fat or liquid
4 cups	= 2 pints, or 1 quart, or 32 ounces
2 quarts (liquid)	= 4 pints or ½ gallon
4 quarts (liquid)	= 8 pints or 1 gallon

4 cups sifted pastry flour   = 1 pound
4 tablespoons sifted all-purpose flour = 1 ounce
2 cups granulated sugar   = 1 pound
2 tablespoons butter, fat or liquid   = 1 ounce
2 cups butter   = 1 pound
½ cup butter   = ¼ pound, or 1 stick
1 cup corn meal   = 6 ounces
1 cup stemmed raisins   = 6 ounces
1 cup cleaned currants   = 6 ounces
1 cup pitted dates   = 6 ounces
Lemon rind: 1 average lemon   = 1½ teaspoons grated
                                          rind
Orange rind: 1 average orange   = 1 tablespoon grated
                                          rind
Nutmeats, shelled or chopped: 1 cup = ¼ pound

Sugar:
    Granulated: 2 tablespoons = 1 ounce
                 1 cup   = 8 ounces
                 2 cups   = 1 pound

    Confectioners, sifted: 2 tablespoons = ½ ounce
                         1 cup   = 4 ounces
                         4 cups   = 1 pound

    Brown, firmly packed: 2 tablespoons = 1 ounce
                         1 cup   = 8 ounces
                         2 cups   = 1 pound

BAKING PROPORTIONS

4 cups flour require:
   1⅓ cups butter for short pastry
   4 tablespoons butter (¼ cup or ½ stick) for biscuit
   6 tablespoons butter (¾ stick) for shortcake
   ½ cup butter for cup cakes
   1 level teaspoon salt
   4 teaspoons baking powder
   1 pint of liquid for batter
   1 teaspoon baking soda to 2 cups sour milk
   1 teaspoon of baking soda to 1 cup of molasses

BAKING TIME

Loaf bread	45 to 60 minutes
Rolls & Biscuits	10 to 20 minutes
Graham Gems	30 minutes
Gingerbread	20 to 30 minutes
Sponge Cake	45 to 60 minutes
Plain Cake	30 to 40 minutes
Cookies	10 to 15 minutes
Bread Pudding	1 hour

BAKING TEMPERATURES

A general baking temperature guide could be misleading—no hard and fast rule can be given, because each oven has its own peculiarities. And, in bread baking, it is always necessary to consider such factors as the shape and size of the loaf and the amounts of sugar, eggs, milk, fat, fruit, etc., added to the dough. A principal point to remember is that in order to obtain best results there is no substitute for continual close supervision.

On your initial attempt follow the temperatures as given in the recipes and make careful note of the results. On subsequent attempts you can then amend the time and temperature to best suit your own oven.

When baking in glassware the oven temperature should always be set at least 25° *lower* than that indicated for metalware.

BAKING PANS & UTENSILS

Loaf Pans: Very small—4½ x 2½ x 2½ inches; Small—7½ x 3½ x 2¼ inches; Medium—8½ x 4 x 2½ inches; Large —9 x 5 x 3 inches

Shallow baking pans: 8 x 8 x 2 inches; 9 x 9 x 2 inches; 9 x 13 x 2 inches; 10 x 15 x 2½ inches

Round spring forms (with or without tubes): 7. 8, 9 and 10 inches

Round layer cake pans: 8 and 9 inches
Baking (cookie) sheet: 10 x 15 inches
Iron popover mold
10-inch tube pan (also called a Bundt or Baba au Rhum pan)
Empty coffee can (3-lb. size) for Easter breads
Muffin tins (gem pans) for 6, 8 and 12 muffins
Ovenware pie pan, 8-inch
Ovenware baking dishes: 1, 1½ and 2-qt. sizes
Brioche tins (optional)
Ovenware casserole
Ovenware custard cups (8)
Iron skillet
Griddle iron
Ring mold, 9-inch size
Bread board
Rolling pin
Wire cake racks (3) for cooling
Set of small, medium and large-size mixing bowls
Individual clay (red earthenware) flower pots: graduated sizes
Electric blender
Hand rotary beater
Flour sifter
Pastry blender
Wooden spoon and fork
Rubber spatula
Large graduated measuring cup, or measuring cups in assorted
    sizes
Measuring spoons in assorted sizes
Biscuit cutters: 2, 2½ and 3-inch sizes
Wire cake tester
Pancake turner
Wire whisk
Nut grinder

SOURCES OF SUPPLY

Stone ground whole grain flours
   Byrd Mill Company, R.F.D. 5, Louisa, Virginia
   Elam's Mills, Broadview, Illinois 60153
Gluten flour
   Dia'mel Brands, Dietetic Food Co., Brooklyn, N.Y.
   Diet Wise Company, R.F.D. 1, Barta, Pennsylvania
Seven-grain wonder meal
   El Molino Mills, Alhambra, California
Soya bean flour or powder
   Fern Soya Foods, Melrose Park, Illinois
Soya date mix
   Nutrafoods Corp., Valley Stream, New York 11582
Rose essence and rose water
   Most drugstores and gourmet stores

BEGINNER'S BAKE-A-BREAD RECIPES

HOT ROLL MIX FOR QUICK BREADS

This chapter embraces a series of experiments we made with packaged hot roll mix with exciting results. For beginning bread bakers who have never worked with yeast and raised doughs the hot roll mix provides a wonderful opportunity to try your hand at it. There is magic in this little package! It produces an ideal enriched bread, sweet bread or hot rolls; a perfect blend of ingredients, resulting in a soft, satiny smooth dough. The directions on the package are practically foolproof. Do not rush, but take your time, improvise, have fun and let your imagination run riot. You are bound to come up with unusual ideas of your own; the variations are endless. Knead the dough, at times lifting it, French baker fashion, and dropping it hard on the board surface to break the air bubbles and cut the kneading time. Give the dough its due rising time; slow gentle rising will result in better flavor, tenderness and volume, while fast rising will only result in a heavier and less flavorful bread.

The hot roll mix does not have to be just hot rolls. The delightful French Herb Bread, the Apricot Coffee Loaf, and the Fragrant Orange Nut Bread and Cinnamon Tea Loaf are just wonderful. Try these quick and easy uncomplicated recipes.

APRICOT COFFEE LOAF
(From Hot Roll Mix)

¾ cup lukewarm water
yeast from package of hot roll mix
1 teaspoon sugar
2 eggs, beaten
1 package (13¾-ounce) hot roll mix

1½ cups Apricot Filling
½ cup coarsely chopped walnuts
1 tablespoon grated orange rind
Chocolate Rum Frosting

Pour lukewarm water into a mixing bowl. Sprinkle with dry yeast and sugar. Stir. Cover and set aside for 5 minutes until it begins to foam. Add beaten eggs; mix. Add ½ package hot roll mix. Beat well with a wire whisk until well blended, then gradually add the rest of the mix. Mix with a spatula until the dough leaves the sides of the bowl. If it is slightly sticky, sprinkle 1 tablespoon flour over all. Turn out onto a lightly floured board and knead for 5 minutes. Place the dough in a warm buttered bowl, turning the dough until it is completely greased. Cover with a clean cloth. Set aside in a warm place until doubled in bulk (about 45 minutes). Punch down and let rise again until doubled. Punch down once more, turn out onto a lightly floured board and roll out into a 10″ x 12″ rectangle. Spread with Apricot Filling (see below); sprinkle with nuts and orange rind. Roll up short side. Secure ends. Shape and fit into a well-buttered and lightly floured 9″ x 5″ x 3″ loaf pan, seam side down. Cover and let rise until the dough reaches the top of the baking pan, or until doubled. Bake in a preheated 375° F. oven for 35 to 40 minutes or until done. Cool in pan for 15 minutes. Loosen sides with the flat side of a silver knife. Turn out onto a wire rack until cold. Spread with Chocolate Rum Frosting.

APRICOT FILLING: Combine 1½ cups cooked and pureed dried apricots with 1 tablespoon sugar and 1 tablespoon brandy. Beat until smooth; if too thick, add a little more brandy. Spread on dough, leaving an inch border around the edge of the dough. (Prepared apricot puree or apricot lekvar is available in small tins in most supermarkets, or in 1-pint glass jars in Hungarian grocery stores.)

23

CHOCOLATE RUM FROSTING: Melt 3 ounces semisweet chocolate with 1 tablespoon hot coffee. Beat until smooth and free from lumps. Add 1 tablespoon rum, and 1 to 2 tablespoons confectioners sugar; beat well. The frosting should not be too thin. Spread over top of cooled loaf. Let stand until the frosting is set before slicing.

CINNAMON TEA LOAF

¾ cup lukewarm water
package yeast from the box
  of hot roll mix
1 teaspoon sugar
1 egg
1 package (13¾-ounce) hot
  roll mix

2 to 3 tablespoons soft butter,
  not melted
⅓ cup sugar
1½ teaspoons cinnamon
  sugar
½ cup raisins
½ cup chopped nuts

Pour lukewarm water into a mixing bowl. Add yeast and 1 teaspoon sugar. Cover. Let stand for 5 minutes until the yeast begins to foam. Add beaten egg and ½ package hot roll mix. Beat well with a wooden spoon, then gradually add remaining mix. Mix until the dough leaves the sides of the bowl. Knead on a lightly floured board for 5 minutes. Turn into a warm, buttered bowl, turning the dough until thoroughly greased. Cover with a clean cloth. Set aside in a warm place until doubled in bulk. Turn out onto a lightly floured board; roll into an 18″ x 12″ rectangle and spread with soft butter. Combine sugar with cinnamon, sprinkle over the butter, then add the raisins and nuts. Roll up long side. Seal seams and ends. Cut in half and fit into two 7½″ x 3½″ x 2″ well-buttered and lightly floured loaf pans, seam side down. Cover; let rise until doubled in bulk. Bake in a 375° F. oven for 35 minutes or until golden brown. Cool in pans for 10 minutes. Turn out onto wire cooling racks. Drizzle with white icing or sprinkle with a soft cloud of powdered sugar.

FRENCH HERB BREAD
(From Hot Roll Mix)

¾ cup lukewarm water
yeast from hot roll mix
   package
1 teaspoon sugar
1 egg plus 1 egg yolk
2 teaspoons grated carrot
1 teaspoon very finely
   chopped fresh parsley

½ teaspoon crushed basil
   leaves
½ teaspoon crushed
   rosemary
1 13¼-ounce package hot
   roll mix
1 egg white, beaten with 1
   tablespoon water
coarse salt (kosher type)

Pour lukewarm water into a mixing bowl. Sprinkle with the dry yeast and sugar. Stir. Cover and set aside for 5 minutes until it begins to foam. Add beaten egg and egg yolk; mix. Then add the grated carrot and herbs. Beat with a wire whisk until well blended. Add ½ package hot roll mix. Mix well with a wooden spoon, then gradually add the rest of the hot roll mix. Mix with a spatula until the dough leaves the sides of the bowl. If it is sticky, sprinkle 1 tablespoon flour over all. Turn out onto a lightly floured board and knead for 5 minutes. Place the dough in a warm, buttered bowl, turning the dough until it is completely greased. Cover. Set aside in a warm place until doubled in bulk (about 45 minutes). Punch down, and let rise again until doubled. Knead and shape into a loaf. Place in a buttered and lightly floured 9" x 5" x 3" loaf pan. Cover and let rise until doubled in bulk. Bake in a preheated 375° F oven for 35 minutes or until golden brown. Tap the loaf; when it gives off a hollow sound it is done. Beat egg white with water, brush top of loaf with the egg-white mixture and sprinkle with coarse salt. Return to oven until the glaze is dry (5 to 8 minutes). Cool for 10 minutes, then turn out onto a wire cake rack.

GARLIC BREAD
(Refrigerator Biscuits)

3 packages refrigerator biscuits (10 in a package)
1 stick soft butter or
margarine

2 cloves garlic, crushed
½ cup grated Romano or
Parmesan cheese
dash paprika

Butter generously an 8-inch ring mold with a center tube. Open 1 package of refrigerator biscuits at a time. Spread them out on a paper towel or plate. Blend softened butter with garlic. Spread each biscuit with the garlic butter; arrange them on edge, one against the other, until the ring is full. This will take the entire three packages of biscuits. Spread the top with softened garlic butter and sprinkle with grated cheese and paprika. Bake in a hot oven (425° F.) until puffed and golden brown, about 25 minutes. Place a serving plate over top, invert, and turn out, very carefully, leaving the round biscuit loaf intact. Break off hot biscuits as needed. Makes an attractive presentation for the company dinner table.

FRAGRANT ORANGE NUT BREAD
(From Hot Roll Mix)

¾ cup lukewarm water
package yeast from the box
of hot roll mix
1 teaspoon sugar
1 egg plus 1 egg yolk, beaten
1 tablespoon grated orange
rind
1 tablespoon orange juice

1 tablespoon chopped
candied orange peel
1 package (13¾-ounce) hot
roll mix
1 tablespoon sugar
½ cup chopped walnuts
1 egg white beaten with 1
tablespoon cold water

Pour lukewarm water into a mixing bowl. Add the yeast and 1 teaspoon sugar. Cover. Let stand for 5 minutes until the yeast begins to foam. Add beaten egg, orange rind, orange juice and candied orange peel. Mix well. Combine hot roll mix with 1 tablespoon sugar and walnuts. (If a sweeter bread is desired, add another tablespoon of sugar.) Add half of the amount to the yeast mixture. Beat well with a wooden spoon, then gradually add remaining mixture. Mix until the dough leaves the sides of the bowl. Knead on a lightly floured board for 5 minutes. Turn into a warm, buttered bowl, turning the dough until thoroughly greased. Cover with a cloth. Set aside in a warm place until doubled in bulk. If a second rising is desired, for a lighter bread, punch down, cover and let rise again until doubled in bulk. Turn out onto a lightly floured board and shape into a loaf. Bake in a buttered 9" x 5" x 3" loaf pan. in a 375° F. oven for 35 to 40 minutes or until golden brown. Remove from oven, brush with beaten egg white, return to oven until the top is glazed a golden brown (5 to 8 minutes). Cool in tin for 10 minutes, then complete cooling on a wire rack. When ready to serve sprinkle with powdered sugar or drizzle with white icing.

NOTE: If two smaller loaves are desired, divide dough in half, shape into two small loaves, bake in buttered and lightly floured 7½" x 3½" x 2" baking pans.

BROWN-AND-SERVE ONION ROLLS

1 package brown-and serve-rolls (any brand)	coarse salt (kosher type)
⅔ stick soft butter	3 chopped scallions or 1 small chopped onion

Brush rolls with soft butter. Sprinkle with a little coarse salt and chopped onions. Bake in a hot oven according to directions on the package.

VARIATIONS:

1. Brush rolls with soft butter, sprinkle with garlic salt and a little paprika. Bake as directed on the package.
2. Brush rolls with butter, sprinkle with grated Cheddar cheese. Bake as directed on the package.
3. Brush rolls with beaten egg yolk mixed with 1 tablespoon water. Sprinkle thickly with sesame seeds. Bake as directed on the package.
4. Brush rolls with butter, sprinkle with coarse salt and caraway seeds. Bake as directed on the package.

REFRIGERATOR BISCUIT CHEESE LOAF

2 packages refrigator biscuits
½ cup melted sweet butter
½ to ¾ cup coarsely grated Cheddar cheese

Separate biscuits. Arrange one layer in two rows in the bottom of an 8-inch loaf pan. Brush with melted butter and sprinkle with half of the grated cheese. Arrange another layer of biscuits on top, brush again with melted butter and sprinkle top generously with grated cheese. If there are any biscuits left over, make another layer, or 1 row in the center of the loaf, brushing top with melted butter and sprinkling with grated cheese. Bake in a hot oven, according to directions on the package, until golden brown. Cool 10 to 15 minutes. Turn loaf out on a bread board. Serve warm, breaking off biscuits as needed. *Do not use a knife.*

STICKY BISCUITS
(Refrigerator Biscuits)

2 packages refrigerator
  biscuits
½ cup soft sweet butter
½ cup soft brown sugar

1 tablespoon cinnamon sugar
½ cup very coarsely chopped
  pecans or walnuts
3 to 4 tablespoons honey

Arrange biscuits in a well-buttered 8-inch square baking pan.
Spread tops with soft butter, brown sugar, cinnamon sugar
and nuts. Dribble honey over top. Bake in a hot oven according to directions on package. Watch carefully; if the oven
is too hot, after 15 minutes, turn heat down to 350° F. as the
top may burn easily. Bake until the biscuits and the top are
golden brown. Serve warm or cold.

YEAST BREADS

HINTS ON BAKING YEAST BREADS

In baking yeast breads, all utensils and ingredients should always be kept at room temperature before using.

Yeast, which is a delicate living plant, should be treated tenderly. When yeast is mixed with lukewarm water and sugar it forms carbon dioxide gases which foam and bubble. When this foaming yeast is mixed with the dough, it lifts the moist warm dough and makes it light and porous.

Two types of yeast are available; dry granular and the compressed cakes. In our recipes we have used the granular type, although either may be used. If the cake yeast is used, the water with which it is mixed must be warm instead of luke-warm as with dry yeast. In both cases the water must be just right, for water too hot or too cool will kill the yeast action. The dry granular packaged yeast will keep indefinitely for weeks when stored in a cool place. The cake yeast must always be refrigerated. If you use the cake yeast for the recipes, remember that one cake equals one package of the dry granular yeast.

Salt adds zest to bread, but too much may interfere with the action of the yeast.

Sugar acts as food for the yeast and hastens its foaming action. It also adds flavor and a beautiful brown crust.

Shortening, especially fresh butter, improves the flavor, adds to the tenderness and keeping quality of the bread. Use with a light hand, as too much may slow up fermentation.

ALMOND BREAD

1 package dry granular yeast
⅓ cup lukewarm water
2 teaspoons sugar
1 cup scalded milk, cooled
1 stick sweet butter or
   margarine (¼-pound)
1 tablespoon honey
⅓ cup finely ground
   almonds

1 egg
3 cups flour
½ teaspoon baking powder
½ teaspoon salt
2 tablespoons hot water
1 tablespoon sugar
⅓ cup very coarsely chopped
   almonds
1 teaspoon cinnamon sugar

Dissolve yeast in water; add sugar. Stir. Cover and let stand in a warm place until doubled in volume. In a large mixing bowl add the milk, butter, honey and ground nuts. Stir until the butter is melted. Add foaming yeast. Mix. Add egg, flour, baking powder and salt. Turn out onto a lightly floured board. Knead, with just enough flour on the board to keep the dough from being sticky, about 10 minutes. Turn into a warm, greased bowl, turning dough to grease top. Cover. Let rise in a warm place until doubled in bulk; punch down. Knead until smooth and elastic, about 5 minutes. Shape into a ball. Turn into a greased and lightly floured round (Pyrex) bowl. Cover. Let rise again until doubled. In the meantime boil 2 tablespoons water with 1 tablespoon sugar for 1 minute or until the sugar is thoroughly dissolved. Cool. Brush top of loaf lightly with the syrup; sprinkle with nuts and cinnamon sugar. Bake at 400° F. for 15 minutes. Reduce heat to 375° F. and continue to bake 20 to 25 minutes longer or until the bread is golden brown. Tap bread; if it sounds hollow it is done. Cool 5 minutes. Turn out on a wire rack.

NOTE: This is a beautiful round bread, topped with chunky bits of almonds and lightly spiced with cinnamon. It is delicious served with Vanilla Butter, marmalade or jam. To toast, slice bread ½-inch thick, spread on a cookie sheet, toast in a 350° F. oven for a few minutes until golden brown.

VANILLA BUTTER: Soften 1 stick sweet butter. Blend well with 1 teaspoon vanilla sugar, or mix with a few drops of pure vanilla flavor. Return to refrigerator until chilled and firm.

VANILLA SUGAR: Store 1 cup sugar in a small jar with a 1-inch piece vanilla bean, or, if desired, just sprinkle a few drops of pure vanilla flavor onto the sugar. Cover tightly. Shake well. Store until needed.

ANADAMA BREAD

An old New England recipe, originated by a fisherman who had a lazy wife and often had to do his own cooking. Of the many versions of this story the most popular one is that his wife always gave him corn meal mush and molasses for dinner. One day she left the house in the midst of preparing the mush. The husband desperately mixed the mush with flour and yeast and set it to bake as bread, saying to himself, "Anna, damn her." The bread was so delicious that the neighbors pleaded with him for the recipe which has long since passed into general use and known now as Anadama Bread.

2 cups water	2 packages dry granular
½ cup corn meal	yeast
2 tablespoons butter	½ cup lukewarm water
½ cup dark molasses	1 tablespoon sugar
2 teaspoons salt	6 cups flour
	¼ cup warm melted butter

Boil the 2 cups water and gradually add the corn meal in a slow stream, stirring constantly until the mixture is smooth. Add 2 tablespoons butter, the molasses and salt; let stand until lukewarm. Add the yeast to the ½ cup lukewarm water, sprinkle with sugar, cover and let stand until foaming and doubled in volume. Add to corn meal mixture. Stir in the flour, gradually, just enough to make a stiff dough. Knead well for 10 minutes. Place in a warm greased bowl, cover and let rise until doubled in bulk. Cut through dough several times with a knife. Cover and let rise again for 45 minutes or until doubled in bulk. Toss lightly on a floured board. Knead and mold into two loaves. Place in greased and lightly floured bread pans. Cover and let rise again until doubled in bulk. Bake in a 400° F. oven for 20 minutes; reduce heat to 375° F. and continue to bake until the loaves are golden brown. Brush bread with warm melted butter and turn on sides on a cooling rack to cool.

FRAGRANT CASSEROLE YEAST BREAD

1 package dry granular yeast
1 cup lukewarm water
2 teaspoons sugar
2 scant teaspoons salt

4 cups flour
½ teaspoon garlic powder
soft butter
garlic salt

Soften yeast in lukewarm water, add sugar. Stir. Cover and set aside until foaming and doubled in volume. Add salt, 2 cups flour and garlic powder. Beat well until thoroughly blended. Add remaining flour to make a soft thick batter. Place in a warm greased bowl, cover and let rise until doubled in bulk. Punch down, place in a well-greased and lightly floured 1½ quart casserole. Cover and let rise again until doubled in bulk. Bake at 375° F. to 400° F. for 35 minutes or until golden brown. (When baking in glass lower heat by 25°.) Remove from oven, brush with butter, sprinkle with garlic salt. Return to a slow oven for a few minutes. Cool on wire cake rack.

BREAD OF MY CHILDHOOD

This is a long-time favorite, often varied by using more eggs or just egg yolks, occasionally a pinch of saffron for an exotic color, or even a pinch of nutmeg to tease the palate. Slice ¾-inch thick and toast *lightly* for the most fragrant toast ever! Crisp on the outside and tender on the inside.

2 packages dry granular yeast
⅓ cup lukewarm water
2 teaspoons sugar
2 cups milk, scalded
1 stick sweet butter or
   margarine (¼-pound)
4 tablespoons golden orange
   blossom honey

3 egg yolks, beaten
1½ teaspoons salt
6 cups unbleached flour
1 egg yolk beaten with 2
   teaspoons water
poppy seeds

Dissolve yeast in lukewarm water; add sugar. Stir. Cover and set aside until foaming and doubled in volume. In a large mixing bowl stir together the scalded milk, butter and honey. Cool to lukewarm. Add beaten egg yolks, salt and 2 cups flour. Beat vigorously with a wooden spoon until bubbly and well blended. Add the remaining flour, one cup at a time, just enough to make a soft, but firm dough. Turn out onto a lightly floured board. Knead for at least 10 to 15 minutes, occasionally dropping the dough hard onto the board. Place in a warm greased bowl, turning to grease top. Cover with a light clean towel and set in a warm place until doubled in bulk. Punch down with a floured fist and let rise again. Cut down, turn out into a lightly floured board and shape into 2 medium size loaves. Place in greased and lightly floured 8" x 4" x 2½" bread pans. Cover and let rise in a warm place until doubled in bulk or until the dough reaches the top of the pans. Brush with beaten egg yolks and sprinkle with poppy seeds. Bake in a 400° F. oven for 10 minutes. Reduce heat to 350° F. and continue to bake 35 to 40 minutes longer or until the loaves are golden brown and tests done. (Tap bread—if is sounds hollow the bread is done.)

GOLDEN EGG BREAD
(Baked in Red Clay Flower Pots)

Baking in clay flower pots simulates a brick oven. The clay retains. the heat in just the same way, producing wonderful golden crusts and a fine crumbly texture to the bread.

2½ packages dry granular yeast
½ cup lukewarm water
2 teaspoons sugar
1¾ cups lukewarm water
¼ teaspoon powdered saffron
2 tablespoons honey
½ stick butter or margarine
4 eggs plus 1 egg yolk
7 cups unbleached flour
2 teaspoons salt
½ teaspoon baking powder
½ cup white raisins
1 egg white, slightly beaten with 2 teaspoons cold water
1 teaspoon poppy seeds

In a small bowl dissolve yeast in ½ cup of lukewarm water; add sugar, stir. Cover and set aside until foaming and doubled in volume. Pour 1¾ cups lukewarm water into a large bowl; add saffron and stir until dissolved, then add the honey and butter. Stir until the butter is dissolved. Beat in eggs, one at a time; add the foaming yeast mixture. Add 3 cups flour; beat vigorously until the batter is smooth. Combine salt, baking powder, raisins and remaining flour; add to yeast mixture, 2 cups at a time, until the dough clears the sides of the bowl. The dough may be slightly sticky. If so, add another tablespoon flour. Turn out onto a lightly floured board. Knead for 10 to 15 minutes, sprinkling dough occasionally with a little flour. Knead into a smooth elastic ball. Place in a warm greased bowl. Cover and set aside in a warm place until doubled in bulk. Punch down and let rise again until doubled. Turn out onto a lightly floured board, knead lightly for 5 minutes. *Grease generously,* three prepared (see note) flower pots and sprinkle lightly with flour. Cut three rounds of aluminum foil to fit bottom of flower pots. Grease well on both sides and cover bottom holes. Divide dough into three parts, leaving out small pieces of dough for each top. Knead and shape divided dough into three balls. Place one in each pot. Brush with egg white. Pinch off 9 little pieces from reserved piece of dough. Roll into little balls, and arrange three little balls on top of each bread. Brush again with egg white

35

and sprinkle with poppy seeds. Cover and set aside until doubled in bulk. Bake in a preheated 425° F. oven for 10 minutes. Reduce heat to 375° F. and continue to bake until golden brown, about 35 to 40 minutes. Place on cooling racks, in the pots, and let cool for 10 minutes. Then remove *carefully* from flower pots and let cool on racks.

FLOWER POTS: Scour flower pots with hot water and dry well. Oil each pot and place in a 275° oven for 2 hours until well seasoned. Dry well with soft paper towels. When ready to use, oil or grease with butter, sprinkle lightly with flour and use as directed. The size of the flower pots used in the recipe is 4 inches high by 4½ inches top diameter. Any leftover dough may be refrigerated for loaf bread or rolls.

MY MOTHER'S FAMOUS EGG TWIST

2 packages dry granular yeast
½ cup lukewarm water
2 teaspoons sugar
2 cups hot water
2 tablespoons orange blossom honey
pinch saffron dissolved in 1 tablespoon hot water

4 tablespoons melted butter or peanut oil
2 teaspoons salt
3 eggs plus 1 egg yolk
7 to 7½ cups flour
1 egg white, slightly beaten with 2 teaspoons cold water
poppy seeds

Dissolve yeast in lukewarm water, add sugar; stir. Cover and set aside until foaming and doubled in volume. Pour the hot water into a large mixing bowl. Add honey, saffron, butter or oil, and salt. Mix well. Cool to lukewarm. Add yeast mixture and eggs. Beat well until thoroughly blended. Add 3 cups flour, one at a time, beating well after each addition. Add 3 more cups flour, beating vigorously until the batter becomes very thick. Now, add just enough of the remaining flour to make a soft but moderately stiff dough. Turn out onto a lightly floured board and knead until the dough is smooth and elastic,

36

about 10 minutes. Shape into a ball. Place into a warm and well-greased bowl, turning to grease top. Cover and set aside in a warm place until doubled in bulk. Punch down, cover and let rise again until doubled. Turn out onto a lightly floured board and knead again for 5 minutes. Divide dough into 6 parts. Roll each of the 6 equal pieces into 12-inch "ropes." Fasten 3 ropes together at top (by pressing them with your thumb) and braid. Repeat with 3 remaining ropes. Place loaves well apart on a greased and lightly floured large baking sheet, or fit into two greased and lightly floured loaf pans (9" x 5" x 3"). Cover and let rise until doubled in bulk. Glaze with egg white. Sprinkle with poppy seeds. Bake at 400° F. for 10 minutes, then reduce heat to 375° F. and continue to bake 35 minutes longer or until the loaves are golden brown.

PRIZE WINNING FRENCH BREAD

1½ packages dry granular yeast
1 teaspoon sugar
½ cup lukewarm water
2 cups hot water

2 tablespoons melted butter
2 tablespoons sugar
1 tablespoon salt
7 cups unbleached flour
corn meal for pans

Dissolve yeast and 1 teaspoon sugar in ½ cup lukewarm water. Stir. Cover and set aside until foaming and doubled in volume. In a large mixing bowl, put 2 cups hot water; add butter, sugar and salt. Cool to lukewarm. Add foaming yeast, and beat in 2 cups flour, mixing well after each addition. Cover and let stand for a few minutes. Add more flour until a stiff dough is formed. Turn out onto a lightly floured board, using just enough flour to knead the dough. Knead well, about 10 minutes, until the dough is smooth and elastic. Several times during the kneading process you may, French baker fashion, lift the dough up and bang it down hard on the board. Vigorous long kneading makes the dough fine and regular. Shape the dough into a ball and place into a warm greased bowl. Cover with buttered wax paper, then with a clean light towel. Set aside in a warm place until doubled in bulk (about 1¼ to 1½ hours). Turn out onto a lightly floured board, cut in half, and knead well until all the air bubbles have been worked out. Shape into two long loaves, shaping and tapering ends. Gash top, diagonally, ¼-inch deep, about 2 inches apart. Place on a greased baking pan sprinkled lightly with cornmeal. Cover, set aside in a warm place, free from drafts, until doubled in bulk, about 1 hour. Bake in a 350° F. oven for 40 to 45 minutes for crusty loaves. For a crisp golden brown crust, brush top of bread with a little salt water before baking, and once or twice during baking. Sprinkle with sesame seeds if desired. Cool on wire racks.

CRUSTY GARLIC BREAD

2 packages dry granular yeast
⅓ cup lukewarm water
2 teaspoons sugar
¾ cup flour
2 cups hot water, cooled to lukewarm

1 teaspoon salt
½ teaspoon garlic powder
6 cups unbleached flour
2 cloves fresh garlic, crushed
⅓ stick soft butter

Sprinkle yeast over lukewarm water, add sugar. Stir. Cover and set aside for 2 to 3 minutes until bubbly. Then add ¾ cup flour; mix and form into a ball. Make a criss-cross cut across the top and float the ball in a warm bowl containing 2 cups lukewarm water. Cover and let stand for 5 to 10 minutes, then add the salt, garlic powder and enough flour to make a soft smooth dough. Beat well with a wooden spoon. Turn out onto a lightly floured board and knead until smooth and elastic, sprinkling a little flour from time to time on the board. Place in a warm, well-greased bowl, turning to grease top. Cover. Let rise in a warm place free from drafts until doubled in bulk. Punch down and knead again. Shape into two long loaves, tapering ends. Make a deep gash atop the center of each loaf. Place the two loaves on a greased and lightly floured baking sheet. Cover and let rise again until doubled in bulk. Bake in a 400° F. oven for 10 minutes; reduce heat to 375° F. and continue to bake until crusty, about 30 minutes. Cool. Combine crushed garlic with the soft butter and brush warm loaves with the garlic butter. Return to oven for 5 minutes. Let cool on wire racks. When ready to serve, cut bread into 2-inch chunks. Wrap chunks in foil and place in a hot oven for 10 minutes until toasted a light golden brown. Serve hot!

MILK BREAD

2 cups scalded milk
2 tablespoons sweet butter or margarine
2 tablespoons honey
1 teaspoon salt
1 package dry granular yeast

⅓ cup lukewarm water
2 teaspoons sugar
5½ to 6½ cups flour
1 egg white, slightly beaten with 2 teaspoons cold water

Place scalded milk in a large mixing bowl. Add butter, honey and salt. Sprinkle yeast over lukewarm water, add sugar. Cover and set aside until foaming and doubled in volume. When the milk mixture has cooled to lukewarm add the foaming yeast mixture. Stir in 3 cups flour, one at a time, beating vigorously until the batter is smooth. Add remaining flour gradually, just enough to make a soft but firm dough. Knead on a lightly floured board until the dough is smooth and elastic, about 10 minutes. Place in a warm, greased bowl; cover and set aside in a warm place until doubled in bulk. Punch down, cover and let rise again until doubled. Knead for a few minutes. Divide dough in half and shape into two loaves. Place in greased and lightly floured bread pans. Cover and let rise until doubled in bulk, or until the dough reaches the top of the pans. Brush with egg white and bake in a 400° F. oven for 10 minutes; reduce heat to 350° F. and continue to bake until the loaves are golden brown, about 30 to 35 minutes. Cool. Remove from pans and return to oven for 5 to 10 minutes until nice and crusty. Let cool on wire racks.

NOTE: Baked bread should be removed from pans after 5 to 10 minutes to prevent sweating and softening of the crust. For a crustier bread remove from pans and place in hot oven for 5 to 10 minutes, as directed above.

SPICED ONION BREAD

1 package dry granular yeast
⅓ cup lukewarm water
1 tablespoon sugar
2 cups scalded milk
1 stick butter or margarine
  (¼-pound)
2 tablespoons sugar
6 cups flour

1 teaspoon salt
⅛ teaspoon freshly grated
  black pepper
good dash of onion powder
1 tablespoon minced scallion,
  white part only
1 egg yolk, beaten with 2
  teaspoons water

Dissolve yeast in lukewarm water, add 1 tablespoon sugar. Cover and set aside until foaming and doubled in volume. In a large bowl, combine scalded milk with butter and sugar. Stir. Cool to lukewarm. Add foaming yeast mixture. Gradually add half of the flour; beat well. Add the remaining flour, salt, pepper, onion powder and minced onion. Mix into a soft dough. Turn out onto a lightly floured board and knead 10 minutes, until smooth and elastic. Turn into a warm, greased bowl, turning to grease top. Cover. Let stand in a warm place until doubled in bulk. Punch down. Shape into 2 loaves. Place in greased and lightly floured 9" x 5" x 3" loaf pans. Brush lightly with egg yolk mixture. Bake in a 425° F. oven for 10 minutes; reduce heat to 375° F. and continue to bake 30 minutes longer or until the bread is a nice golden brown, and tests done. Cool on wire racks.

NOTE: For an extra appetizing twist, after brushing loaves with beaten egg, sprinkle lightly with a little onion soup mix before baking.

FARMHOUSE POTATO BREAD

1 package dry granular yeast
½ cup scalded milk, cooled
   to lukewarm
2 teaspoons sugar
2 eggs
½ cup warm, unseasoned
   mashed potatoes
½ teaspoon salt

⅓ stick soft butter or
   margarine
3 cups flour
½ teaspoon baking powder
1 egg yolk mixed with 2
   teaspoons cold water
1 tablespoon sesame seeds

Sprinkle yeast over lukewarm milk; add sugar. Cover and set aside until foaming and doubled in volume. In a large mixing bowl, combine eggs, mashed potatoes, salt and butter. Beat until well blended. Add foaming yeast, 2 cups flour, and baking powder. Blend. Knead about 10 minutes until the dough is smooth and elastic. Place in a warm, buttered bowl, turning to grease top. Cover. Let rise in a warm place until doubled in bulk. Punch down and let rise again until doubled. Knead and shape into a loaf and place in a greased and lightly floured 9" x 5" x 3" bread pan. Cover and let rise in a warm place until doubled in bulk. Brush top with beaten egg yolk and sprinkle with sesame seeds. Bake at 400° F. for 5 to 10 minutes. Reduce heat to 375° F. and continue to bake until the loaf is golden brown, about 30 to 35 minutes. Cool. Turn out onto a wire cake rack.

NOTE: A good rule to remember when baking bread or cakes is to use flour with a light hand, using a scant cup of flour rather than an overflowing one. Too much flour will result in heavy loaves and cakes.

FAMOUS BYRD MILL PUMPERNICKEL

2 packages dry granular yeast
½ cup lukewarm water
1 tablespoon sugar
2 cups boiling water
1½ tablespoons salt
4 tablespoons dark molasses

1 cup mashed potatoes
7 cups rye flour
½ cup corn meal
2 cups whole wheat flour
(may need a little more)

Soften yeast in ½ cup lukewarm water. Add sugar. Mix. Cover and set aside until foaming and doubled in volume. In a large mixing bowl stir together boiling water, salt, molasses and unseasoned mashed potatoes. Cool to lukewarm. Add the foaming yeast. Add rye flour, corn meal and whole wheat flour, just enough to make a stiff dough. Mix well with hands or a large wooden spoon, and let stand for 10 to 15 minutes. Turn out onto a bread board sprinkled lightly with whole wheat flour. Knead well for 10 minutes. Place the dough in a warm, well-greased bowl, turning to grease the top. Cover with a light towel and let rise in a warm place free from drafts for 1½ hours or until doubled in bulk. Place on a floured board and knead again for 10 minutes. Let rise again, covered, in a warm place for 45 minutes, or half as big again. Place on a lightly floured board and knead lightly for a few minutes. Divide dough in half and shape into round loaves. Place in greased and lightly floured round casseroles or on a baking sheet. Cover and let rise again for 30 minutes. Bake in a preheated 375° F. oven for 1¼ hours or until the bread is firm and golden brown. If a thick, crisp crust is desired, brush top of loaves with water, before baking, and several times during baking.

NOTE: Pumpernickel baked in round casseroles or pyrex bowls will hold the shape better than if baked on a baking sheet. Will yield two large or 3 smaller loaves.

SEEDED RYE BREAD

We often thicken pot roast gravy with a tantalizing and fragrant slice of fresh baked seeded rye softened in chicken broth and mashed until satiny smooth. The mashed rye bread is then squeezed dry and stirred into the gravy until it thickens. This addition gives the gravy a wonderful aroma and flavor and it is delicious!

2 cups hot water
2 tablespoons butter or margarine
2 teaspoons salt
2 tablespoons molasses
1 teaspoon caraway seeds
1 teaspoon poppy seeds

1½ packages dry granular yeast
⅓ cup lukewarm water
1 teaspoon sugar
2½ cups unbleached flour
3 cups rye flour
1 egg, beaten with 1 tablespoon water

In a large bowl, mix the hot water, butter, salt, molasses and seeds. Stir well. Cool to lukewarm. Dissolve yeast in warm water, add sugar. Cover and set aside until foaming and doubled in volume. Add to the first mixture. Add the unbleached flour and rye alternately, beating well until the dough is a solid mass. It will be slightly sticky. Turn out onto a floured board. Knead for 10 minutes, adding a little flour from time to time. If the board becomes sticky, scrape clean, sprinkle with a little flour and continue to knead until the dough is smooth and elastic. Turn into a warm greased bowl, turning to grease top of dough. Cover. Set aside in a warm place until doubled in bulk. Punch down and turn out onto a lightly floured board. Shape into 1 large or 2 medium size loaves. Turn into buttered and lightly floured bread pans. Cover and let rise until the dough reaches the top of the pans. Place a pan of hot water in the oven underneath the bread. Bake in a 400° F. oven for 5 to 8 minutes; reduce heat to 350° F. and continue to bake for 45 minutes or until the bread is golden brown. If desired, brush bread before baking with beaten egg yolk, and sprinkle top with caraway seeds. Cool 5 minutes. Remove from pans, place on wire racks until cold.

NOTE: For a crisp, crusty top remove baked bread from pans and return to oven for 8 to 10 minutes until the bread is crisp.

43

HIGH PROTEIN SOYBEAN DATE BREAD

2 packages dry granular yeast
¼ cup lukewarm water
2 teaspoons sugar
2 cups hot water
¾ cup instant non-fat dry milk
2 tablespoons honey

2 teaspoons salt
2 tablespoons soft butter or margarine
½ cup Soya Date Mix*
1 cup soybean flour
5 cups unbleached flour

Dissolve yeast in lukewarm water, add sugar; stir. Cover and set aside until foaming and doubled in volume. Boil water, cool to lukewarm and add instant non-fat dry milk. Stir. Add honey, salt, butter and Soya Date Mix. Stir well. Add foaming yeast mixture, then the soybean flour and 2 cups unbleached white flour. Beat vigorously until the batter is thoroughly blended. Add remaining white flour, using just enough to make a soft but moderately firm dough. Turn out onto a lightly floured board and knead for 10 minutes or even a little longer, until the dough is smooth and elastic. Shape into a ball and place in a warm, well-greased bowl, turning dough to grease top. Cover and set aside in a warm place until doubled in bulk. Punch down, cover and let rise again. Punch down, turn out onto a lightly floured board and knead for 5 minutes. Divide dough into 3 parts. Knead into 3 balls. Shape into loaves. Place in three greased and lightly floured 7" x 4" x 2½" bread pans. Cover and let rise until doubled in bulk, or until the dough reaches the top of the pans. Brush top with melted butter or slightly beaten egg white. Bake in a 400° F. oven for 15 minutes, then reduce heat to 350° F. and continue to bake 35 to 40 minutes longer or until done. Cool on wire cake racks.

SOYA DATE MIX: A delicious, nutritious high protein wheat-free cereal mix, with added dehydrated ripe date bits. The soybean granules add a nutty flavor and a crunchy bite. (See Sources of Supply.)

GOLDEN TEA BREAD

1 package dry granular yeast
⅓ cup lukewarm water
2 teaspoons sugar
¼ cup flour
1 stick sweet butter or margarine (¼ pound)
3 tablespoons orange blossom honey

1 teaspoon grated lemon rind
1 teaspoon brewed tea
¼ teaspoon salt
3 eggs
2 cups flour
Lemon Icing (if desired)

Sprinkle yeast over lukewarm water, add sugar and ¼ cup flour. Stir. Cover, and let stand in a warm place until light and bubbly. Cream softened butter with honey. Add lemon rind, tea and salt. Beat in eggs, one at a time. Add bubbly yeast mixture and flour. Beat well for 10 to 15 minutes. Pour the spongy dough into a well-greased and lightly floured loaf pan or into an 8-inch tube springform. Cover, keep in a warm place until doubled in bulk. Brush top lightly with little melted butter for a golden gloss, if desired. Bake in a preheated 350°F. oven for 40 minutes or until golden. Cool 10 minutes. Turn out on a wire cake rack.

NOTE: This versatile bread may be topped with lemon flavored icing for a quick coffee cake. With a bit of imagination, many of the yeast breads may be turned into last-minute desserts by using sweet toppings, brandied or rum syrups, crushed berries or any favorite fresh or frozen fruits. The best part is that it takes only minutes and success is always assured.

Lemon Icing: Blend together 1 cup confectioners sugar, 1 to 2 tablespoons lemon juice, and 2 teaspoons freshly brewed strong tea. Beat until smooth. If too thin, add a little more sugar. Dribble over bread.

QUICK AND EASY WHITE BREAD

2 packages dry granular yeast
⅓ cup lukewarm water
2 teaspoons sugar
2 cups scalded milk
2 tablespoons sugar or honey
2 teaspoons salt

1 tablespoon instant mashed potato mix, mixed with ¼ cup lukewarm water
2 tablespoons soft butter or margarine
6 cups unbleached white flour
warm melted butter

Dissolve yeast in lukewarm water, add 2 teaspoons sugar; stir. Cover and set aside until foaming and doubled in volume. In a large mixing bowl combine the milk, sugar, salt, instant mashed potato mix dissolved in lukewarm water, and butter or margarine. Mix well. Cool to lukewarm. Add yeast mixture and 2 cups flour and beat until the batter is smooth. Add 2 more cups of flour, beating well, then just enough flour to make a soft but firm dough. Turn out onto a lightly floured board and knead for 10 minutes until smooth and elastic. Shape into a ball and place in a warm, well-greased bowl, turning the dough to grease top. Cover and let rise in a warm place until doubled in bulk (about 1 to 1½ hours). Punch down. Divide dough in half and shape into two smooth balls. Let rest 10 minutes. Shape into two loaves. Place in greased and lightly floured 8- or 9-inch bread pans. Cover and let rise again until doubled in bulk, about 1 hour. Brush tops with warm melted butter. Bake in a 400°F. oven for 25 minutes, reduce heat to 375°F. and continue to bake until the loaves are golden brown and test done. Cool on wire cake racks.

NOTE: Oven temperatures vary. If the oven is too hot, reduce heat to 375°F. after first 15 minutes.

OLD-FASHIONED WHITE BREAD
WITH WHEAT GERM

2 packages dry granular yeast
½ cup lukewarm water
1 tablespoon sugar
1½ cups hot water
1 stick sweet butter or margarine (¼ pound)

2 teaspoons salt
2 tablespoons light honey
½ cup wheat germ
6½ cups flour
1 egg beaten with 2 teaspoons water

Sprinkle yeast over the lukewarm water; add sugar. Stir. Cover and let stand until foaming and doubled in volume. In the meantime place hot water in a large mixing bowl, add butter and cool to lukewarm. Add salt and honey. Mix well, then add the foaming yeast mixture; blend. Add wheat germ and 2 cups flour; beat well until thoroughly blended. Continue to add flour until a soft but firm dough is formed. Turn the dough out onto a lightly floured board and knead until satin smooth and elastic, about 10 minutes. Place in a warm, well-greased bowl, turning the dough until greased on all sides. Cover with a clean, light cloth and set aside in a warm place until doubled in bulk. Punch down dough and turn out onto a lightly floured board. Divide dough in half. Knead each for a few minutes, shaping each piece into a loaf. Place the dough seam side down in two well-greased and lightly floured 9" x 5" x 3" loaf pans. Cover and set aside in a warm place until doubled in bulk. Brush with beaten egg. Bake in a 400°F. oven for 10 minutes; reduce heat to 375°F. and continue to bake 30 minutes longer or until loaves sound hollow when tapped with fingers. Cool on wire racks; turn loaves on sides, so air can circulate around them.

ENRICHED WHITE BATTER BREAD

1 package dry granular yeast
¼ cup lukewarm water
1 teaspoon sugar
1¼ cups lukewarm water
½ cup instant non-fat dry
  milk

2 tablespoons soft butter or
  margarine
2 teaspoons salt
3 cups flour
1 tablespoon wheat germ
melted butter

Sprinkle yeast over the ¼ cup lukewarm water; add sugar and stir. Set aside until foaming and doubled in volume. In a large mixing bowl, stir dry milk, butter and salt into the 1¼ cups lukewarm water. Stir well. Add foaming yeast mixture; add flour and wheat germ. Beat 3 minutes at medium speed on electric mixer, or beat vigorously by hand. Scrape sides of bowl. Cover. Let rise in a warm place until doubled in bulk, about 45 minutes. Stir down batter, beating for 5 minutes. Spoon batter evenly into one greased and lightly floured 9" x 5" x 3" bread pan, or into two smaller pans if desired. Cover and let rise again for 45 minutes or until the dough reaches the top of the pan. The batter will be rather thick and sticky. Bake in a 375°F. oven for 45 minutes or until golden brown. Test by tapping bottom and top crust; if the loaf sounds hollow it is done. Remove from pan. Brush top with melted butter, sprinkle with a little wheat germ if desired, and return to oven for 5 minutes. Cool on wire rack.

PROSPECTOR'S SOURDOUGH BREAD

Sourdough, or wild yeast, although not of American origin, has become an item steeped in Americana because of its storied association with the early Alaska prospectors. These pioneers were called "sourdoughs" because they carried the sourdough starter pots strapped to their packs so that they could bake bread wherever they encamped for the night, without worrying about where and how to find yeast for their loaves.

SOURDOUGH STARTER:

1 package dry granular yeast
⅓ cup lukewarm water
2 teaspoons sugar

1 cup lukewarm water
2 teaspoons salt
1 cup unbleached white flour

Sprinkle dry yeast over ⅓ cup lukewarm water. Add sugar, stir. Cover and let stand for 5 minutes until the mixture begins to foam. Add 1 cup lukewarm water, salt and flour. Beat well with a whisk or rotary beater until well blended. Pour into a large wide-mouthed jar. Cover lightly and let stand in a warm place for 2 to 3 days until the starter is a bubbly foaming mass. After a day or two the liquid will rise to the top, mix gently with a fork to blend sourdough mixture.

SOURDOUGH BREAD

1 cup starter
½ cup scalded milk, cooled
   to lukewarm or ½ cup
   lukewarm water
3 tablespoons soft butter or
   margarine

2 tablespoons sugar
2½ to 3 cups unbleached
   white flour
1 egg yolk, beaten with 1
   tablespoon water

In a large mixing bowl, combine 1 cup starter, milk or water, butter or margarine. Beat well with a wooden spoon until thoroughly blended. Add sugar and 1 cup flour. Mix well. Then gradually add remaining flour until a soft but firm ball is formed. Turn out onto a floured board and knead for 10 minutes until the dough is smooth. Turn into a warm greased bowl. Cover and set aside in a warm place until doubled in bulk, about 1 hour. Punch down with a wooden spoon, cover

49

and let rise again until doubled in bulk. Turn out onto a floured board and knead for 5 minutes. Shape into a ball. Place in a well-greased and lightly floured *ovenproof* 1½ quart round bowl, or if desired, shape into a loaf and bake in a well greased 9-inch loaf pan. Cover and set aside in a warm place until doubled in bulk. Brush with beaten egg yolk for a beautiful glossy crust. For an attractive top, slash with a sharp knife making a crisscross on top of round loaf. Bake in a preheated 400°F. oven for 35 to 40 minutes or until done. Tap loaf; when it sounds hollow it is done. Cool on wire rack. If a crisper crust is desired, remove from bowl or pan and return bread to oven for 10 minutes.

SOURDOUGH BREAD I F

SOURDOUGH STARTER:

1 cup unbleached flour
1 cup water, room
temperature

3 rounded teaspoons sugar

Combine flour, water and sugar. Beat with a whisk or rotary beater until thoroughly blended. Pour into a wide-mouthed jar (large enough to allow the starter to expand). Let stand, covered lightly, in a warm place for 2 to 3 days until the mixture is bubbly. Mix with a fork, beating slightly, every day.

SOURDOUGH BREAD

1 cup sourdough starter
1½ packages dry granular yeast
1 rounded tablespoon sugar
1¼ cups lukewarm water
2 tablespoons shortening (butter or margarine)
2 cups rye flour

2½ cups unbleached or all-purpose flour plus ½ cup for board
2 teaspoons salt
½ teaspoon baking soda
1 teaspoon caraway seeds (optional)
egg yolk beaten with 1 tablespoon water

Put sourdough starter in a large mixing bowl. In the meantime dissolve yeast and sugar in the lukewarm water. Cover lightly and let stand for 10 minutes until the mixture begins to foam. Add to sourdough starter; mix, then add the shortening. Gradually add rye flour and 1 cup white flour. Beat vigorously with a wooden spoon for 5 minutes. Add salt and baking soda to remaining flour together with the seeds. Mix and add to sourdough mixture. Beat well. Knead on a floured board for 5 minutes; then turn into a warm greased bowl. Cover with a light towel and set aside in a warm place until doubled in bulk, about 1 to 1½ hours. Turn out onto a floured board and knead until smooth and free from stickiness. Shape into two round loaves. Place in two well-greased and lightly floured ovenproof 1 quart bowls. Cover and set aside in a warm place until doubled in bulk. Bake in a preheated 400°F. oven for 45 to 50 minutes until golden brown. Tap loaves; when they sound hollow they are done. For a beautiful glossy golden brown, brush loaves with beaten egg yolk before placing in oven. Cool on wire racks.

SOURDOUGH BREAD II

SOURDOUGH STARTER:

1 cup rye flour
1 cup water

1 tablespoon sugar

Combine mixture in a glass wide-mouthed jar. Let stand, covered lightly, in a warm place for 2 to 3 days until fermented and bubbly.

SOURDOUGH BREAD ☞

1 cup sourdough starter
1 package dry granular yeast
1½ cups lukewarm water
2 teaspoons sugar

2 cups rye flour
4 cups all-purpose flour
2 teaspoons salt
½ teaspoon baking soda

Put the sourdough starter in a large mixing bowl. In the meantime dissolve yeast in lukewarm water, add sugar. When it begins to foam add to sourdough starter. Add 4 cups flour (2 cups rye and 2 cups all-purpose flour). Stir well with a wooden spoon for 3 to 5 minutes. Turn into a large, warm, well-buttered mixing bowl. Cover with a light cloth and set aside in a warm place until doubled in bulk (about 1½ to 2 hours). Add salt and baking soda to 1 cup of remaining all-purpose flour and stir into dough. Mix well. Turn out onto a floured board and knead in remaining 1 cup flour until the dough is smooth and free from stickiness. Shape into 2 round or 2 oblong loaves. Place on a greased and lightly floured baking sheet. Cover and let rise in a warm place until doubled in bulk. Brush loaves with water. Slash the top with a sharp knife, making a criss-cross on top of loaves. Place a shallow pan of hot water in the bottom of the oven. Then bake the loaves in a preheated 400°F. oven for 45 to 50 minutes until golden brown. Tap loaves; when they sound hollow, they are done. If a crisper crust is desired, remove bread from baking sheet, return to oven for 5 to 10 minutes until nice and crusty. Cool on wire racks.

SWEET YEAST BREADS

Sweet yeast breads and coffee cakes are made from a sweeter, richer and softer yeast dough than bread. It is enriched with butter, eggs, sweet or sour cream, dried fruits, raisins, currants, and a variety of nuts. The sweet butter used as a shortening and the milk to add flavor and food value are essential to good bread and yeast cakes. A good flour, unbleached if possible, and fresh or dry granular yeast of good quality, are also requisite for best results. Fruit juices, freshly grated orange and lemon rind, honey or molasses, and pure cream-of-tartar baking powder for extra leavening add interesting variety to everyday bread and sweet bread.

In the old days, recipes were rarely used, as most of the women baked by "ear." During the holidays the dough was sweetened and filled with candied and dried fruits and assorted nuts. Often, little prizes were hidden in the dough, to delight the youngsters in the family. Fancy Easter breads were shaped into bunnies or beautiful nests filled with colorful eggs and jelly beans.

With a little bit of imagination, and the change of the shape of the baking pans, the dough can be formed into interesting and unusual shapes and sizes. Although some of the sweet breads, such as bundts, kugelhopfs, brioches, panetones, sweet twists, babas au rhum, wreaths and coffee rings, have their own traditional shapes, they can be baked successfully in any shape baking pans. If a new, heavy type baking pan is used, season it first with oil and place in a preheated 275°F. oven for 1 hour. It should be wiped with soft paper towels or a soft cloth. Grease and lightly flour when ready to use. For best results and a more delicate flavor we prefer to grease baking tins with sweet butter.

BASIC SWEET DOUGH

2 packages dry granular yeast
¼ cup lukewarm water
1 teaspoon sugar
1 cup scalded milk
½ cup sugar
½ teaspoon salt

½ stick sweet butter
2 eggs
1 teaspoon grated orange rind
1 teaspoon grated lemon rind
5 cups flour
⅓ cup flour for the board

Sprinkle yeast over warm water. Add 1 teaspoon sugar. Stir. Cover and set aside until foaming and doubled in volume. In a large mixing bowl, combine the scalded milk, sugar, salt and butter. Mix well. Cool to lukewarm. Add foaming yeast mixture and eggs. Beat vigorously with a wooden spoon. Add orange and lemon rind and 2 cups flour. Beat well. Now add just enough flour to make a soft pliable dough. Turn out onto a lightly floured board and knead until the dough is smooth and elastic. Place in a warm, well-greased bowl, turning dough until thoroughly greased on all sides. Cover with a sheet of buttered wax paper, then with a soft linen towel. Set aside in a warm place until doubled in bulk, about 1 to 1½ hours. When light and spongy, punch down with a floured fist. Turn out onto a lightly floured board and knead 5 to 8 minutes. Cover with a clean cloth or a bowl and let the dough rest for 10 minutes. Shape into loaves, braids or rings. Brush with warm melted butter or beaten egg yolk. Cover and let rise again until doubled in bulk. Bake in a preheated 375°F. oven for 35 to 40 minutes or until golden brown. If desired, raisins, currants, chopped nuts, or chopped candied fruits may be added to the dough. Cool on wire cake racks. Sprinkle with a soft cloud of soft powdered sugar or dribble with lemon-flavored white icing.

NOTE: To give yeast cakes a lighter texture and a more tender crumb, add 1 teaspoon pure cream-of-tartar baking powder to the flour. There is an excellent one on the market and it may be found in all shopping areas.

ADELE'S MERINGUE YEAST KUCHEN

½ pound sweet butter, room temperature
3 tablespoons sugar
3 eggs, separated
1 package dry granular yeast
⅓ cup lukewarm water
1 teaspoon sugar

2⅓ cups flour
¾ cup sifted sugar
½ cup chopped nuts
½ cup soft brown sugar
½ cup plump raisins
2 tablespoons cinnamon sugar

Cream butter with the 3 tablespoons sugar. Add egg yolks one at a time until well blended. Sprinkle yeast over lukewarm water; add 1 teaspoon sugar. Stir. Cover and set aside until the yeast begins to foam and doubles in volume. Add to creamed mixture. Add half of the flour and beat vigorously until well blended. Add rest of flour and continue to beat with a wooden spoon until a soft smooth dough is formed. Turn out onto a lightly floured board and knead for 5 to 8 minutes. Place in a warm, buttered bowl. Cover with a sheet of buttered wax paper, then with a soft linen towel. Set aside in a warm place until doubled in bulk. Punch down. Cover with buttered wax paper and refrigerate over night. Next day, let stand at room temperature for 15 minutes, then roll dough out on a lightly floured board into a ⅓-inch thick rectangle. Beat egg whites until they hold soft peaks; gradually add ¾ cup sugar in a slow stream, and continue to beat until the meringue is the consistency of whipped cream. Spread over dough. Sprinkle with chopped nuts, brown sugar, raisins and cinnamon sugar. Roll up lengthwise, as for a jelly roll. Fit into a well-buttered and lightly floured 9- or 10- inch tube spring form. Cover and let rise in a warm place until doubled in bulk. Bake in a 350°F. oven for 40 to 45 minutes or until done. Cool 15 minutes, then remove rim from spring form. Place on a wire cake rack until cold. Sprinkle top with powdered sugar or spread with white icing if desired. This is an elegant coffee cake, rich with butter and eggs, and enhanced with a delectable meringue filling.

ALMOND SWEET BREAD

2 packages dry granular yeast
½ cup lukewarm water
2 teaspoons sugar
4 tablespoons soft butter or corn oil
2 cups lukewarm water
½ teaspoon almond flavor
3 eggs, slightly beaten

½ cup sugar
8 scant cups flour
¾ cup coarsely chopped almonds
1 egg yolk
1 tablespoon water or milk
2 cubes sugar, crushed, *or* Almond-Flavored White Icing

Sprinkle yeast over ½ cup lukewarm water. Add 2 teaspoons sugar. Cover and set aside for 5 minutes or until the mixture foams and doubles in volume. Place butter or corn oil in a large mixing bowl. Add 2 cups lukewarm water, almond flavor, eggs and sugar. Beat until well blended, then add the yeast mixture. Mix. Add 3 cups flour and ½ cup almonds; beat well, then gradually add enough flour to make a soft dough. Turn dough out onto a lightly floured board and knead for 10 minutes until satiny smooth. The longer the kneading the better. Turn the dough into a warm, buttered bowl, turning dough until it is thoroughly greased on all sides. Cover with a buttered sheet of wax paper, then with a clean, light kitchen towel. Set in a warm place until doubled in bulk. Punch down, knead again for a few minutes, and return to a clean buttered bowl to rise again until doubled in bulk—about 1 hour. Turn out onto a lightly floured board. Knead for 1 minute. Divide dough into two parts. Knead and shape into 2 loaves. Place in two 9" x 5" x 3" loaf pans or 3 smaller loaf pans. Cover and set aside once more until doubled in bulk. Beat egg yolk with water or milk, and brush top of loaves with the mixture. Crush sugar. Sprinkle top with remaining ¼ cup chopped almonds and crushed sugar cubes. Bake in a 400°F. oven for 10 minutes. Reduce heat to 375°F. and continue to bake until golden brown, about 35 minutes. To test loaves for doneness, remove from pans, and tap bottom and sides with fingers; when it gives off a hollow sound the loaves are done. This is an unusually rich and delicious sweet bread with a hint of pure almond flavor.

Cool in pans for 10 minutes, then turn out onto wire cake

racks. Spread with almond-flavored white icing, if the crushed sugar-nut topping isn't used.

ALMOND-FLAVORED WHITE ICING: Blend 1 cup confectioners sugar with 2 teaspoons water and about 10 drops pure almond flavor. Beat until smooth. When the loaves are cold, spread with the almond icing. Sprinkle top with toasted coarsely chopped almonds.

ICEBOX COFFEE CAKE

¾ cup scalded milk
½ cup sweet butter or margarine (¼ pound)
⅓ cup sugar
1 teaspoon salt
2 packages dry granular yeast
⅓ cup lukewarm water

2 teaspoons sugar
2 eggs plus 1 egg yolk
1 tablespoon grated orange rind
4 cups flour
Sesame Brown Sugar Topping

Pour the scalded milk into a large mixing bowl. Stir in butter, ⅓ cup sugar and salt. Cool to lukewarm. Sprinkle yeast over ⅓ cup lukewarm water; stir in 2 teaspoons sugar. Cover and set aside until it begins to foam and doubles in volume. Add yeast mixture to scalded milk mixture. Add eggs and egg yolk; beat well with a wooden spoon. Add orange rind and 2 cups flour. Beat until the batter is smooth, then add remaining flour, 1 cup at a time, until the mixture is well blended. Scrape down dough from sides of the bowl; cover with buttered wax paper and refrigerate overnight. When ready to use, let stand at room temperature for 10 minutes. Punch down, pat dough evenly into a well-buttered and lightly floured 9- or 10-inch tube spring form. Cover and let rise in a warm place until doubled in bulk. Sprinkle topping evenly over dough. Bake at 400°F. for 10 minutes; reduce heat to 350°F. and bake 30 to 40 minutes or until done.

SESAME BROWN SUGAR TOPPING: Combine ⅓ cup flour with ½ cup soft brown sugar, 2 tablespoons soft butter, 2 teaspoons cinnamon sugar, ½ cup chopped walnuts, and

2 tablespoons sesame seeds. Mix well with fingers. Brush top of coffee cake with melted butter, then sprinkle brown sugar topping evenly over top. Pat gently with fingers so that it will adhere to dough. Proceed as directed above.

FRUIT AND NUT SWEET BREAD

2 packages dry granular yeast
½ cup lukewarm water
2 teaspoons sugar
⅔ cup evaporated milk
¾ cup boiling water
2 tablespoons butter
¾ cup quick oatmeal
½ cup good molasses

1 teaspoon salt
5 cups flour
½ teaspoon baking powder
1 tablespoon grated lemon
   rind
½ cup mixed candied fruits
½ cup chopped mixed nuts

Combine yeast with lukewarm water, add sugar. Stir. Cover. Set aside for 5 minutes or until the yeast foams and doubles in volume. Into a large mixing bowl, pour the evaporated milk and boiling water. Add butter, oatmeal, molasses and salt. Beat well. Cool to lukewarm. Add foaming yeast to molasses-oatmeal mixture. Add half of the flour sifted with the baking powder. Beat well with a wooden spoon. Gradually add remaining flour sifted over the lemon rind, fruits and nuts. Mix and beat until well blended. Cover and set aside in a warm place until doubled in bulk, about 1 to 1½ hours. Punch down and divide in half. Place in 2 greased and lightly floured 8" x 4" x 2½" loaf pans. Cover and let rise again until the dough reaches the top of the pans. Bake at 400°F. for 5 minutes; reduce heat to 375°F. and continue to bake 35 to 40 minutes or until the loaves are golden brown. Cool 10 minutes in pans; let cool completely on wire racks. Sprinkle with a thick cloud of powdered sugar.

REMINDER: Tap bottom of loaf with fingers—if it gives off a hollow sound, the loaves are done. If a crustier, crisper loaf is desired, remove from pans when done, return to oven for 10 minutes.

HONEY KAFFEE KLATSCH CAKE

1 package dry granular yeast
¼ cup lukewarm water
1 teaspoon sugar
½ cup scalded milk
¼ cup honey
½ stick sweet butter, melted
½ teaspoon salt
1 egg, beaten
2 cups flour

½ cup currants
1 tablespoon grated orange
   rind
2 tablespoons honey
1 tablespoon cinnamon sugar
⅓ cup coarsely chopped
   walnuts
Rum-Flavored White Icing

Soften yeast in lukewarm water and sprinkle with sugar. Stir. Cover and set aside for 5 minutes until it begins to foam. In a large mixing bowl, combine scalded milk, ¼ cup honey, butter and salt. Stir and cool to lukewarm. Add egg, mix well, then the foaming yeast. Stir well with a wooden spoon. Add 1 cup flour and continue to beat until well blended. Sift remaining 1 cup flour over currants and orange rind, and add to batter. Beat until smooth. Cover with a sheet of buttered wax paper, then with a light kitchen towel. Let rise in a warm place until the mixture is spongy and doubled in bulk, about 1 hour. Stir down. Spoon half of the batter into a well-greased and lightly floured 8-inch tube spring form or into an 8" x 8" x 2" baking pan. Dribble 2 tablespoons honey over top of batter; sprinkle with cinnamon sugar and nuts. Top with remaining batter. Cover. Let rise until doubled in bulk. Bake in a 375°F. oven for 35 minutes or until done. Cool. Spread top with icing.

RUM-FLAVORED WHITE ICING: Combine 1 cup confectioners sugar with 1 tablespoon rum. Beat until smooth. If icing is too thin, add a little more sugar. For a very smooth icing, sift confectioners sugar twice into a bowl before adding the rum.

GOLDEN POPPY SEED COFFEE CAKE

1 package dry granular yeast
⅓ cup lukewarm water
1 teaspoon sugar
½ cup melted butter or margarine
⅓ cup sugar
2 eggs plus 1 egg yolk, beaten
1 scant teaspoon salt

1 tablespoon grated lemon rind
1 cup scalded milk
3 tablespoons poppy seeds
3 tablespoons white raisins
4½ to 5 cups flour
1 egg yolk, beaten with 1 tablespoon water or milk
3 cubes sugar, crushed

Sprinkle dry yeast over lukewarm water, add 1 teaspoon sugar. Stir. Cover and set aside until foaming and doubled in volume. In a large mixing bowl, combine the butter, ⅓ cup sugar, eggs, salt, lemon rind, milk, poppy seeds and raisins. Blend well. Cool to lukewarm. Add foaming yeast. Blend in 3 cups flour and beat vigorously until the batter is smooth; then add just enough flour to make a soft, easy-to-handle dough. Turn out onto a lightly floured board and knead for 10 minutes until satiny smooth. Place in a warm, buttered bowl. Cover with buttered wax paper, then with a light kitchen towel. Set aside in a warm place until doubled in bulk. Turn out onto a lightly floured board and knead for 1 minute. Divide dough into 6 equal parts, roll each part into a ball, then roll into strips about 10 inches long. Place three strips together, side by side, and pinch top together. Braid. Secure ends. Repeat with remaining three strips. Place on a buttered and lightly floured baking sheet or fit into 9" x 5" x 3" loaf pans. Cover. Let rise in a warm place until doubled in bulk. Brush with beaten egg yolk. Sprinkle with crushed sugar. Bake in a 375°F. oven for 35 to 40 minutes until golden brown. Cool on wire cake racks.

OLD FASHIONED SPICED PRUNE LOAF
(The Kind Grandmother Used To Make)

2 packages dry granular yeast
⅓ cup lukewarm water
2 teaspoons sugar
½ cup sugar
⅓ teaspoon cinnamon
½ teaspoon salt
1¾ cups scalded milk
4 tablespoons melted butter

2 eggs, slightly beaten
6½ to 7 cups flour
¼ teaspoon nutmeg
pinch ginger
¾ cup soft, pitted prunes
   (snip into pieces with a
   scissors)
powdered sugar or white icing

Sprinkle yeast over lukewarm water; add 2 teaspoons sugar. Cover and set aside until the yeast begins to foam and doubles in volume. In a large mixing bowl, combine the ½ cup sugar with the cinnamon and salt. Add milk. Stir. Cool to lukewarm, then add the yeast mixture. Stir well. Add butter and eggs. Beat vigorously until thoroughly blended, then add 2½ cups flour, nutmeg and ginger. Beat again, then add just enough flour together with the sliced prunes to make a soft dough. Beat well with a wooden spoon. Turn out onto a lightly floured board and cover; let rest for 10 minutes. Knead dough for 10 minutes until smooth. Divide dough into 2 equal parts. Cover with soft cloths or paper towels for ½ hour. Shape into loaves and place in greased and lightly floured 9" x 5" x 3" loaf pans. Cover and let rise until doubled in bulk. Bake at 400°F. for 10 minutes; reduce heat to 375°F. and continue to bake 35 to 40 minutes or until the bread is golden brown, and tests done when tapped with fingers (if it gives off a hollow sound the bread is done). Cool 5 minutes, remove from baking pans. Cool on wire racks away from drafts. Sprinkle with powdered sugar or spread with white icing if desired.

RAISIN AND NUT SWEET YEAST BREAD

2 packages dry granular yeast
⅓ cup lukewarm water
2 teaspoons sugar
1 cup scalded milk
½ stick sweet butter
½ cup sugar
1 teaspoon salt
1 tablespoon grated lemon rind

2 eggs, beaten
4½ to 5 cups flour
½ teaspoon baking powder
½ cup currants
½ cup white raisins
⅓ cup dark raisins
⅓ cup chopped nuts
1 tablespoon cinnamon sugar

Sprinkle yeast over lukewarm water. Add 2 teaspoons sugar and stir. Cover and set aside until it begins to foam and doubles in volume. Scald milk (do not boil). In a large mixing bowl combine milk, butter, ½ cup sugar, salt and lemon rind. Stir until dissolved. Cool to lukewarm and add foaming yeast and eggs. (If the eggs are small, add an extra egg yolk.) Beat well. Blend flour with baking powder and add just enough of the flour to make a soft dough. Turn out onto a lightly floured board and knead for 10 minutes until satiny smooth. Place the currants on the board and knead into the dough, repeat with the raisins until all have been kneaded into the dough. Shape into a ball and place in a warm buttered bowl. Grease top. Cover and let rise until doubled in bulk, about 1 to 1½ hours. Punch down. Divide dough into two equal portions. Shape into loaves or balls. Place loaves in two buttered and lightly floured 8" x 4" x 2½" loaf pans, or the balls into two Pyrex (1-quart) mixing bowls. Cover and let rise again until doubled in bulk. Brush top with melted butter or beaten egg yolk. Sprinkle with nuts and cinnamon sugar. Bake in a 375°F. oven for 40 minutes or until golden brown. Remove from pans or bowls, cool on wire cake racks.

RAISIN STREUSEL KUCHEN

2 packages dry granular yeast
½ cup lukewarm water
2 teaspoons sugar
1 cup scalded milk
1½ sticks sweet butter or
  margarine
½ cup sugar

6 large egg yolks
1 tablespoon grated lemon
  rind
½ teaspoon salt
½ teaspoon baking powder
5 cups flour
Raisin Streusel Topping

Sprinkle yeast over lukewarm water. Add 2 teaspoons sugar; stir. Cover. Set aside for 5 to 8 minutes until the yeast mixture begins to foam and doubles in volume. In a large mixing bowl, combine the scalded milk, butter and ½ cup sugar. Mix. Cool to lukewarm. Add yeast mixture, egg yolks and lemon rind. Sift salt, baking powder and flour together. Add 2½ cups flour and beat thoroughly until the batter is smooth. Add rest of flour, gradually, beating well after each addition. Brush top with warm melted butter. Cover and let rise in a warm place until doubled in bulk. Punch down, cover and let rise again for 30 minutes. Punch down. Spread dough in two shallow, well-buttered and lightly floured baking pans (8½" x 4½" x 2½"). Sprinkle with Raisin Streusel Topping. Cover and let rise again for 30 minutes. Bake in a 375°F. oven for 30 to 35 minutes or until done. Cool. Cut into squares and serve slightly warm.

RAISIN STREUSEL TOPPING: Blend together ½ cup soft brown sugar, ½ teaspoon nutmeg, 4 tablespoons flour, 1 tablespoon grated lemon rind, 3 tablespoons soft butter or margarine, ½ cup plump Sultana raisins (white), and ½ cup chopped walnuts. Spread topping over batter; sprinkle with 2 teaspoons cinnamon sugar. Pat lightly with fingers.

QUICK LOAF BREADS

Quick breads are so called to distinguish them from yeast breads, which require more time for preparation and baking. The quick breads are made either from batters or quick doughs, leavened with *baking soda* or *baking powder*. They should be prepared quickly, and placed in a preheated oven at once. Batters require less heat then doughs, which are baked in a hot oven. Too much heat will cause bubbles, and also cracks on top of the bread. Have the necessary bread pans ready, greased and lightly floured, so that the batter or dough may go into the oven as quickly as possible. The secret of success in preparing quick breads is in following the recipe exactly, paying special heed to the simple rules of mixing the ingredients. Small loaves are ready if they feel gently firm to touch. Larger loaves should be tested by running a cake tester or toothpick in the center of the loaf—if the skewer or toothpick comes out sticky, the loaf is not baked enough, but if it comes out clean the breads are done. Let stand about 5 minutes before removing them from the bread pans. They will then be easier to handle. Cool on wire cake racks. It is best to lay them to rest on one side across the top of the pans so that the air gets around the bottom and sides of the loaves. When cold return to clean, dry tins. Cover with wax paper or plastic wrap. Leftover quick bread may be sliced and toasted, or placed in damp brown paper bags and reheated in the oven for about 10 to 15 minutes, for a wonderful fresh tasting bread. However, all quick breads are at their best when served fresh the day they are baked.

REMINDER: Heat the oven to the correct temperature before you begin to mix the batter or dough.

SPICED APPLESAUCE LOAF CAKE

1 stick butter or margarine
  (¼ pound)
1 cup sugar
1 egg, beaten
1 cup applesauce
½ cup chopped walnuts
⅓ cup raisins
pinch nutmeg
¼ teaspoon cinnamon

¼ teaspoon allspice
1 teaspoon grated lemon rind
1¾ cups flour
1¾ teaspoons baking soda
½ teaspoon baking powder
1 beaten egg white
2 teaspoons cinnamon-
  flavored powdered sugar

Cream butter and sugar until light and fluffy. Add beaten egg, applesauce, walnuts, raisins, spices, lemon rind, flour, baking soda and baking powder. Mix until well blended. Fold in beaten egg white. Turn into a greased and lightly floured loaf pan. Bake in a 350°F. oven for 35 to 40 minutes or until the loaf tests done. Sprinkle top with the cinnamon-flavored powdered sugar while still warm.

APRICOT BUBBLE LOAF

2 cups flour
½ cup sugar
2 teaspoons baking powder
pinch salt
1 stick sweet butter
  (¼ pound)
1 egg

¼ cup milk
8 soft dried apricots, cut into
  quarters
½ cup melted butter
½ cup sugar, mixed with 1
  teaspoon cinnamon

Sift dry ingredients (except cinnamon sugar) into a large bowl. Cut butter in with a pastry blender until the mixture is crumbly. Stir in the egg and milk to make a soft dough. Break off pieces the size of a large walnut. Roll each between the palms of the hands, press flat, place a piece of apricot in the center, then roll into a ball. Dip in melted butter, then roll in cinnamon sugar. Arrange a layer of the little balls in the bottom of a well-greased and lightly floured loaf pan. Top with another layer of filled apricot balls. Bake in a 375°F. oven for 20 minutes; reduce heat to 350°F. and continue to bake 20 minutes longer or until the loaf is golden brown. Cool 10 minutes. Turn out onto a wire cake rack. When ready to serve break off portions and spread with sweet butter or jam. (Do not use a knife.)

BLUSHING PINK LOAF CAKE

1 cup sugar
½ cup melted butter
2 eggs, beaten
1 cup tomato soup, undiluted
2 cups flour
1 teaspoon baking soda
1 teaspoon baking powder
⅓ teaspoon nutmeg
pinch cloves

pinch cinnamon
½ cup chopped nuts
⅓ cup sliced dates
Topping
1 package softened cream cheese
2 tablespoons sweet cream
1½ cups powdered sugar
1 teaspoon grated lemon rind

Mix sugar with butter, beat until smooth and creamy, add eggs and continue to beat until well blended. Add tomato soup. Mix thoroughly. Sift flour together with the dry ingredients; add nuts and dates, and fold into the creamed soup-mixture. Bake in a well-greased and lightly floured loaf pan in a 325°F. oven for 1 hour or until the loaf tests done. Cool. Blend softened cream cheese with sweet cream, sugar and lemon rind. Beat until the frosting is light and fluffy. When the loaf is thoroughly cooled, spread with the cream-cheese topping.

SUNDAY BREAKFAST LOAF

3½ cups flour
3½ teaspoons baking powder
⅔ cup sugar
1 cup ground hazelnuts or almonds

½ teaspoon salt
1 egg
2 tablespoons soft butter
1 cup milk
white icing or powdered sugar

66

In a large mixing bowl, combine flour, baking powder, sugar, nuts and salt. Mix with a fork. Add egg, butter and milk. Beat with an electric mixer or a wooden spoon until thoroughly blended. Spoon into a greased and lightly floured loaf pan. Let stand for 20 minutes. Then bake in a 325°F. oven for 30 to 35 minutes or until done. Cool. Dribble with white icing or sprinkle with a soft cloud of powdered sugar.

COFFEE KLATSCH CARAWAY LOAF

2 cups flour
2 teaspoons baking powder
½ teaspoon salt
1 cup sugar plus 1 tablespoon
1 stick butter, melted
 (¼ pound)
½ cup orange juice
1 tablespoon grated orange rind
2 eggs, plus 1 egg yolk
1 teaspoon caraway seeds
1 beaten egg white

Combine flour, baking powder, salt and sugar. Add melted butter, orange juice and rind, beat well. Then add eggs, one at a time, beating well after each addition. Fold in caraway seeds and beaten egg white. Turn into a greased and lightly floured loaf pan. Bake in a 350°F. oven for 35 to 45 minutes or until the top is gently firm to touch and the loaf tests done.

GOLDEN CARROT LOAF

4 eggs, separated
1 cup sugar
2 tablespoons grated orange rind
2 tablespoons orange juice
1 *small* tender carrot, grated
2 tablespoons melted butter
¾ cup chopped walnuts
pinch nutmeg
⅔ cup cake flour
powdered sugar (optional)

Beat egg yolks over warm water until thick and lemon colored. Add sugar gradually, beating constantly after each addition. Add orange rind, juice, grated carrot and butter. Mix well, then add the walnuts, nutmeg and cake flour. Mix. Fold in stiffly beaten egg whites. Turn batter into a greased and lightly floured loaf pan or into a well-greased and lightly floured tube spring form. Bake in a 350°F. oven for 35 minutes or until the loaf is golden brown and tests done. Sprinkle with powdered sugar, if desired.

SOUR CREAM CHOCOLATE LOAF

1 cup sugar
2 eggs
1 cup sour cream
½ teaspoon baking soda
1 teaspoon baking powder

½ teaspoon salt
2¼ cups flour
4 tablespoons grated chocolate
powdered sugar (optional)

Beat sugar and eggs until very light. Add sour cream and baking soda, mix. Add baking powder, salt and flour. Beat until well blended. Turn into a greased and lightly floured loaf pan. Sprinkle top with grated chocolate. Swirl chocolate through the batter with the tines of a fork, giving an instant marble effect. Bake in a 350°F. oven for 35 to 40 minutes or until the loaf tests done. Cool. Sprinkle with a soft cloud of powdered sugar, if desired.

SPICED CHOCOLATE LOAF

2 cups flour
½ teaspoon ginger
¼ teaspoon mace
¼ teaspoon nutmeg
¼ teaspoon cloves
¼ teaspoon cinnamon
½ teaspoon salt
½ cup buttermilk

½ cup molasses
1½ teaspoons baking soda
1 tablespoon water
2 squares (ounces) melted chocolate
2 tablespoons shredded candied citron
⅓ cup soft dates, sliced

Sift together flour, spices and salt. Combine buttermilk and molasses with the baking soda dissolved in 1 tablespoon water.

Add with melted chocolate, citron and dates to the flour-spice mixture; beat thoroughly until the batter is well blended. Bake in a 9″ x 5″ x 3″ well-greased and lightly floured loaf pan at 350°F. for 30 to 40 minutes or until the loaf tests done. Cool. Sprinkle with a soft cloud of powdered sugar, if desired.

DANISH COFFEE LOAF

1 cup sugar
1 stick sweet butter
4 eggs
2 tablespoons grated orange rind
1 tablespoon shredded citron
1 tablespoon chopped candied pineapple or orange peel
2 tablespoons orange juice

½ teaspoon crushed cardamom seeds
2½ cups flour
2 teaspoons baking powder
1 cup milk
½ cup coarsely chopped nuts
¼ cup orange juice
2 cups confectioners sugar

Cream sugar and butter until well blended. Add eggs one at a time, beating until the mixture is smooth and fluffy. Add orange rind, citron, candied pineapple or candied orange peel, and 2 tablespoons orange juice. Mix well. Combine crushed cardamom seeds, flour and baking powder and stir in alternately with the milk. Blend. Spoon batter into a greased and lightly floured loaf pan. Bake in a 350°F. oven for 30 to 35 minutes, or until done. Mix orange juice with confectioners sugar to form an icing. Spread over cooled loaf and sprinkle top with nuts.

HARLEQUIN BREAD

1 cup sugar
1 cup milk
2 cups flour
1½ teaspoons baking powder
pinch salt
2 tablespoons soft butter

1 egg, beaten
½ teaspoon cinnamon
4 slices jellied cranberry, cubed
1 teaspoon cinnamon sugar

69

Combine all ingredients except jellied cranberry. Cut jellied cranberry into tiny cubes. Fold gently into the batter, being *very careful* not to crush them. Turn into a greased and lightly floured loaf pan, or into an 8-inch square baking pan. Sprinkle top of batter with 1 teaspoon cinnamon sugar. Bake in a 350°F. oven for 25 to 30 minutes or until golden brown and the loaf tests done.

SPICED HONEY LOAF

3 eggs
1 cup sugar
1 cup honey
1 generous tablespoon tart orange marmalade
1 cup hot black coffee
2 tablespoons melted butter
2 teaspoons double-acting baking powder

3 cups presifted flour
1 teaspoon baking soda
½ teaspoon salt
¼ teaspoon nutmeg
½ teaspoon cinnamon
¼ teaspoon ginger
pinch cloves or allspice
½ cup chopped almonds

Beat eggs until thick and lemon colored, about 10 minutes. Add sugar, gradually, beating after each addition. Add honey, marmalade, coffee and melted butter. Blend well. Combine all dry ingredients and add gradually to the egg mixture. Continue to beat into a smooth batter. Grease and lightly flour 2 medium-size loaf pans and sprinkle with chopped almonds. Spoon batter onto the nuts. Sprinkle top with 2 tablespoons chopped almonds. Bake in a 350°F. oven for 35 to 40 minutes or until the top is gently firm to touch and loaves test done. Cool 10 minutes, then turn out on wire racks to cool.

MARBLE NUT BREAD

½ cup granulated sugar
½ teaspoon salt
4 teaspoons baking powder
3 cups flour
1 teaspoon grated lemon rind
1½ cups milk

1 egg, slightly beaten
½ cup coarsely chopped walnuts
3 tablespoons melted butter
1 teaspoon cocoa
1 tablespoon grated chocolate

70

In a large mixing bowl, combine sugar, salt, baking powder and flour; blend. Add lemon rind, milk and the beaten egg. Dust walnuts with a little flour and add to batter, together with the melted butter. Mix. Turn into 2 medium-size greased and lightly floured loaf pans. Sprinkle top with cocoa, stir gently through the batter with the tines of a fork. Add grated chocolate and swirl gently through top of batter. Bake in a 350°F. oven for 35 to 40 minutes or until the top is gently firm to touch and the loaves test done. Top with a soft cloud of powdered sugar, if desired.

PEANUT BUTTER BREAD

½ cup plus 1 tablespoon
  chunky peanut butter
⅓ cup sugar
1 egg, beaten
2 cups flour

½ teaspoon salt
4 teaspoons baking powder
1 cup milk
½ cup toasted peanuts,
  coarsely chopped

Cream peanut butter with sugar; add egg and continue to beat until the mixture is smooth. Add flour, salt, and baking powder alternately with the milk. Beat well. Fold in ¼ cup chopped peanuts. Turn into a greased and lightly floured loaf pan. Sprinkle top with remaining ¼ cup peanuts. Bake at 350°F. for 40 to 50 minutes or until the top is gently firm to touch and the loaf tests done.

TOASTED PEANUTS: Add a delightful flavor to the peanuts by toasting them *lightly*. Spread peanuts in a baking pan, toast in a low oven (300°F.) until crisp and of a delicate color. Cool, chop coarsely.

QUICK PLANTATION BREAD

½ cup sugar
1 egg plus 1 egg yolk
1¼ cups milk
2 tablespoons melted butter
3 cups biscuit mix

½ apple, cored and cut into small cubes
½ banana, cubed
1 tablespoon citron, cut into small cubes
½ cup chopped nuts

Blend sugar, eggs, milk, butter and biscuit mix. Beat until the mixture is smooth. Sprinkle cubed apple and banana with a little flour, and fold gently into the batter. Add citron and chopped nuts. Bake in a greased and lightly floured square pan in a 350°F. oven for 30 to 35 minutes or until done. *Serve warm.* Cut into 2½-inch squares. Split in half, add dabs of cold sweet butter and serve at once. At its best served fresh the day it's baked.

POPPY SEED LOAF

½ stick butter or margarine
1 cup sugar
2¼ cups cake flour
2½ teaspoons baking powder
½ teaspoon salt
¼ teaspoon nutmeg

1 cup milk
1 teaspoon grated orange rind
1 tablespoon orange juice
⅓ cup poppy seeds
⅓ cup finely chopped nuts
⅓ cup white Sultana raisins
3 egg whites, stiffly beaten

Cream shortening with sugar until smooth. Combine dry ingredients and add alternately with the milk. Beat until well blended. Add orange rind, juice, poppy seeds, nuts and raisins, and lastly fold in the stiffly beaten egg whites. Spoon into a greased and lightly floured 9″ x 5″ x 3″ loaf pan. Bake at 350°F. for 35 to 40 minutes or until the loaf is golden brown and tests done. Cool thoroughly before slicing. This loaf has excellent keeping qualities. It is especially delightful served with Tangy Apricot Spread.

TANGY APRICOT SPREAD: Soften 1 stick sweet butter (¼ pound), and combine with 2 tablespoons apricot jam, 2 tablespoons Seville orange marmalade, 1 teaspoon grated lemon rind, 1 teaspoon lemon juice and 1 tablespoon sherry. Beat until smooth. Pack into a small glass dish. Chill. When ready to serve, let stand at room temperature for several minutes for easy spreading.

BYRD MILL FOXHUNTERS PANBREAD

Foxhunters meal is a natural, flavorful wholegrain meal, stone ground in a 228-year old Virginia mill. (See Sources of Supply.) It contains all the natural vitamins and minerals.

2 eggs	2 tablespoons brown sugar or honey
1 cup milk	1½ cups Foxhunters meal
4 tablespoons butter or margarine	2½ teaspoons baking powder
	1 teaspoon salt

Beat eggs. Add milk, butter or margarine, and sugar or honey. Stir in the Foxhunters meal, baking powder and salt. Stir only enough to dampen dry ingredients. Do not beat. Let stand for a few minutes while greasing pan. Pour batter into an 8-inch square baking pan. Bake in a 425°F. oven for 20 minutes or until done. If desired, instead of the pan-bread, drop mixture by spoonfuls into greased muffin tins and bake until a delicate golden brown.

ALL-RAISIN BREAD

3 cups flour	2 eggs, slightly beaten
5 teaspoons baking powder	1 cup milk
1 scant teaspoon salt	6 tablespoons melted butter
½ cup plump dark raisins	1 tablespoon grated orange rind
⅓ cup white Sultana raisins	powdered sugar or white icing
⅓ cup currants	

73

Sift dry ingredients together; add dark and light raisins and currants. Mix with a fork until all the raisins are completely coated with the flour mixture. Add eggs to milk, mix well and blend together with the dry ingredients. Add melted butter and orange rind. Beat together. Fill 8" x 4" x 3" greased and lightly floured loaf pans ⅔ full of batter. Let stand for 20 minutes before baking. Bake in a 350°F. oven for 35 to 45 minutes or until the top is gently firm to touch and golden brown. Test with a toothpick; if it comes out clean the loaf is done.

NOTE: For an exotic twist and extravagant touch, substitute the meats of soft *lichee nuts* in place of the raisins. Remove pits, and snip the soft fruity meats in halves or thirds with a sharp scissors. Sift the flour over a generous ½ to ⅔ cup of the lichees; reserve a few and arrange on top of batter. Sprinkle lightly with a little sugar flavored with a pinch of ginger and 1 tablespoon of chopped candied ginger.

SALLY LUNN LOAF

1 egg	3½ cups flour
1 scant cup sugar	2 teaspoons baking powder
3 tablespoons butter	½ teaspoon salt
1 cup milk	½ cup currants (optional)

Beat egg with sugar; add butter, and cream well. Then add the milk alternately with the flour, baking powder and salt. Blend well. If currants are desired, mix with a little flour and fold into the batter. Bake in a greased and lightly floured loaf pan at 350°F. for 30 to 35 minutes or until done. Serve warm. Have ready a small pot of whipped sweet butter and favorite jam.

QUICK SESAME SEED TEA LOAF

1 stick sweet butter
  (¼ pound)
3 eggs
1 cup sugar
½ teaspoon vanilla
1 teaspoon grated lemon rind
1 cup milk

2 cups flour
3½ teaspoons baking powder
½ teaspoon salt
2 tablespoons sesame seeds
1 tablespoon cinnamon sugar
1 tablespoon sesame seeds

With an electric mixer, cream butter and eggs at low speed for 2 minutes. Add sugar gradually then vanilla, lemon rind and milk. Increase speed and beat until well-blended. Mix flour with baking powder and salt and add a little at a time. Continue to beat until thoroughly mixed. Fold in 2 tablespoons sesame seeds. Turn into a greased and lightly floured 9" x 5" x 3" loaf pan. Sprinkle top with cinnamon sugar and remaining sesame seeds. Bake in at 350°F. for 30 to 40 minutes or until the loaf tests done. Cool on wire cake rack before slicing.

DELICATE STREUSEL LOAF

1 cup flour
2 teaspoons baking powder
1 tablespoon grated lemon
  rind
¾ cup sugar
¾ stick sweet butter
3 eggs, separated

STREUSEL TOPPING:
4 tablespoons flour
4 tablespoons soft butter
½ cup soft brown sugar
½ teaspoon cinnamon
4 tablespoons finely chopped
  nuts

Batter: Combine flour and baking powder; add lemon rind. Cream sugar and butter thoroughly and gradually add the egg yolks, one at a time; beat until well blended. Fold in flour mixture, ⅓ at a time, beating well after each addition. Fold in stiffly beaten egg whites. Spoon into a well-greased and lightly floured 9" x 5" x 3" loaf pan. *Streusel Topping:* Mix the flour, butter, brown sugar, cinnamon and nuts until the mixture is crumbly. Sprinkle mixture on top of batter and pat gently with fingers so that the streusel mixture will adhere to the top of the batter. Bake in a 350°F. oven for 30 to 40 minutes or until the loaf tests done. Allow to cool in pan for 20 minutes.

QUICK AND EASY VIRGINIA GRITS BREAD

A different, unusually delicious bread to serve warm with pot roast gravy or dribbled with melted sweet butter. Grits, which resemble a white, coarse corn meal, are available even in northern supermarkets.

2 cups milk	½ teaspoon salt
½ cup grits	1 beaten egg
2 tablespoons butter	1 teaspoon sugar

In a saucepan, bring milk to boiling point. Slowly add the grits. Cook, stirring constantly, for 15 minutes until the grits begin to thicken. When thick, remove from heat and beat in the butter, salt, egg and sugar. Grease a 9-inch skillet with butter, heat in a hot oven for 5 minutes. Pour grits mixture into the hot bubbling butter and bake 30 minutes in a 400°F. oven.

WHOLE WHEAT NUT BREAD

1 stick butter	4 teaspoons baking powder
1 scant cup sugar	¾ cup coarsely chopped nuts
2 eggs, beaten	2 cups flour
1 cup milk	1 cup whole wheat flour
½ teaspoon salt	1 tablespoon cinnamon sugar

Cream butter and sugar until fluffy. Add eggs and milk. Mix well. Combine salt, baking powder, ½ cup chopped nuts, white flour and whole wheat flour. Blend well. Fill greased and lightly floured 8" x 4" x 2½" loaf pans half full with the batter. Sprinkle with remaining ¼ cup walnuts and cinnamon sugar.

Cover with wax paper and let stand for 20 minutes. Bake in a 350°F. oven for 35 to 45 minutes or until the top is gently firm to touch and golden brown.

REMINDER: Small loaves of quick bread are ready if they feel gently firm to touch—larger loaves should be tested by running a cake tester or toothpick in the center of the loaf. If it comes out sticky the loaf is not baked enough, but if it comes out clean the loaf is done.

CORN & SPOON BREADS, JOHNNY CAKES & HUSH PUPPIES

CORN BREAD

Two cupfuls Indian, one cupful of wheat
One cupful sour milk, one cupful sweet,
One good egg that you will beat;
Half a cupful of molasses, too;
Half a cupful sugar add thereto;
With one spoonful of butter new,
Salt and soda each a spoon;
Mix up quickly and bake it soon;
Then you'll have corn bread complete.
Best of all corn bread you meet.
It will make your boy's eyes shine
If he is like that boy of mine;
If you have a dozen boys
To increase your household joys,
Double, then, this rule, I should,
And you'll have two corn cakes good,
When you've nothing nice for tea,
This the very thing will be.
All the men that I have seen
Say it is, of all cakes, queen;
Good enough for any king
That a husband home can bring;
Warming up the human stove, cheering
Up the hearts you love;
And only Tyndall can explain
The links between corn bread and brain,
Get a husband what he likes,
And save a hundred household strikes.
                              —Lydia Millard (1908)

CORN BREAD

Long before America became a nation, the Indians had already taught the use of corn meal to the early American housewife. And it was not long before the quickly and easily made corn bread became—and still remains—a favorite in American households.

The early settlers found that grinding corn on genuine Buhr stones protected the rich, full-bodied flavor of the grain. The old-fashioned water-ground corn, while yielding a coarse meal, produces a far more flavorful bread than the finer steel-cut variety.

Basically, the corn meal for many of the recipes is cooked first until thick and smooth, and then beaten with eggs, butter, milk and various other ingredients into a well-blended batter. It is then usually baked in shallow baking pans or in oven-to-table baking dishes.

The pans should be greased more thoroughly for corn bread than for that made from all-purpose flour. To cut warm corn bread heat a sharp knife.

GOLDEN BATTER CORN BREAD
(With Grains of Rice)

Instant rice is ideal for this recipe, since each grain cooks tender and separate. Soft gummy rice will result in a heavy bread.

2 tablespoons melted butter
1 cup cooked rice
½ teaspoon salt
2 eggs, beaten
1 cup milk

½ cup yellow corn meal
1 teaspoon baking powder
2 teaspoons freshly grated carrot

Combine all ingredients. Mix well with a wooden spoon. Spoon batter into a buttered and lightly floured shallow 8-inch square baking pan. Bake at 350°F. for 30 minutes, or until the top is gently firm to touch, and a delicate golden brown. Makes an unusual corn bread with a pudding-like consistency. Serve warm dribbled with melted butter.

COUNTRY CORN BREAD WITH BACON BITS

1 cup corn meal
½ teaspoon salt
1 teaspoon sugar
½ teaspoon baking soda
1 scant teaspoon baking
   powder

1 egg
½ cup buttermilk
2 strips bacon, cooked until
   crisp and broken into bits

Dry the crisp bacon bits with a soft paper towel until completely free from grease. Combine all ingredients except bacon. Beat well. Fold in the bacon bits. Turn into a shallow, 7-inch square baking pan. Bake in a 400°F. oven until golden brown, about 20 to 25 minutes. Serve warm.

FAVORITE COUNTRY CORN BREAD
(With Fresh Corn Kernels)

½ cup flour
½ cup plus 2 tablespoons
   yellow corn meal
1 tablespoon sugar
1 scant teaspoon salt

2 eggs
1½ cups milk
1 cup fresh corn kernels
3 tablespoons melted butter
   or margarine

In a large mixing bowl, combine flour, corn meal, sugar and salt. Blend well. Beat the eggs until thick, add the milk, and continue to beat until well blended. Add corn kernels and butter. Mix. Add the egg-corn mixture gradually to the dry ingredients. Stir briskly. Pour into a warm, buttered oven-to-table baking dish. Bake at 375°F. for 35 minutes or until the corn bread is golden brown. Serve hot with gobs of sweet butter.

NOTE: If fresh corn is out of season, use well-drained canned corn kernels. For a change in taste and flavor, add a dash of freshly ground black pepper, 1 teaspoon freshly minced parsley and 1 tablespoon freshly grated carrot.

PIRI BROWN'S COUNTRY STYLE CORN BREAD

¾ cup yellow corn meal
1 cup all purpose flour
2½ teaspoons baking powder
½ teaspoon baking soda
½ teaspoon salt
1 egg plus 1 egg yolk

½ cup milk
¾ cup thick sour cream
1 teaspoon caraway seeds
2 tablespoons melted sweet
butter

Combine all dry ingredients except caraway seeds. Blend beaten eggs with milk and sour cream. Add gradually to the dry mixture; then the caraway seeds and melted butter. Heat a buttered and lightly floured 8-inch square baking pan, add batter and bake in a 425°F. oven until golden brown and gently firm to touch. Serve hot.

BYRD MILL FEATHERLIGHT CORN BREAD

2 eggs
4 cups buttermilk
4 cups yellow corn meal
1 cup unbleached flour

2 teaspoons baking soda
2 teaspoons salt
3 teaspoons sugar

Beat eggs until very light with a rotary beater or wire whisk. Add to buttermilk. Mix in corn meal. Sift together the flour, soda, salt and sugar. Blend into the corn meal mixture. Cover dough lightly with a sprinkling of cornmeal and let rise in a warm place for 1½ to 2 hours. When dough is light, place in shallow square well-buttered baking dishes. Bake in a 350°F. oven for 1 hour or until golden brown. Cut into squares and serve warm. If desired, pass a small bowl of thick, cold sour cream and use as a topping, sprinkled lightly with cinnamon sugar.

NOTE: For leftover corn bread, split squares, toast lightly and spread with fresh whipped sweet butter and favorite jam.

HONEY CORN BREAD

1 quart fresh buttermilk
2¼ cups yellow corn meal
1 teaspoon baking soda
½ teaspoon salt

2 tablespoons golden orange blossom honey
3 eggs

Combine all ingredients. Beat until smooth. Spoon into a well-buttered shallow baking pan. Bake at 400°F. for 30 to 40 minutes or until golden brown. Although the batter will be thin it bakes into a firm delicious corn bread.

MOLASSES CORN BREAD

1 cup plus 2 tablespoons flour
1 cup corn meal
½ teaspoon salt
2½ teaspoons baking powder
1 level teaspoon baking soda

2 eggs, beaten
1½ cups buttermilk
3 tablespoons melted butter
4 tablespoons dark unsulfured molasses

Combine flour, corn meal, salt, baking powder and baking soda. Add the beaten eggs to the buttermilk, butter and molasses. Blend. Add gradually to dry ingredients, beating well after each addition. Turn into a shallow well-buttered baking dish. Bake in a 400°F. oven for 35 minutes or until firm and golden brown. Cool. Cut into squares; serve topped with Molasses Butter.

MOLASSES BUTTER: Soften ¼ pound sweet butter, whip with a rotary beater until light and fluffy. Gradually add 3 tablespoons molasses. Blend well.

NUTTY CORN BREAD

2 eggs
1 tablespoon melted butter
1¼ cups milk
½ cup finely ground walnuts
2 cups yellow corn meal
⅓ cup flour

½ teaspoon salt
1 teaspoon baking soda
1 teaspoon baking powder
1 tablespoon sugar
⅓ cup coarsely chopped walnuts

Beat eggs until thick. Add butter and milk. Gradually add the finely ground walnuts, corn meal and flour. Mix the salt, baking soda, baking powder and sugar, and add to the corn meal mixture. Blend well. Place batter in a buttered and lightly floured shallow 8- or 9-inch square baking pan. Sprinkle top with coarsely chopped nuts. Bake in a 400°F. oven for 25 minutes or until golden brown.

PEANUT CORN BREAD

1 cup yellow corn meal
1 cup flour
2 teaspoons baking powder
2 eggs
1 cup milk
2 tablespoons sugar
pinch salt
3 tablespoons melted butter or margarine
½ cup coarsely chopped salted peanuts

Combine corn meal, flour, and baking powder. In a large mixing bowl, beat eggs until thick and lemon colored; add milk, sugar, salt and butter. Gradually add dry ingredients, beating well after each addition. Fold in chopped peanuts. Spoon batter into a warm buttered baking dish. Bake in a 400°F. oven for 30 minutes or until firm and golden brown. Cut into squares and serve warm.

NOTE: If desired, this may be served with a peanut butter spread. Beat ½ to ¾ cup peanut butter with 1 to 2 tablespoons milk or light cream until very smooth.

QUICK CORN BREAD

2 cups yellow corn meal
1 teaspoon baking soda
½ teaspoon salt
2 tablespoons melted butter
1 egg, well beaten
1 cup buttermilk
cold sweet butter for topping
coarse salt (kosher type)

Combine all ingredients except the sweet butter for topping and the coarse salt, using just enough buttermilk to make a thick batter. Pour into a well-buttered shallow 8-inch square baking pan. Bake in a 400° to 425° F. oven until golden brown. Serve topped with bits of cold butter, and sprinkled lightly with coarse salt.

SOUTHERN SOFT CORN BREAD

1 cup cold boiled rice
½ cup yellow corn meal
2 eggs plus 1 egg yolk, beaten

4 cups milk
½ teaspoon salt
1 tablespoon melted butter

Combine all ingredients and beat well together. Spoon into a well-buttered baking dish. Bake in a 350°F. oven until thick and custardlike, and the top is a nice golden brown. Serve hot in the same dish as baked.

SOUTHERN SWEET CORN MEAL BATTER BREAD

1 cup yellow corn meal
1 tablespoon butter
1 teaspoon salt
1 cup boiling water

3 tablespoons sugar
2 eggs, beaten
2 cups buttermilk
¾ teaspoon baking soda

In a mixing bowl, combine corn meal, butter, salt and boiling water. Beat vigorously until well blended. Add sugar, eggs and buttermilk, beating all the while. Stir in baking soda at the last minute. Pour at once into a buttered baking dish. Bake in a 400°F. oven for 45 minutes or until firm and golden brown. Serve from baking dish with plenty of whipped butter and warm honey or maple syrup.

SPOON BREAD

Spoon bread, a delicious, soft, custardlike bread is served from the pan or dish in which it was baked, and *spooned* into individual serving dishes. Many family recipes are secretly guarded, cherished, and passed on from mother to daughter. Delicious and feather-light in texture, spoon bread is excellent served dribbled with warm melted butter, warm maple syrup, honey or molasses.

CRUNCHY SPOON BREAD

2 cups yellow corn meal
½ teaspoon salt
1 cup boiling water
3 tablespoons butter or margarine

2 teaspoons baking powder
2 eggs, separated
1½ cups milk
1 tablespoon brown sugar
Corn Flake Topping

Scald corn meal and salt with boiling water. Add butter. Cover and set aside until cool. With a wire whisk beat in baking powder, egg yolks, milk and brown sugar. Beat thoroughly. Fold in stiffly beaten egg whites. Turn into a buttered shallow baking dish. Sprinkle with Corn Flake Topping. Pat lightly with fingers. Bake in a 375°F. oven for 30 to 40 minutes or until golden brown. Spoon portions into individual dishes. Serve warm.

CORN FLAKE TOPPING: Toss together in a mixing bowl until well blended 1 cup cornflakes, 1 tablespoon cinnamon sugar, 1 tablespoon brown sugar and 1 tablespoon coarsely chopped nuts.

GEORGIA SPOON BREAD

4 egg yolks
6 tablespoons sugar
1 stick butter (¼ pound)
½ teaspoon salt
pinch nutmeg
1 cup corn meal

1 cup flour
2 teaspoons baking powder
3 cups milk
4 egg whites, beaten stiff with a pinch of salt

Beat egg yolks over warm water until thick and lemon colored. Add sugar and continue to beat until well blended. Beat in softened butter with a rotary or electric beater until creamy. Sift dry ingredients; add alternately with the milk to the butter-yolk mixture. Fold in stiffly beaten egg whites. Pour into a well-buttered casserole. Bake in a 350°F. oven for 45 to 50 minutes, or until firm and golden brown.

PIQUANT SPOON BREAD

2 cups yellow corn meal
2 cups scalded milk
1 tablespoon melted butter
1 teaspoon sugar

1 teaspoon onion salt
1 teaspoon dry onion flakes
2 eggs, separated
2 teaspoons grated cheese

Pour corn meal in a thin stream into the scalded milk, stirring vigorously with a wooden spoon until the mixture is smooth and free from lumps. (If lumps persist, beat with a rotary beater.) Cook over medium heat until the mixture thickens. Add butter, sugar, salt, and onion flakes. Mix well. Beat in egg yolks. Beat egg whites until they hold soft peaks, then gently fold into batter. Spoon into a buttered baking dish and sprinkle top with grated cheese. Bake in a 350°F. oven for 35 to 45 minutes until golden brown. Serve hot from baking dish.

LOUISA, VIRGINIA SPECIAL SPOON BREAD

3 cups milk
1 cup Byrd Mill corn meal
salt

2 tablespoons butter or
margarine
2 tablespoons sugar
2 eggs, separated

Scald milk; add corn meal, salt, butter and sugar. Cook until thick and smooth, stirring constantly. Remove from heat, beat vigorously, cool for a few minutes, then add the egg yolks, beating all the while. Fold in stiffly beaten egg whites. Spoon into a well-buttered casserole and bake in a 350°F. oven for 45 minutes or until golden brown. Serve hot with plenty of warm melted butter and maple syrup.

WHITE CORN MEAL SPOON BREAD

2 cups milk
1 cup water
1 cup white corn meal
1 teaspoon salt

1½ teaspoons baking powder
4 eggs, separated
2 tablespoons melted butter
or margarine

Combine and scald milk and water. Add to corn meal, stirring until very smooth. Cook over hot water (in a double boiler) until thick. Cool slightly. Add salt, baking powder, egg yolks and melted butter. Beat well. Fold in stiffly beaten egg whites. Turn into a hot, well-buttered casserole. Bake in a 375°F. oven for 40 to 45 miuntes or until the top is firm and golden brown. Spoon onto warm serving plates. Serve with warm maple syrup and melted butter.

CORN MEAL APPLE PONE

1 cup corn meal
1 cup boiling water
1 egg, beaten
1 teaspoon sugar

1 cup chopped apples
1 tablespoon melted butter
½ teaspoon salt
2 teaspoons baking powder

Place corn meal in a bowl and scald with the boiling water. Stir until smooth. When cold add beaten egg and beat vigorously for 5 minutes. Stir in the sugar, apples, butter, salt and baking powder. Mix well. Bake in a well-greased 8-inch, shallow square baking pan in a 350°F. oven for 25 to 30 minutes or until the top is golden brown. Serve the pone warm. Pass a pitcher of sweet cream or warm syrup, or sift a soft cloud of powdered sugar over the pone. Delicious!

CREOLE JOHNNY CAKE

3 eggs
3 cups yellow corn meal
2 to 3 tablespoons sugar

1 teaspoon salt
2 tablespoons melted butter
2 cups milk

Beat eggs over warm water for 5 minutes. Add corn meal, sugar and salt. Beat again, until well blended. Add melted butter, then the milk. Mix well. Drop by heaping spoonfuls on a well-greased baking sheet, about ½-inch thick. Leave a little space between each one. Bake at 325°F. for 30 minutes.

During baking time, brush with melted butter from time to time. Split while still hot, add a dab of cold butter and serve at once.

NOTE: Watch carefully so as not to over-bake. For crispness and golden color baste often with melted butter. This recipe produces a rich and crisp Johnny cake.

MARY'S JOHNNY CAKE

½ cup flour
2 cups yellow corn meal
2 teaspoons baking power
½ teaspoon salt
2 tablespoons brown sugar

1 egg
1 cup milk
2 tablespoons melted butter
or margarine
2 tablespoons sesame seeds

In a large mixing bowl, combine flour, corn meal, baking powder, salt and brown sugar. Mix well. Add beaten egg, milk and butter. Blend. Spoon into a buttered 8″ square baking dish. Sprinkle top with sesame seeds. Press down lightly with fingers. Bake in a 400° to 425°F. oven for 20 minutes, reduce heat to 350° and continue to bake until golden brown. Cut into squares and serve while still warm.

HUSH PUPPIES

Hush puppies originated around campfires in the south, where fishermen gathered and waited to bring in their daily catch. Many a tall story was told around the blazing fires. While frying the batter in deep hot fat, their hungry barking dogs sniffing the appetizing aroma of the frying cornpones, were only quieted when the little fried cakes were thrown out to them with a loud warning, "HUSH, PUPPIES." A great southern favorite served hot from the pan with fish dinners.

1 teaspoon baking soda	pinch salt
1½ cups buttermilk	1 small onion, diced, *or*
1½ cups yellow corn meal	½ cup minced scallions
½ cup flour	pinch cracked black pepper

Mix baking soda with buttermilk, then mix with corn meal and flour to form a stiff batter. Add salt, onion and pepper. Drop batter in spoonfuls in hot deep fat (375°F.). Do not crowd. Cook until browned.

ANOTHER METHOD:

2 teaspoons baking powder	1½ cups milk
1 teaspoon salt	½ cup water
2 cups corn meal	1 medium onion, diced, *or*
pinch nutmeg	½ cup minced scallions
pinch cracked black pepper	

Combine baking powder, salt, corn meal, nutmeg and pepper together. Stir in milk, water, and chopped onion. Mix into a soft dough. If necessary add a little more corn meal, so that the soft dough will be easy to handle. Dip hands in flour and form 5-inch long pones. (They should look somewhat like frankfurter rolls, with tapered ends.) Fry in deep hot fat, (375°F.) turning with a spatula until browned on all sides. Drain on soft paper towels. Serve hot. Either method produces appetizing, flavorful hush puppies.

NATURAL WHOLE GRAIN BREADS

OLD-FASHIONED BUCKWHEAT "HEALTH" BREAD

2 scant cups Old Fashioned
    Elam's Buckwheat Flour
1 tablespoon wheat germ
2 teaspoons baking soda
1½ teaspoons cream of tartar
4 tablespoons raw brown
    sugar or honey

1 egg, beaten
1 cup milk
4 tablespoons sweet butter or
    margarine, softened
½ cup plump white Sultana
    raisins

Sift dry ingredients together in a mixing bowl. Add beaten egg, milk and butter or margarine. Beat well with a wooden spoon. Fold in raisins. Bake in a greased and lightly floured loaf pan in a 350°F. oven for 35 to 45 minutes or until the loaf is golden brown and tests done.

NOTE: Old Fashioned Buckwheat Flour, raw sugar and wheat germ is available in all health or specialty food stores, or direct from Elam's Mills (see Sources of Supply). These items are organically grown and are not sprayed with any chemicals. The bread has a delicate nutty flavor and makes excellent toast. Organically grown dates, nuts, prunes or figs, cut into small pieces, may be used in place of the Sultana raisins. All the types of flour used in this chapter are milled and stone-ground on genuine old-fashioned burstones, to protect the rich full-bodied flavor of the whole grains. Nothing is taken from or added to the flour—no bleaching agents, chemicals or preservatives.

WHOLE GRAIN COUNTRY BREAD F

2 cups warm milk
2 packages dry granular yeast
1 teaspoon salt
½ cup dark unsulphured molasses
2 tablespoons soft butter or margarine

2 cups unbleached white flour with added wheat germ
1 cup rye flour
1 cup unbleached white flour
1 cup whole wheat flour
3 tablespoons melted butter

Combine warm milk, yeast, salt and molasses in a large mixing bowl. Stir. Cover and let stand until the mixture is bubbly. Add softened butter and 2 cups unbleached white flour with added wheat germ. Beat for 10 minutes at low speed in an electric mixer. Then add rye flour and beat by hand with a wooden spoon; add remaining flour to make a soft dough. Turn out onto a lightly floured board; grease hands with a little butter or margarine and knead until the dough is smooth and easy to handle. Place in a warm, well-greased bowl, turning dough until the top is greased. Cover with wax paper, then with a cloth and let stand in a warm place until doubled in bulk. Punch down. Cover and let rise again. Punch down, turn out onto a lightly floured board, divide in half, shape into two loaves, and place them in 9" x 5" x 3" loaf pans. Cover, let rise until doubled in bulk. Bake in a 300°F. oven for 1 hour or until golden brown. If the bread sounds hollow when tapped, it is done. Brush top with warm melted butter. Cool in tins for 10 minutes. Cool on wire racks.

NOTE: Unbleached white flour with wheat germ added (Byrd Mill) contains the natural nutritious wheat germ, one of nature's richest sources of vitamins. Excellent flour for baking bread, muffins, cake, cookies and pastry.

Whole Grain flours may be obtained from specialty food or health food stores, or direct from Byrd Mill (see Sources of Supply). These whole grain flours are made from the choicest fresh milled grains, and contain no bleaches or preservatives. They should be kept in a cool place or refrigerated, even in your deep freeze. Before using let stand at room temperature.

⨍ ENRICHED GLUTEN BREAD

4 cups skim milk
¾ cup instant non-fat dry
  milk
1½ packages dry granular
  yeast

¼ cup lukewarm water
1 teaspoon salt
4 cups gluten flour
2 egg whites, slightly beaten
1 teaspoon wheat germ

Scald milk, do not boil. Remove from heat, cool slightly. Stir
in non-fat dry milk until dissolved. Cool to lukewarm. Dissolve
yeast in ¼ cup lukewarm water, stir. Cover and let stand until
foaming. Add salt. Add gluten flour gradually, 1 cup at a time,
beating well after each addition. Add the slightly beaten egg
whites. Spoon the thick batter into two 8″ x 4″ x 2½″ loaf
pans, greased and lightly floured. Sprinkle top with wheat
germ. Cover with a clean cloth. Set aside in a warm place and
allow to rise for 1 hour. Bake at 375°F. for 50 to 60 minutes
or until done.

NOTE: The idea of including recipes in this book for gluten
breads was suggested to us by Alfred and Dora McCann
during a recent radio interview. This charming and well-
informed WOR radio team, nationally famous as The Mc-
Canns, told us that they were constantly receiving inquiries for
gluten flour products, especially from those maintaining diets.
It seems that few recipes of this type are available even though
a great many dieters find gluten breads and muffins both
necessary and valuable to their diets. Benefiting from the
McCann's experience and acting on their advice, we have
included a number of recipes for gluten products in this book.

⨍ GLUTEN BREAD

1 scant cup lukewarm water
⅓ cup instant non-fat dry
  milk
1 teaspoon salt
1½ teaspoons dry granular
  yeast

1 tablespoon sugar
3½ to 4 cups gluten flour
1 tablespoon melted butter or
  margarine
warm melted butter
1 teaspoon sesame seeds

Pour lukewarm water into a mixing bowl, add dry milk. Stir quickly until dissolved. Add salt, yeast and sugar. Stir. Cover and let stand until foaming and very light. Beat in 1 cup gluten flour, add 1 tablespoon melted shortening. Beat vigorously until the batter is smooth. Add remaining flour and beat well until the dough leaves the sides of the bowl. Turn out onto a lightly floured board, sprinkling the board with a little gluten flour as the dough will be slightly sticky. Knead dough until smooth and elastic, about 10 minutes. Place dough in a warm greased bowl, turning the dough to grease top. Cover, set aside in a warm place until doubled in bulk, about 1½ hours. When light, turn out onto a lightly floured board, knead for 2 minutes, then shape into a round or oblong loaf. Brush top with warm melted butter and sprinkle with sesame seeds if desired. Cover and let rise again until doubled in bulk. Bake in a 400°F. oven for 40 to 45 minutes. Cool thoroughly before slicing.

GLUTEN FLOUR: Practically sodium-free, gluten flour is especially prepared for low-starch and low-sodium diets. Salt may be omitted if not permitted in diet. Available in most health food and specialty shops, or order direct from mill (see Sources of Supply).

QUICK-AND-EASY GLUTEN BREAD

1 cup lukewarm water
1½ packages dry granular yeast
1 teaspoon sugar
½ pound gluten flour
¼ teaspoon salt

Combine lukewarm water, yeast and sugar. Stir. Cover and set aside until foaming and doubled in volume. Add flour and salt, and mix thoroughly. When the dough leaves the sides of the bowl, turn out onto a lightly floured board and knead until smooth. Place in a warm greased bowl. Cover with a soft clean cloth and let rise in a warm place for 1 hour or until doubled in bulk. Shape into a loaf and bake in an 8" x 4" x 2½" greased and lightly floured loaf pan at 375°F. for 40 to 45 minutes.

SALT-FREE BREAD

Despite the lack of salt, this an unusually palatable bread with real flavor appeal.

1 stick sweet butter or salt-free margarine
2 tablespoons honey
2 packages dry granular yeast
⅓ cup lukewarm water
1 tablespoon sugar

2 cups scalded milk, cooled to lukewarm
2 eggs
6 cups unbleached flour
1 slightly beaten egg, plus 1 tablespoon water
poppy seeds

Soften butter and blend well with the honey. Sprinkle yeast over the lukewarm water; add sugar. Cover. Set aside in a warm place until it begins to foam and doubles in volume. Add the milk to the creamed butter mixture. When cool, add eggs and yeast mixture. Add flour, gradually kneading the dough into a soft ball. Turn out onto a lightly floured board, and knead for 10 minutes. Place in a warm greased bowl, turning to grease top of the dough. Cover with wax paper, then with a clean cloth. When doubled in bulk, punch down; let rise again until doubled in bulk. Punch down again and knead for 5 minutes. Shape into two loaves and place in two greased and lightly floured 9" x 5" x 3" loaf pans. Brush tops with beaten egg. Cover and let rise again until doubled. Bake in a 425°F. oven for 10 minutes. Reduce heat to 375°F. and continue to bake until a delicate golden brown, about 30 to 40 minutes. Tap bread—if it sounds hollow it is done. Cool in pans for 10 minutes. Turn out on wire racks to cool thoroughly. If a crustier bread is desired, remove from pans and return to oven for 10 minutes.

NUTRITIOUS SEED BREAD

2 cups unbleached white flour
  with added wheat germ
½ cup sugar
3 teaspoons baking powder
½ teaspoon salt
2 teaspoons crushed sun-
  flower seeds

3 teaspoons sesame seeds
1 teaspoon caraway seeds
½ cup white Sultana raisins
2 eggs
milk

Sift together dry ingredients, mix. Add seeds and raisins. Mix again. Beat eggs with milk; gradually add to the dry ingredients. Stir until the dough leaves the sides of the bowl. The dough will be slightly sticky. Turn into a greased and lightly floured 9" x 5" x 3" loaf pan. Sprinkle top with a little cinnamon sugar, if desired. Bake in a 350°F. oven for 45 to 55 minutes or until the bread tests done. Turn out of pan and cool on a wire rack.

NOTE: Sunflower and sesame seeds are available in most specialty and health food stores. An excellent source of proteins, vitamins and minerals, these tasty seeds add a nutty flavor to the bread and toast to a crisp golden brown.

SEVEN GRAIN PROTEIN BREAD

You will never know how really good bread can taste until you try this recipe.

2 cups hot water
2 tablespoons honey
½ stick sweet butter or
  margarine
2 teaspoons salt
2 packages dry granular
  yeast
½ cup lukewarm water

2 teaspoons sugar
3 eggs
1 cup 7-grain Wonder Meal
6½ cups unbleached flour
½ cup wheat germ
1 egg yolk beaten with 1
  tablespoon water

Pour the hot water in a large mixing bowl and add the honey, butter and salt. Cool to lukewarm. Sprinkle yeast over the ½ cup lukewarm water; add sugar. Cover and set aside until foaming and doubled in volume. Add foaming yeast to lukewarm honey-water mixture. Add eggs. Beat with a wire whisk. Add Wonder Meal, and half of the unbleached flour. Beat well with a wooden spoon. Gradually add the remaining flour and wheat germ until a soft dough is formed. Turn out onto a lightly floured board and knead for 10 to 15 minutes; flour hands while kneading. Slap the dough on the board, baker fashion, about 10 times to break the air bubbles. (This also reduces the kneading time.) Place the dough into a large, warm and well-greased bowl. Turn dough several times until all sides are greased. Cover with wax paper, then with a clean cloth, and set in a warm place, free from drafts, until doubled in bulk. Punch down with a floured fist and let rise again until doubled. Turn out onto a lightly floured board and knead gently for 5 minutes. Cut dough into nine even pieces. Roll each piece into a ball. Place three balls in each of three well-greased and lightly floured 8″ x 4″ x 2½″ loaf pans. Cover and set aside in a warm place until doubled in bulk. (The dough should reach the rim of the bread pans.) Brush with beaten egg yolk and sprinkle with poppy seeds, if desired. Bake in a preheated 425°F oven for 10 minutes. Reduce heat to 375°F. and continue to bake about 30 to 40 minutes longer or until the loaves are golden brown. Tap bread with fingers; if it sounds hollow the bread is done. If a well-crusted bread is desired, remove bread from pans, then return to oven (350°F.) for 10 minutes. Cool on wire racks or place bread across top of pans. Slice when cold. This also makes excellent golden toast.

NOTE: When we prepared this recipe, we used freshly ground flour from a local mill, and natural uncooked sunflower honey. The flour has a light beige tinge and the wheat germ has a rich nutty flavor which enhances the texture and flavor of the bread. However, the different kinds of flour used in all these recipes are available, freshly ground, through mail order. See Sources of Supply.

WONDER MEAL is a carefully milled combination of seven grains: wheat, corn, barley, oats, rye, soybeans, and rice bran, and is available through El Molino Mills, Alhambra, California, or at your local health or specialty food stores. Although its primary use is as a cereal, we have found it superb for use in baking breads and muffins. If desired, add ½ cup plump dark raisins, and sliced dates to the flour mixture for an unusual variation.

NUTTY SWISS BIRCHER MUESLI BREAD

2 eggs
¾ stick sweet butter
1 cup sugar
pinch salt
grated rind of 1 small lemon
1 tablespoon rum

½ cup milk
3 teaspoons baking powder
2 cups unbleached white
flour
½ cup Swiss Bircher Muesli
powdered sugar

In a large mixing bowl, beat together eggs, butter, sugar, salt, lemon rind, rum and milk. Stir in the baking powder, flour and Bircher Muesli. Beat thoroughly with a wooden spoon until the batter is well blended. Turn into a well-greased and lightly floured 8″ x 4″ x 2½″ loaf pan. Bake in a 350°F. oven for 45 minutes or until golden brown and the bread tests done. Cool in pan for 10 minutes, then complete cooling on a wire cake rack. Sprinkle with powdered sugar if desired.

SWISS BIRCHER MUESLI: An unusual blend of crushed hazelnuts, almonds, wheat germ, apples, raisins, oat flakes, whole wheat, rye and millet grains, sweetened with raw sugar. Available in most food markets and specialty food stores in 2½ oz. packages or in cereal size boxes.

SWISS PROTEIN BREAD

2 packages dry granular
yeast
⅓ cup lukewarm water
1 tablespoon sugar
½ cup scalded milk, cooled
to lukewarm
¾ cup sour cream
2 tablespoons honey

1 teaspoon salt
2 tablespoons butter or
margarine
⅓ cup Swiss Bircher Muesli
4 cups unbleached white
flour
½ cup wheat germ
1 teaspoon baking powder

Dissolve yeast in lukewarm water; add sugar. Cover. Let stand for 5 minutes until the yeast is foaming and doubled in volume. In a large mixing bowl, add lukewarm milk to sour cream, honey, salt and butter. Stir with a wooden spoon. Add the yeast mixture, Swiss Bircher Muesli, 2 cups flour, wheat germ and baking powder. Beat vigorously, then add remaining flour. Beat until a soft ball is formed. Knead on a floured board for 10 minutes. Place in a warm, greased bowl, turning to grease top of dough. Cover with wax paper, then with a cloth. Set aside in a warm place until doubled in bulk, about 1 to 1½ hours. Turn out onto a lightly floured board and knead until the dough is smooth and elastic. Return to warm, buttered bowl. Cover and let rise again until doubled. Punch down again, knead a minute or two, then shape into two medium-size loaves. Place in greased and lightly floured 8" x 4" x 2½" loaf pans. Cover and let rise until the dough reaches the top of the pans. Bake in a 425°F. oven for 10 minutes, then reduce heat to 375°F. and continue to bake 35 to 40 minutes longer or until loaves are golden brown. Tap bread—if it sounds hollow, it is done. Cool in pans for 10 minutes, then cool thoroughly on wire racks.

WHEATLESS FRUIT BREAD

This loaf keeps very well in the refrigerator; it is quite moist. Slice when cold and spread with whipped butter or favorite jam.

2½ cups Elam's Stone
   Ground Whole Rye Flour
1 teaspoon salt
2 teaspoons baking powder
½ cup sliced figs
⅓ cup plump dark raisins

3 soft prunes, sliced
½ teaspoon baking soda
1½ cups warm water
¼ cup molasses or honey
2 tablespoons oil, melted
   butter or margarine

Combine flour, salt, baking powder, figs, raisins and prunes. Mix soda, warm water and molasses in a 1-pint measuring cup. Add oil, butter or margarine. Blend, then pour gradually into the flour mixture. Mix. Spoon into a well-greased and lightly floured 8" x 4" x 2½" loaf pan. Bake at 350°F. for 50 to

60 minutes or until done. Loosen sides of loaf with the flat side of a silver knife, and turn out onto a wire rack to cool.

NOTE: Stone Ground Whole Rye Flour has the rich full-bodied flavor of natural whole grain. Carefully milled between old-fashioned burstones, it protects and retains all the natural minerals and vitamins so important in producing wholesome bread, and contains no chemical preservatives. (See Sources of Supply.)

WHOLE WHEAT BREAD

1¼ cups lukewarm water
½ stick soft butter
3 tablespoons sugar
1½ teaspoons salt
⅓ cup honey
¾ cup scalded milk
½ cup wheat germ
2 packages active dry
   granular yeast

⅓ cup lukewarm water
1 teaspoon baking powder
   mixed with
3 cups stone ground whole
   wheat flour, unsifted
3 cups unbleached white
   flour
½ cup warm melted butter
   (for brushing tops)

In a large mixing bowl combine 1¼ cups lukewarm water, butter, sugar, salt and honey. Stir until well blended. Pour scalded milk over wheat germ; cool to lukewarm. Dissolve yeast in ⅓ cup lukewarm water; let stand until foaming and add to honey-wheat germ mixture. Beat well with a wooden spoon. Add and mix well, alternately, the whole wheat and unbleached flours, and beat until a smooth dough is formed. Turn out onto a lightly floured board and knead until the dough is elastic—at least 10 minutes. (Kneading develops elasticity and a wonderful tranquil spirit!) Place dough in a warm, buttered bowl, turning the dough to grease the top. Cover with a warm, damp tea-towel. Let rise in a warm place until doubled in bulk. Punch down, and for a lighter bread, let rise again until doubled in bulk. Punch down, divide in half, and shape into two loaves. Place in two well-greased and lightly floured 9" x 5" x 3" loaf pans. Cover, set aside in a warm place and let rise until doubled in bulk. Bake in a pre-heated 400°F. oven for 15 to 20 minutes; reduce heat to

375°F. and continue to bake 25 to 30 minutes longer or until the bread is done. Remove from pans, and cool on wire racks. Brush tops with warm melted butter.

NOTE: A fine mixture of whole wheat flour may be purchased in health and specialty food stores. Use directly out of the package, without sifting. Or try to find a local mill, where the flour is ground to order. This grade of whole wheat flour imparts a sweet, nutty old-fashioned flavor to the bread. Nothing adds more to the goodness and digestibility of whole wheat bread than good freshly ground grains and thorough baking.

WHOLE WHEAT NUT BREAD

½ cup butter or margarine
1 cup raw brown sugar
2 eggs
1 cup milk
½ teaspoon salt
4 teaspoons baking powder

1 cup chopped mixed nuts
2 cups stone ground whole wheat flour
1 cup unbleached white flour with wheat germ

Cream butter with sugar until well blended. Beat in eggs and milk. Add salt, baking powder, mixed nuts, whole wheat flour and the unbleached white flour with wheat germ. Fill two well-greased 8″ x 4″ x 2½″ loaf pans, half full with the batter. Let stand for 20 minutes. Bake in a 350°F. oven for 40 to 45 minutes or until the loaf tests done.

NOTE: Whole Wheat Stone Ground Flour imparts a delicious flavor to bread, pastries and cookies. The bread makes excellent golden crisp toast. The flour keeps well, refrigerated.

FRUIT BREADS & KUCHENS

SPICED APPLE LOAF

3 tablespoons soft butter
1 cup sugar
2 eggs
⅔ cup flour
½ teaspoon salt
⅓ teaspoon cinnamon
⅓ teaspoon allspice
pinch mace or nutmeg
3 teaspoons baking powder

2 teaspoons grated lemon
rind
½ cup chopped walnuts or
pecans
2 medium-size apples, pared
and cut into tiny cubes
1 teaspoon flour
1 teaspoon cinnamon sugar

Blend butter with sugar and beat well until smooth and creamy. Add eggs and continue to beat until well blended. Add flour, salt, spices, baking powder, lemon rind and nuts. Sprinkle the apple cubes with the flour and cinnamon sugar; fold gently into the batter. Pour batter into a greased and lightly floured 8" x 4" x 2½" loaf pan, or into a shallow 8" square baking pan. Bake in a 350°F. oven for 30 to 35 minutes or until the loaf tests done. Cool. Sprinkle thickly with a cloud of Spiced Powdered Sugar if desired.

SPICED POWDERED SUGAR: Combine ⅓ cup powdered sugar with a pinch of nutmeg, cinnamon and ginger. Blend well.

BANANA NUT BREAD

½ cup butter or margarine
1 cup sugar
2 eggs
3 bananas, mashed
2½ cups flour
pinch nutmeg

1 teaspoon baking soda
1 teaspoon baking powder
½ teaspoon salt
2 teaspoons candied ginger,
chopped
½ cup chopped walnuts

101

Cream butter and sugar. Add the eggs and beat until the mixture is light and fluffy. Add mashed bananas. Combine flour, nutmeg, baking soda, baking powder, salt; add to creamed mixture. Add chopped ginger and nuts. Mix well. Spoon into a greased and lightly floured 9" x 5" x 3" loaf pan. Bake in a 375°F. oven for 45 minutes or until golden brown and the loaf tests done.

NOTE: For a quick dessert, cut the banana nut bread into thick slices, and top with sliced bananas and rum-flavored whipped cream.

FRESH BLUEBERRY LOAF

1 stick sweet butter
½ cup sugar
2 eggs. beaten
¾ cup milk
2 cups flour
3 teaspoons baking powder
½ teaspoon salt
1 cup perfect blueberries
1 teaspoon flour
1 teaspoon cinnamon sugar
Blueberry Topping

Blend butter with sugar and beat well until smooth and creamy. Add eggs and continue to beat until well-blended. Add milk alternately with the flour, baking powder and salt, beating well after each addition. Combine blueberries with the 1 teaspoon flour. Fold carefully into the batter, being careful not to crush the berries; use a gentle folding motion with a rubber spatula. Turn into a greased and lightly floured 8" x 4" x 2½" loaf pan or into a 8" square baking pan. Sprinkle top of batter with the cinnamon sugar. Bake at 375°F. for 30 to 35 minutes. Cool. Turn out onto a wire cake rack to complete cooling process. Spread with Blueberry Topping if desired.

TOPPING: Combine 1 cup perfect sugared blueberries with ¾ cup very cold sour cream. Serve separately as a luscious topping.

PAT JOHNSON'S FRESH CRANBERRY BREAD

2 cups sifted flour
½ teaspoon salt
1½ teaspoons baking powder
½ teaspoon baking soda
1 cup sugar
1 beaten egg
2 tablespoons melted butter

2 tablespoons hot water
½ cup orange juice
1 cup fresh cranberries cut
  in halves
½ cup chopped pecans
grated rind of 1 orange

Sift flour, salt, baking powder, baking soda and sugar. Then combine beaten egg, butter, hot water and orange juice; add to dry ingredients and mix well. Fold in cranberries, pecans and orange rind. Blend well with a wooden spoon. Pour batter into a greased loaf pan lined with well-greased wax paper. Bake in a 325°F. oven for 1 hour to 1¼ hours. Test with a toothpick—if it comes out clean, it is done. Cool. Wrap in wax paper and store for 24 hours before serving.

DATE MARBLE LOAF

½ cup soft butter
⅞ cup sugar
2 eggs
2 cups flour
2 teaspoons baking powder
½ teaspoon salt
¾ cup milk

½ teaspoon vanilla
10 soft dates, pitted and
  snipped with a scissors
1 teaspoon flour
1 tablespoon sweet cocoa
⅓ cup powdered sugar
1 teaspoon cocoa

Blend butter with sugar and beat well until smooth and creamy. Add eggs and continue to beat until well blended. Mix flour, baking powder and salt and add alternately with the milk to the creamed mixture, beating well after each addition. Add vanilla. Sprinkle snipped dates with the 1 teaspoon flour; fold into batter. Turn into a greased and lightly flour 8" x 4" x 2½" loaf pan. Sprinkle top with 1 tablespoon cocoa and swirl with the tines of a fork, creating a marbled effect. Bake in a 350°F. oven for 30 to 40 minutes or until the loaf tests done. Cool. Sprinkle top of cooled loaf with ½ of the powdered sugar, then with the 1 teaspoon cocoa and lastly with the remaining powdered sugar.

FRUIT AND NUT HOLIDAY LOAF

1 stick butter (¼ pound)
1 scant cup sugar
2 eggs
½ cup milk
1¾ cups flour
3 teaspoons baking powder
½ teaspoon salt
⅓ cup plump raisins
⅓ cup mixed candied fruits, cubed
6 dates, sliced

Cream butter with sugar. Add eggs and beat well until the mixture is light and fluffy. Add milk; mix well. Sift flour, baking powder and salt over raisins, candied fruits and dates; blend well. Combine with creamed mixture. Turn into a greased and lightly floured loaf pan. Bake in a 350°F. oven for 35 to 40 minutes or until the loaf tests done. Cool 10 minutes. Turn out onto a wire cake rack. Cool thoroughly before slicing. Sprinkle with cinnamon sugar or powdered sugar.

HOT SPICED MOLASSES LOAF
WITH CANDIED FRUITS

4 tablespoons butter
½ cup sugar
1 egg
½ cup milk
½ cup molasses
½ teaspoon allspice
½ teaspoon powdered ginger
½ teaspoon salt
½ teaspoon baking soda
½ teaspoon baking powder
1¾ cups flour
1 teaspoon grated orange rind
¼ cup chopped candied ginger
½ cup candied fruits, cubed
½ cup (3-ounce package) softened cream cheese, mixed with
1 teaspoon chopped candied ginger

Blend butter with sugar and beat well until smooth and creamy. Add egg and continue to beat until well blended. Mix the milk and the molasses, and add alternately with the mixed and sifted dry ingredients to the creamed mixture. Fold in grated orange rind, candied ginger and candied fruits. Turn into a 8" x 4" x 2½" greased and lightly floured loaf pan. Bake at 350°F. for 30 minutes or until the loaf tests done. Remove from oven and spread top with the creamed cheese. Return to oven for 1 minute. Cool for a few minutes. Serve at once.

NOTE: If desired, bake in an 8" or 9" shallow square baking pan, greased, lined with wax paper and greased again. Cut into squares while still warm and serve topped with the cream cheese and candied ginger.

GOLDEN ORANGE BREAD

3 cups flour
¾ cup sugar
5 teaspoons baking powder
½ teaspoon salt
2 tablespoons dark plump raisins
2 tablespoons white raisins

2 eggs, beaten
½ cup water
½ cup orange juice
grated rind of 2 oranges
6 tablespoons melted butter
Orange Sugar

Sift flour, sugar, baking powder and salt together. Add raisins. Blend well. Add eggs, water, and orange juice; mix. Beat in the melted butter and grated orange rind and continue to beat for 1 minute until the batter is smooth and well blended. Spoon batter into 2 medium-size well-greased and lightly floured loaf pans. Sprinkle with Orange Sugar. Let stand for 20 minutes. Bake in a 375°F. oven for 35 to 40 minutes or until the loaves test done. Cool before slicing.

ORANGE SUGAR: Combine ¼ cup sugar with the grated rind of 1 small orange. Blend well.

NOTE: The raisins need not be washed. They should always be thoroughly dry for fruit breads are oftentimes made heavy by the use of moist fruits. Packaged raisins are usually thoroughly processed and may be used without further preparation. This rule also applies to dried fruits.

SPICED PRUNE LOAF

½ cup butter (¼ pound)
1 cup sugar
2 eggs
2½ cups cake flour
2 teaspoons baking powder
½ teaspoon allspice
⅓ teaspoon powdered cloves

1 teaspoon baking soda
12 soft pitted prunes, sliced
1 tablespoon chopped candied ginger
1 cup buttermilk
2 teaspoons cinnamon sugar

Cream butter and sugar together thoroughly. Add eggs and continue to beat until well blended. Mix the dry ingredients (except cinnamon sugar) together and sift over the sliced prunes and ginger. Add alternately with the buttermilk to the creamed mixture. Blend well with a wooden spoon. Turn into a greased and lightly floured 9″ x 5″ x 3″ loaf pan or, if desired, into a greased 9″ tube spring form. Bake in a 350°F. oven for 35 to 45 minutes or until the loaf tests done. Cool 15 minutes. Turn out onto a wire cake rack to cool. Sprinkle top of loaf with cinnamon sugar, while still warm, if desired.

NOTE: The new soft ready-to-eat pitted prunes are moist and tender and ready to use right out of the package. For easier handling, snip them with a scissors.

FRESH RASPBERRY TEA LOAF

A cherished old recipe used in my dear mother's kitchen so many, many years ago—but tucked away in a "special file" until now. Pass this heirloom recipe on to your children!

2 cups flour
⅓ cup sugar
½ teaspoon salt
4 teaspoons baking powder
2 teaspoons grated lemon
    rind

1 egg
⅓ cup melted butter
¾ cup milk
⅔ cup fresh firm raspberries

Sift the flour, sugar, salt, and baking powder into a bowl. Add lemon rind. Beat egg, butter and milk together until well blended. Add all at once to the dry ingredients. Do not over-mix—blend just enough to moisten the flour. Sprinkle berries lightly with a little flour and fold gently into the batter. Turn into a well-greased and lightly floured 8″ loaf pan or into a shallow 8″ square baking pan. Bake in a preheated 375°F. oven for 25 to 30 minutes or until the loaf tests done. Cool. An unusually fragrant tea loaf, excellent served while still warm, accompanied by small pots of cold fresh sweet butter or cold thick sour cream blended with sugared raspberries.

FRESH SWEET BUTTER:

Pour ½ pint heavy sweet cream into a 1 pint bowl. Chill rotary beater before using. Beat until the whipped cream turns slightly yellow and becomes buttery. Continue to beat until thick. Pour off excess liquid, place in a small bowl. Cover with plastic wrap and refrigerate until ready to use. This unusually festive spread, made in minutes, produces the best sweet butter ever and right out of your own kitchen without using a back-breaking churn!

APPLE STREUSEL KUCHEN

½ cup butter
4 tablespoons sugar
1 egg
4 tablespoons milk
1 teaspoon grated lemon rind
1 cup flour
1 teaspoon baking powder
½ teaspoon salt

3 apples, cored, pared and
    sliced
Topping: 3 tablespoons
    brown sugar
1 tablespoon flour
2 tablespoons soft butter
1 tablespoon cinnamon sugar
4 tablespoons chopped nuts

107

Cream butter, sugar and egg. Beat until fluffy. Add milk, lemon rind, flour, baking powder and salt. Mix with a wooden spoon into a thick batter. Spread in a well-greased and lightly floured 9-inch baking pan. Spread sliced apples over the top of batter. *Topping:* Combine brown sugar, flour, butter, cinnamon, sugar and nuts. Mix with fingers until crumbly. Sprinkle over sliced apples. Pat gently with fingers. Bake in a 350°F. oven for 35 to 40 minutes or until the apples are tender and the kuchen is done.

CRANBERRY KUCHEN

4 tablespoons sweet butter
1 cup soft brown sugar
1 to 1½ cups whole cranberry sauce
1 generous tablespoon grated orange rind
½ cup chopped nuts
¼ teaspoon allspice

½ stick butter
½ cup sugar
1 egg, beaten
1½ cups flour
2½ teaspoons baking powder
pinch salt
½ cup milk

Melt 4 tablespoons butter in a 9″ square baking pan. Add brown sugar, simmer gently over low heat for 5 minutes. Remove from heat. Break up cranberry sauce with a fork, mix with grated orange rind, nuts and allspice. Spread over butter-sugar mixture. In the meantime prepare batter: Cream ½ stick butter with ½ cup sugar. Add egg and continue to beat until the mixture is light and fluffy. Add flour, baking powder and salt, alternately with the milk. Mix with a wooden spoon until blended. Spoon batter, very carefully, over the cranberry mixture. Bake in a moderate (350°F.) oven for 25 to 30 minutes or until golden brown. Turn out at once onto a large serving plate, so that the sticky cranberry mixture is on the top. Serve warm with or without topping.

SUGGESTED TOPPING: Beat 1 cup heavy sweet cream with 2 tablespoons confectioners sugar. Add 2 tablespoons whole cranberry sauce. Stir gently until the cream is a light pink. Chill until ready to use.

DUTCH PEACH KUCHEN

2 cups sifted flour
1½ teaspoons baking powder
pinch salt
2 tablespoons butter
1 egg

¼ cup milk
4 firm ripe peaches, pared
   and sliced
1 tablespoon cinnamon sugar
Peach Whipped Cream

Combine flour, baking powder and salt. Sift into a mixing bowl.
Cut in butter with a pastry blender or fingers. Add beaten egg
and milk. Beat into a thick batter. Spread in a shallow 9" or
10" buttered and lightly floured baking dish. Press peaches
into the top of the batter in even rows. (Canned peaches may
be used if necessary, but they must be very well drained.)
Sprinkle with cinnamon sugar. Bake in a 400°F. oven for
15 minutes. Reduce heat to 350°F. and continue to bake 10 to
15 minutes longer or until the peaches are tender and the
kuchen nicely browned. Cut into squares and serve with
favorite topping, or with Peach Whipped Cream.

PEACH WHIPPED CREAM: Pare 2 ripe peaches, mash
with a fork, and fold into sweetened whipped cream. Prepare
the mashed peaches at the last moment and serve at once, or
sprinkle peaches with a little lemon juice to prevent discoloring.

GLAZED PEAR KUCHEN

½ cup butter
4 tablespoons sugar
1 egg
4 tablespoons milk
1 teaspoon baking powder
pinch salt

1 cup flour
1 to 2 teaspoons grated
   orange rind
6 to 8 perfect canned pear
   halves, well drained
⅓ cup currant jelly, melted

Cream butter, sugar and egg until light and fluffy. Add milk;
mix well. Add sifted dry ingredients and grated orange rind.
Beat well with a wooden spoon until the batter is thick and
smooth. Spread in a 9-inch well-buttered and lightly floured
ovenproof glass baking dish. Drain pears and dry with soft

paper towels. Arrange evenly on top of batter. Bake in pre-heated 350°F. oven for 25 minutes or until the kuchen is nicely browned. Melt currant jelly, brush over top of pears. When thoroughly cooled refrigerate for 5 to 10 minutes until glaze is set. Serve topped with brandy-flavored whipped cream, if desired.

TO SERVE: Cut into squares, each containing a half pear, and top with a rosette of brandy-flavored whipped cream; or for an unusual gourmet dessert, omit the currant glaze. Heat 3 tablespoons rum, ignite and pour flaming over the pears. Top each with hot chocolate sauce and whipped cream.

PURPLE PLUM KUCHEN

2 tablespoons sugar
½ teaspoon salt
2½ teaspoons baking powder
1 cup flour
½ stick butter
⅓ cup milk
1 tablespoon grated orange rind

12 purple plums (fresh Italian plums)
½ cup soft brown sugar
pinch mace
⅓ teaspoon allspice
2 tablespoons soft butter
1 tablespoon flour
⅓ cup chopped walnuts

Combine 2 tablespoons sugar, the salt, baking powder and flour. Cut in ½ stick butter with a pastry blender until crumbly. Add milk and orange rind, stirring just enough to blend ingredients. Spread the thick batter in a 8″ or 9″ square baking dish. Cut plums in halves, remove pits, and arrange plums over batter, cut side down. Combine soft brown sugar with spices, 2 tablespoons butter, 1 tablespoon flour and the nuts. Mix until crumbly. Sprinkle over plums. Bake in a 375°F. oven for 25 to 35 minutes or until the plums are tender. Serve warm, topped with thick sour cream sprinkled lightly with cinnamon sugar, or brandy-flavored whipped cream.

110

TROPICAL RUM KUCHEN

½ cup butter
5 tablespoons fine sugar,
  sifted
1 egg
4 tablespoons milk
2 teaspoons baking powder
pinch salt
1 cup flour
pinch ginger

2 teaspoons grated orange rind
2 to 3 bananas, ripe but firm
1 tablespoon sweet butter
2 tablespoons brown sugar
3 tablespoons good dark
  Jamaica rum
Ginger-Flavored Whipped
  Cream

Cream ½ cup butter, the fine sugar and egg. Add milk. Beat
well. Add sifted dry ingredients, then the orange rind. Beat
with a wooden spoon until the batter is thick and smooth.
Spread in a well-buttered and lightly floured 9" baking dish.
Slice bananas lengthwise and arrange evenly over top of batter.
Dot with bits of butter, sprinkle with brown sugar. Bake in a
375°F. oven for 25 to 30 minutes. Heat rum, ignite, and pour
flaming over top of kuchen. Cut into squares and serve warm
or cold topped with Ginger-Flavored Whipped Cream.

GINGER-FLAVORED WHIPPED CREAM: Beat 1 cup
heavy sweet cream until thick, add 2 tablespoons confectioners
sugar, a pinch powdered ginger, and 1 tablespoon finely
chopped candied ginger. Chill until ready to serve.

NOTE: We prefer to bake fresh fruit kuchens in ovenproof
glass baking dishes, which can be used for serving "from oven
to table."

111

GINGERBREADS

The interesting ginger root grows in the shape of a hand, actually a palm with fingers. It is used either fresh, especially in Chinese cookery, or dried and pulverized for medicinal or culinary use. Best known is Jamaica ginger, which is found in the West Indies and is also grown and highly prized in the Orient.

It is said that gingerbread was brought to America by the Pilgrims. The Puritan housewife brought along her prized recipes, sharing them with friends. The recipes were often mixed with corn meal, dried-pumpkin flour, wheat flour and ginger.

In the early nineteenth-century America, highly spiced gingerbread was used to prevent seasickness. As much as a teacup of powdered ginger might be used in a single recipe, and the gingerbread or ginger cookies were taken along on a long sea-voyage to sooth intestinal upsets and to stimulate the appetite.

Still an American favorite, gingerbread is served most times unfrosted, or unadorned with toppings. However, it is excellent dressed up with a variety of frostings, exotically flavored whipped cream, fruit sauces, whipped cream cheese and spiced applesauce. For more eye-appeal and interest, gingerbread may be baked in square, round, oblong, loaf or cupcake pans. The end result, whether fancy shapes or plain; will have the same delicious flavor.

EGGLESS APRICOT GINGERBREAD

1 cup sugar
1 cup molasses
½ cup soft sweet butter
1 cup sour cream
1 teaspoon powdered ginger
pinch mace
pinch cinnamon
½ cup chopped nuts

6 to 8 soft apricots, snipped
   with a scissors
3½ cups flour, sifted
2 teaspoons baking soda
   dissolved in
2 tablespoons cold water
Cream Cheese-Chutney
     frosting

In a large mixing bowl combine sugar, molasses, soft butter, sour cream and spices. Beat by hand or with an electric mixer (if possible) until all the ingredients are well blended. Blend nuts and apricots with the flour, and add gradually to the creamed mixture. Add the baking soda mixture last. Beat hard for 2 to 3 minutes. Pour batter into a well-buttered and lightly floured 8" or 9" tube spring form. Bake in a 350°F. oven for 30 to 40 minutes or until the top is gently firm to touch and tests done. Cool. Remove outer rim of springform and complete cooling gingerbread on a wire cake rack.

CREAM-CHEESE CHUTNEY FROSTING: Cream 6 ounces cream cheese until very light and fluffy. Blend until very smooth. Add ⅓ cup good chutney and mix well. If there are any large pieces of fruit in the chutney, chop into small pieces. Add 1 to 2 tablespoons sifted confectioners sugar. Mix well. Spread on top of gingerbread when ready to serve.

ANOTHER METHOD: Slice gingerbread about ½-inch thick and pass a bowl of chilled cream-cheese chutney, for an unusual, luscious topping.

CHOCOLATE NUT GINGERBREAD

2 eggs
½ cup molasses
½ cup brown sugar, packed
1 stick sweet butter
  (¼ pound), melted
3 ounces semisweet chocolate,
  melted
2½ cups flour
2 teaspoons baking powder

1 teaspoon ginger
½ teaspoon mace
pinch cinnamon
pinch nutmeg
1 scant teaspoon baking soda
1 cup boiling water, cooled to
  lukewarm
¾ cup chopped walnuts
Spiced Chocolate Frosting

In a large mixing bowl, beat eggs, molasses, brown sugar, butter and chocolate until very smooth. To the flour add baking powder and all the spices, blend well. Add baking soda. Sift the flour mixture over the creamed mixture, beating vigorously, alternating with the lukewarm water. Beat until the batter is satin smooth. Fold in the chopped nuts, reserving 2 tablespoons for the top. Pour into a buttered and lightly floured 9-inch tube spring form. Sprinkle top with the 2 tablespoons nuts. Bake in a 350°F. oven for 30 to 40 minutes or until the top is gently firm to touch and the gingerbread tests done.

SPICED CHOCOLATE FROSTING: Melt 6 ounces semisweet chocolate over warm water with 1 tablespoon coffee. Stir until smooth, remove from heat and beat in 1 tablespoon butter. Add ¼ teaspoon powdered ginger. Blend. Fold in 1 tablespoon thick sour cream. Refrigerate for 10 minutes. Spread over top of cooled gingerbread.

DARK RICH GINGERBREAD

1 cup dark molasses
1 egg, well beaten
1 stick sweet butter
  (¼ pound), melted
1 teaspoon ginger
pinch cloves

1 teaspoon baking soda,
  dissolved in
1 cup hot water
2 cups flour
½ teaspoon instant coffee
1 tablespoon grated dark
  semisweet chocolate

Combine all ingredients in order given. Beat well. Spoon into a shallow buttered and lightly floured 8″ square baking pan. Bake at 350°F. for 30 to 35 minutes or until the gingerbread is gently firm to touch. Cool. Serve topped with spiced apple sauce, if desired.

LAYERED GINGERBREAD

1 cup molasses
1 egg
½ cup melted butter
1 teaspoon powdered ginger
¼ teaspoon mace
¼ teaspoon instant coffee
1 teaspoon baking soda, dissolved in

1 cup hot water, then cooled
2 cups flour
½ teaspoon baking powder
½ cup coarsely chopped nuts
1 cup sweetened and lightly spiced whipped cream

In a large mixing bowl combine molasses, egg, butter, spices, coffee, baking soda dissolved in hot water, flour and baking powder. Beat well. Fold in nuts. Spoon batter into two well-buttered and lightly floured 8″ layer cake tins. Bake at 350°F. for 25 minutes or until the gingerbread is gently firm to touch. Do not overbake, as the edges will become hard and crusty. Cool on wire racks. Whip cream, sweeten to taste and flavor with a pinch of ginger if desired.

NOTE: Chopped candied ginger adds a delightful flavor to the whipped cream. Spread whipped cream between layers and top with whipped cream or with a soft cloud of powdered sugar.

PLANTATION GINGERBREAD

1½ sticks sweet butter,
softened
1 cup soft brown sugar
1 cup maple syrup
3 eggs, beaten
pinch nutmeg
pinch powdered cloves
1 teaspoon powdered ginger
3 cups flour
1 teaspoon baking soda,
dissolved in

1 tablespoon warm water
½ apple, pared, cored and
cubed
½ banana, cut into very small
cubes
1 piece candied ginger,
chopped
⅓ cup powdered sugar,
mixed with
½ teaspoon powdered ginger

Cream butter with brown sugar; beat in maple syrup and eggs. Beat vigorously until well blended. Add spices and flour, gradually, and last, the dissolved baking soda. Sprinkle a little flour over the cubed apple, banana and chopped candied ginger, and fold gently into the batter. Bake in a buttered and lightly floured tube spring form, or in a shallow, well-buttered ovenproof 8″ square baking dish. Bake at 350°F. for 30 to 40 minutes or until done. Cool. Combine powdered sugar with ginger and sprinkle thickly over top of warm gingerbread. Serve slightly warm.

SOUR CREAM GINGERBREAD

1 cup sour cream
5 tablespoons melted sweet
butter
scant ⅔ cup sugar
½ cup molasses
2 eggs
3½ cups flour

½ teaspoon salt
2 teaspoons baking soda
¾ teaspoon powdered ginger
¼ teaspoon mace
½ teaspoon powdered
cinnamon
½ cup dark raisins

Combine sour cream, butter, sugar, molasses and eggs. Beat well. Sift the flour together with the salt, baking soda, ginger, mace and cinnamon; add to sour-cream mixture. Beat well, using an electric mixer if possible, or use a wooden spoon. Sprinkle raisins with a little flour, and fold into the batter. Pour into two well-buttered and lightly floured 7″ or 8″ square baking pans. Bake in a preheated 375°F. oven for 30 minutes or until the top is gently firm to touch and tests done. Cool.

HOT WATER GINGERBREAD

½ cup sugar
½ stick butter, (¼ pound)
1 egg, beaten
1½ cups flour
pinch salt
½ teaspoon ginger
½ teaspoon cinnamon

pinch allspice
1 teaspoon baking soda
½ cup hot water
½ cup dark molasses
1 tablespoon shredded citron
⅓ cup plump dark raisins
powdered sugar (for topping)

Cream sugar and butter until light and creamy. Add beaten egg; mix well. Combine flour, salt, spices and baking soda. Mix hot water with molasses and add alternately with the dry ingredients to the creamed butter mixture. Fold in citron and raisins. Pour batter into a buttered and lightly floured 8″ x 4″ x 2½″ loaf pan. Bake in a 325°F. oven for 30 to 35 minutes or until the gingerbread is lightly firm to touch and shrinks away slightly from the sides of the pan. Sift powdered sugar several times—until it's feather-light—into a bowl. Do not pack. Sprinkle top with a soft cloud of the fluffy powdered sugar.

SEA-VOYAGE WHITE GINGERBREAD

The white gingerbread wafers are made without the traditional molasses, and are excellent baked slowly until a very pale, pale, golden hue.

1 cup butter
1 cup sugar
2 eggs, separated
4 cups flour
2 teaspoons baking powder
pinch salt

2½ teaspoons ginger
1 tablespoon chopped candied ginger
⅓ cup powdered sugar, mixed with ½ teaspoon ginger

117

Cream butter; gradually add sugar, beating the mixture until light and fluffy. Beat egg yolks over warm water until thick and lemon colored. Add the beaten yolks to the creamed sugar-butter mixture. Sift the flour, baking powder, salt and 2½ teaspoons ginger together and stir into the egg mixture, adding about ⅓ of the flour at a time. Last of all fold in the stiffly beaten egg whites. Spread a large sheet of brown or wax paper with butter; place on a baking sheet and sprinkle lightly with flour. Drop gingerbread batter by large spoonfuls, leaving a 2-inch space between each one. Bake in a slow oven, about 275°F. to 300°F., until a pale beige color. Do not brown. Combine powdered sugar with ginger and stir until completely blended. Sprinkle thickly over the warm gingerbread and serve.

EXOTIC BREADS

This chapter introduces a number of recipes, many of foreign origin, which will be found enticingly different in appearance and taste from other recipes in this book. All the recipes are easy to prepare and will produce intriguing "conversation pieces" with an individual charm which both you and your guests will find fascinating.

ALI BABAS

This is the one treasure Ali Baba kept from the Forty Thieves! Semisweet with a tender crumb, these biscuits may be served plain with meals. It is also customary to serve the biscuit warm with honey and fresh sweet butter. But do try this version, with its rich filling of whipped cream and cherry preserves.

1 cup self-rising flour
pinch salt
pinch nutmeg and cinnamon
1 teaspoon grated lemon rind
1 cup milk
2 eggs, slightly beaten
1 tablespoon sugar

½ cup whole dark cherry
  preserves mixed with
1 tablespoon Cherry Kijafa
  or port wine
sweetened whipped cream
powdered sugar

Place flour in a mixing bowl. Add salt. Mix. Make a well in the center and add nutmeg, cinnamon, lemon rind, milk, eggs and sugar. Mix together with a silver knife into a smooth dough. Cover and let stand for 10 minutes. Turn into a well-buttered and lightly floured round baking pan. Start baking in a cold oven. Turn oven on to 350°F. Bake until puffed and a delicate golden brown. Cool. Cut into pie shaped wedges. Split Ali Babas and fill centers with the cherry preserves and whipped cream. Sprinkle top with a soft cloud of powdered sugar.

ALT WIEN SWEETENED EGG BREAD

This very *old* European recipe was a gift to us from a famous chef. The bread is lightly flavored, crisp and sweet. Uniquely delicate, it is an excellent "dunker," served with steaming hot coffee or spiced tea. The ladies often dipped the sliced Vienna bread in cognac or sweet wine—the very nicest way imaginable of having your cake and eating it too!

10 eggs	½ teaspoon pure vanilla
4½ to 5 cups sugar, sifted	½ teaspoon anise flavor
4 cups flour, sifted	powdered sugar

Beat eggs over warm water until thick and lemon colored, about 10 to 15 minutes. Add sugar gradually, beating constantly, until all the sugar has been used up. Mix in the flour, one cup at a time, until the mixture is well blended. Add vanilla and anise flavor. Turn into well-greased and lightly floured long narrow baking tins. Bake in a preheated 375°F. oven until delicately browned. Watch carefully, so that the sweet bread does not burn. If the oven is too hot reduce to 350°F. Cool. Sprinkle with powdered sugar. Slice ½-inch thick, spread on a baking sheet, return to a 250°F. oven and let toast gently for 10 minutes or until a very light golden color.

AMERICAN INDIAN BREAD

2 cups milk	3 eggs, well beaten
3 large or heaping table-spoons corn meal	1 cup filberts or hickory nuts, finely chopped
2 tablespoons maple sugar	2 tablespoons maple sugar
2 tablespoons butter	1 cup hot maple syrup
½ teaspoon salt	

Boil milk, then gradually add the corn meal in a slow stream, stirring constantly. Add 2 tablespoons sugar, butter and salt. Cook gently, stirring from time to time with a wooden spoon until the mixture thickens. Remove from heat, beating all the while until cool. Add eggs, one at a time, beating vigorously after each addition. Fold in chopped nuts. Stir until well blended. Turn into a well-greased and lightly floured 8″ square shallow baking dish. Sprinkle with 2 tablespoons maple sugar. Bake in a 350°F. oven for 30 to 35 minutes or until golden brown. When serving, pass around a bowl of hot maple syrup.

APOSTLES BREAD

This quick hot bread originated many years ago in a Central European monastery, where it is served with rare fruit jams or fragrant marmalade thick with citrus rinds. The bread rounds, not being too sweet, are just right to serve with hot tea or coffee. If desired, omit sugar, and serve plain as a bread for lunch or supper.

2 cups flour
3 teaspoons baking powder
4 teaspoons sugar
1 scant teaspoon salt
4 tablespoons butter or other shortening

2 eggs
½ cup heavy sweet cream
brandy
coarse sugar for topping

Sift the flour, baking powder, sugar and salt together. Then work in the shortening with a pastry blender or fingers. Beat eggs, add cream and mix with flour mixture. Toss on a lightly floured board, roll out ½-inch thick and cut into 5-inch rounds. Brush with brandy; sprinkle with coarse sugar. Bake in a 375°F. oven for 15 minutes. Serve slightly warm.

COARSE SUGAR: Pulverize clear or brown rock candy into coarse particles.

BIBLICAL HARD HONEY BISCUITS

2 cups dark buckwheat honey
4 cups unbleached flour

pinch ginger
pinch powdered cloves

Heat honey until just warm and place in a large mixing bowl. Work in as much flour mixed with the spices as the honey will absorb, making a rather stiff dough so that it can be rolled between 2 sheets of wax paper, about ½-inch thick. Place on a board and let stand, covered, at room temperature for 2 days. Press a springerle rolling pin over the dough, if desired, for a festive appearance, then cut out rounds with a 6-inch sharp tin cover (from a 1-lb. coffee can). For another unusual effect, sprinkle a 6-inch cut glass or pressed glass dish with powdered sugar and press it into the dough. Remove glass dish carefully, and an interesting design will remain pressed into the dough. Bake in a 300°F. oven for 20 to 25 minutes or until the biscuits are a light golden color. Makes about 6 to 8 biscuits.

NOTE: The quality of the honey may differ due to its thickness, or even to certain weather conditions. The recipe may require more or less flour. Start off with a light hand, using less, and continue, using just enough flour, gradually, until it reaches the required thickness. The rich dark buckwheat honey is quite thick. Lighter honey is thinner and may require more flour. These cakes harden, after baking, and will keep indefinitely in a tightly covered container. Historically, these biscuits are not unlike those made in Biblical days with flour and honey; they are still being made in many parts of Israel and North Africa. A pinch of spice, such as ginger, clove, nutmeg or cinnamon, gives off a delicate mysterious aroma with a distinctively unique flavor.

CALIENTE COFFEE LOAF

This superb recipe, favorite fare in elegant European patisseries, will add glamour to your coffee hour. We have secretly cherished this recipe for a long time, now we pass it on to you!

Rose essence or rose water may be found in gourmet stores, pure rose water in most drug stores. Although its use is optional, its perfume is much desired.

2 cups pecans or almonds, *finely* ground
4 zwieback, ground
2 tablespoons flour
6 eggs, separated
½ cup sugar, plus 2 tablespoons
1 tablespoon brandy
1 tablespoon grated orange rind

½ teaspoon rose flavor (rose water or rose essence)
1 tablespoon water
½ teaspoon cinnamon
pinch nutmeg
2 teaspoons baking powder
⅓ cup strong sweet coffee
1 cup sweetened fluffy whipped cream
½ teaspoon instant coffee

Put nuts and zwieback through a food chopper, then combine with the flour in a large mixing bowl. Beat egg yolks over warm water about 10 minutes, until thick and the consistency of whipped cream. Add sugar gradually and continue to beat until all the sugar has been used up. Add brandy, grated orange rind, rose flavor and water, then the spices and baking powder. Blend ingredients together with a wooden spoon. Fold in stiffly beaten egg whites. Bake in a 9" x 5" x 3" well-buttered and lightly floured loaf pan *or* in a 13" x 9" x 2" baking pan. Bake in a 350°F. oven for 30 to 35 minutes or until done. Test with a toothpick; when it comes out clean the loaf is done. Cool on a wire rack. Place the loaf on a large serving dish. Poke tiny holes all over the top of the loaf, then carefully spoon the sweetened dark coffee over the top. Do it sparingly, so that the liquid goes into the little holes, instead of over the top of the entire loaf. Pile sweetened coffee-flavored whipped cream over all.

CHAPATIS
(INDIA)

1 cup whole wheat flour
1 cup unbleached flour
½ teaspoon salt
2 tablespoons melted butter

½ cup coconut milk (see note)
1 teaspoon sugar

Combine all ingredients. Mix well with a wooden spoon until the dough leaves the sides of the bowl. Cover and let stand for 1 hour. Turn out onto a lightly floured board and knead for 5 minutes. Pinch off small balls of dough and roll paper thin into 5-inch rounds. Bake on a greased and lightly floured baking sheet, turning so that they are evenly browned on both sides. Do not overbake. They may also be prepared on a well-greased griddle. Serve with favorite curries.

NOTE: White all-purpose flour is not much used in India. Whole wheat flour is extremely nourishing and is the mainstay of the Indian diet. All breads, with some few exceptions, are unleavened. Chapatis are fresh-made for all meals and served piping hot with a dab of butter. Leftover chapatis are stacked one on top of another and then wrapped in a heavy cloth. To reheat they are placed in a slow oven until they are hot and puffed. Best results are obtained when they are cooked on a hot griddle; they will puff up and rise like the French pommes soufflés. We have streamlined the above recipe for the American kitchen, adding the coconut milk for an exotic flavor. The original Chapatis recipe calls for whole wheat flour, water and salt.

COCONUT MILK: Steep ⅓ cup moist coconut in ½ cup hot milk for 1 hour. Strain.

SNOW CORN BREAD

New snow contains ammonia which causes the batter to rise quickly and acts the same as baking powder. Make certain to gather only fresh, clean fallen snow. An unusual bread, and fun to try—*at least once!*

2 cups yellow corn meal
½ teaspoon salt
pinch freshly ground black
  pepper

4 cups, dry, clean, freshly
  fallen snow
butter

Mix corn meal with salt, pepper and snow in a chilled bowl. Work fast, blending the ingredients quickly with a wooden spoon. Fill a buttered and lightly floured shallow baking dish about ⅞ full. Bake in a hot oven, (400°F.) until the top is crisp and golden brown. This makes an excellent quick corn bread.

SWEET FRUIT BREAD GLAZED WITH RED ROSE SYRUP

2 packages dry granular yeast
½ cup lukewarm water
1 teaspoon sugar
1 cup scalded milk, cooled to lukewarm
½ cup sugar
1 teaspoon salt
½ stick butter
2 eggs plus 1 egg yolk
1 tablespoon grated lemon rind

5 cups presifted flour
5 dates, cut into fourths
1 tablespoon each, chopped candied orange peel and candied pineapple
⅓ cup slivered toasted almonds
½ teaspoon baking powder
Red Rose Syrup

Sprinkle dry yeast over lukewarm water. Add 1 teaspoon sugar; stir. Cover and let stand until foaming and doubled in volume. In a large mixing bowl, combine scalded milk, ½ cup sugar, salt and butter. Stir until dissolved. Add foaming yeast. Add eggs and lemon rind. Beat with a wire whisk or rotary beater. Mix the cut-up dates, candied fruits and nuts with 2 cups flour; add to the egg-yeast mixture. Beat well. Add baking powder and remaining flour, just enough to make a soft pliable dough. When the dough clears the sides of the bowl, turn out onto a lightly floured board. Knead for a least 10 minutes, adding just a light dusting of flour on the board. Form into a ball. Place in a warm buttered bowl, turning the dough several times until completely greased on all sides. Cover with wax paper and then with a cloth. Set aside in a warm place, free from drafts, until doubled in bulk (about 1 to 1½ hours). Punch down with a floured fist, and let rise again until doubled. When light and spongy, punch down, turn out onto a lightly floured board and knead for 3 to 5 minutes. Divide in half and shape into two loaves. Place in well-greased and lightly floured 8″ x 5″ x 2½″ loaf pans. Cover with a cloth. Let rise until

125

doubled in bulk. Brush with slightly beaten egg white. Bake in a preheated 400°F. oven for 10 minutes. Reduce heat to 350°F. and continue to bake 35 to 40 minutes longer or until golden brown. Tap bottom of bread—if it gives off a hollow sound it is done. Cool in pans for 10 minutes, then turn out on wire cooling racks. Glaze with Red Rose Syrup.

RED ROSE SYRUP: 2 large cups Red Rose Petals
grated rind of 1 lemon
2 cups sifted sugar
2 tablespoons sherry
½ cup water

Place red rose petals in a strainer. Spray cold water over all. Drain well. Dry with soft paper towels. Cut off the little white part of the rose petals. In a medium size saucepan, combine the rose petals, lemon rind, sugar, wine and water. Bring to a rolling boil, reduce heat and cook until thick and syrupy. Cool. Place fruit loaves on serving plates. Baste several times with the rose syrup until thoroughly glazed. If desired, pour flaming sherry over the loaves before glazing.

NOTE: Rose jam is available in fine gourmet stores. If desired, in order to save time preparing the syrup, melt ¾ cup rose jam with ⅓ cup rosé wine. Cook until thick and syrupy. Use as the glaze.

SLIVERED TOASTED ALMONDS are available at most supermarkets in 5-ounce tins or in cellophane bags.

HAARD KOEK PETRONELLA
(DUTCH HEARTH BREAD)

This was originally an ancient Roman recipe. The bread, made from crude ingredients, was formed into a round ball, and baked in hot ashes. Somewhere along the way, this recipe found its way to Holland. There, through the ingenuity of the Dutch woman, an unusually palatable bread was baked from more appetizing ingredients. Instead of baking it the modern way in a moderately hot oven the Dutch baked the bread in open hearths. Although we have simplified the baking process, the ingredients remain exactly as given to us by a Hollander. (Since olive oil has too distinctive a flavor we use butter.)

scant ½ cup milk, scalded
   and cooled to lukewarm
1 package dry granular yeast
1 teaspoon sugar
3½ ounces olive oil or melted
   butter
3 eggs
1 tablespoon rum
1 tablespoon orange flower
   water

2 to 3 threads saffron,
   dissolved in 1 tablespoon
   hot water
pinch salt
2¼ cups flour, sifted
egg yolk mixed with 1
   tablespoon water or milk
butter
honey

In a mixing bowl, combine lukewarm milk with the yeast and sugar. Stir. Cover and let stand until foaming and doubled in volume. Add olive oil or butter, beaten eggs, rum, orange flower water and dissolved saffron. Mix well. Add salt, and 1 cup flour. Beat until smooth. Beat in remaining flour until a soft dough is formed. Cover. Set aside in a cool place for 12 hours. Turn out onto a lightly floured board and knead for 10 minutes. Cut the dough into three parts, and roll each part into a long strip. Secure ends of the three strips together and form into a long braid, pinching the ends so that they will not open during baking. Form the braid into a circle. Pinch ends together again. Place on a buttered baking sheet. Brush with beaten egg. Bake in a 350°F. oven for 35 to 45 minutes until golden brown.

PRESSED DESIGN HOLIDAY BISCUIT

½ cup butter (¼ pound)
1 cup sugar, sifted
pinch nutmeg
pinch cinnamon
3 eggs, beaten

1 cup milk
4 cups flour
powdered sugar for pressed
   glass

Cream butter with sugar until fluffy; add spices and eggs, blend well, then add the milk and flour alternately. Roll out on a lightly floured board in a thin sheet. Press a large carved wooden mold or springerle rolling pin into the dough for a fancy effect. For an unusual holiday biscuit sprinkle a small pressed glass dish with powdered sugar, and press gently into the dough, creating a deep, clear design. Remove glass carefully.

NOTE: Many times we cut out each design with a pointed sharp knife and bake them until a delicate golden color. Then we fill them, sandwich fashion, with a delectable brandied dried fruit and nut mixture.

KETEL KOEK WATERREUS
(STEAMED DUTCH SPICED FRUIT BREAD)

Another old Dutch recipe. This produces an unsweetened moist spiced fruit bread, fragrant with brandy, citron and raisins. The mold used for the fruit bread must have a *tightly fitting cover,* for the water in the kettle should reach ⅔ up on the mold. While boiling it will reach nearly to the top of the mold; if the cover is loose the bread will be waterlogged.

1 cup plus 2 ounces flour
2 eggs, beaten
1 cup milk
1 package dry granular yeast
¼ cup currants
½ teaspoon cinnamon and ginger, mixed
¼ cup plump raisins
¼ cup shredded citron
grated rind of 1 navel orange
pinch salt
2 tablespoons brandy

Place the flour in a large shallow bowl. Make a well in the center and add the beaten eggs, milk, yeast, currants, spices, raisins, citron, orange rind and brandy. Sprinkle the salt around the rim of the flour. Mix until a thick batter is formed. Beat vigorously with a wooden spoon for about 10 minutes. Cover. Place the bowl over another bowl filled with hot water for 45 minutes. Fill a well-buttered pudding mold ⅔ full. Cover tightly. Place in a kettle of hot water (the water should be ⅔ the height of the mold) and let cook for 1½ hours. When water starts to evaporate, add more boiling water whenever necessary. When done, remove cover, and place the bread on a warm serving plate. Serve with plenty of warm honey or syrup and fresh sweet butter. If desired, sprinkle thickly with soft powdered sugar. Serve with pitchers of hot, dark, fragrant coffee.

MAMALIGA
(ROUMANIAN CORN BREAD)

A real taste-treat! Serve very hot, and the butter cold. Let butter melt into little golden streams, then top with generous portions of *cold* cottage cheese. The success of this peasant bread depends upon the temperature of the corn bread and cheese. The bread must be *very* hot and the cheese very *cold*. Delicious!

1 cup yellow corn meal	cold sweet butter
salt to taste	cottage cheese *or*
4 cups boiling water	feta cheese
1 tablespoon butter	

Add corn meal and salt to boiling water, *very gradually,* in a very slow stream, stirring constantly with a wooden spoon. Cook until the mixture begins to thicken; keep stirring until very smooth. Beat in butter. Place over hot water, cover and cook gently for 30 minutes until quite thick. Turn out onto a board sprinkled with corn meal. Roll into a round or oblong shape. Place into a well-buttered round or oblong baking dish sprinkled with corn meal. Bake in a preheated 375°F. oven until the top is crisp and brown. Spoon portions onto serving plates, top with bits of butter and then with generous portions of cold cottage cheese or feta cheese.

NOTE: Feta cheese may be found in most gourmet shops and at all Greek grocery stores. Imported from Greece and packed in kegs of milk, it is made from sheep-milk curd, snowy white, soft, sharp and slightly salty. It is a superb, appetizing cheese to use on Mamaliga Bread in place of cottage cheese.

PALACE HONEY BREAD

An exotic honey bread dating back to the Egyptian Kingdom, with the delicate aroma of a mysterious blend of spices, flavored and perfumed with rose water (available in gourmet shops and most drugstores) and rare aromatic liqueurs. It was originally served with "Kaymack," a thick clotted sweet cream boiled long over low heat and stirred constantly until it becomes so thick it can be cut with a knife. As the process is so long and tedious we have substituted the whipped cream flavored delicately with rose liqueur. This adds a piquant, unique flavor, with a hint of oriental glamor.

6 to 8 slices day-old white
   bread
juice of 1½ lemons
1 cup warm water
1 teaspoon rose water
1½ cups fragrant honey
⅓ teaspoon allspice
few grains freshly ground
   black pepper

⅓ teaspoon nutmeg
pinch mace
¼ cup rose liqueur
½ cup chopped pistachio
   nuts
1 teaspoon cinnamon sugar
1 cup sweetened whipped
   cream blended with
2 to 3 teaspoons rose liqueur

Place bread slices in a large shallow dish. Over it, pour the lemon juice mixed with the water. Let stand for 2 minutes, or until the bread is just about softened, but not so soft as to fall apart. Drain off lemon water. Butter a large shallow baking dish. Remove softened bread gently with a broad spatula, and arrange evenly in the dish, covering the bottom of the dish completely. Combine rose water and honey with the spices, beat with a fork until completely blended. Pour the spiced honey over all, then the rose liqueur. Sprinkle with cinnamon sugar and pistachio nuts. Bake in a 350°F. oven for 35 to 45 minutes, until golden brown. The bread should be a dark golden color, with a thick syrupy texture. Watch carefully. Do not burn. Cool. Chill, Cut into squares and serve topped with the chilled rose-flavored whipped cream.

NOTE: Chill whipped cream in the freezing unit for 10 minutes or until slightly frozen; it should have the consistency of a soft mousse.

PUFFED PEASANT BREAD
(Eier Kichlach)

An oriental type biscuit, delicate and unsweetened except for the cinnamon sugar topping. If desired, the cinnamon sugar topping may be omitted, and the biscuits served warm with marmalade or honey, or plain as a bread with salads.

1¾ cups flour	3 eggs
1 teaspoon baking powder	2 to 3 tablespoons cinnamon
½ teaspoon salt	sugar

Sift the flour, baking powder and salt together. Beat eggs over warm water until very light and the consistency of whipped cream. Add to flour mixture. Mix until a soft ball is formed. Turn out onto a lightly floured board. Knead well for 5 minutes. Roll out into a rectangle about ¼-inch thick. Cut out into large rounds or in any desired fancy shapes. Prick all over with a fork, then sprinkle with cinnamon sugar. Bake on a lightly greased and floured baking sheet in a preheated 350°F. oven for 15 to 20 minutes or until puffed crisp and a nice delicate brown.

ROSE PETAL SWEET BREAD

This fabulous bread, perfumed with rose petals and rose flavor, is a long time oriental holiday favorite. It is divine when sliced thickly, sprinkled with rose liqueur and pulverized rock candy or powdered sugar and toasted a lovely delicate golden brown in a moderate oven. Serve hot, and dream of Arabian Nights!

½ cup butter	2¼ cups flour
1 cup sifted sugar	2 teaspoons baking powder
4 eggs	½ cup red rose petals (fresh)
grated rind of 1 small lemon	1 cup milk
grated rind of 1 small navel	½ cup chopped pistachio
orange	nuts or chopped walnuts
½ teaspoon rose essence or	
rose water	

Cream butter with sugar until light and fluffy. Add the eggs, one at a time, beating well after each addition. Add the lemon and orange rind, then the rose flavor (available in gourmet shops and most drugstores). Mix sifted flour and baking powder together and then over the snipped rose petals; stir into the egg mixture alternately with the milk. Mix batter gently with a wooden spoon until the rose petals are well-mixed throughout. Sprinkle half of the nuts into a well-greased and lightly floured tube spring form. Add batter. Sprinkle top with remaining nuts. Bake in a 350°F. oven for 40 to 45 minutes or until the top is gently firm to touch and the bread tests done.

ROSE PETALS: Snip off and discard white part from rose petals. Place petals in a strainer and let a spray of cold water run over all. Place on paper towels and pat dry very gently. Snip with scissors and add to flour. Use dark red rose petals if possible, as more accent is placed on the deep red rather than the pale pink, white or yellow petals.

SEPHARDIC KUCHEN WITH RUM CHOCOLATE BUTTER

4 packages dry granular yeast
1 cup lukewarm water
3 teaspoons sugar
1 cup sweet butter, softened
1¼ cups sugar, sifted
2 teaspoons salt
3 whole eggs
3 egg yolks

3 egg whites, stiffly beaten with a pinch of salt
grated rind of 1 small orange
2 tablespoons candied rose petals, broken into coarse bits
4 cups flour
3 egg whites
Rum Chocolate Butter

Dissolve yeast in lukewarm water, add 3 teaspoons sugar. Stir. Cover and set aside until foaming and doubled in volume. In a large mixing bowl, cream butter with 1 cup sugar until light and fluffy, then add whole eggs, egg yolks, orange rind and candied rose petals. Mix well with a wooden spoon. Then add the foaming yeast mixture and 2 cups flour. Beat well into a smooth batter. Add remaining flour. Beat egg whites until they hold soft peaks; gradually add ¼ cup sugar and continue beating until the consistency of whipped cream. Fold into the batter with a rubber spatula. Cover and let rise in a warm place until doubled in bulk. Beat down with a large wooden spoon. Spoon thick batter into a 9″ or 10″ well-buttered and lightly floured savarin or kuchen baking pan. Cover and let rise again until doubled in bulk. Bake in a preheated 375°F. oven for 10 to 15 minutes, reduce heat to 350°F. and continue to bake 30 to 40 minutes longer or until golden brown and the kuchen tests done. Cool in baking pan for 10 minutes. Turn out onto a wire cooling rack until cold. Slice and spread with Rum Chocolate Butter if desired.

RUM CHOCOLATE BUTTER: ½ pound soft sweet butter *(do not melt)*
¼ to ⅓ cup thick chocolate sauce
3 tablespoons good dark rum or brandy

Cream butter with the chocolate sauce, add rum. Beat well until smooth. Pack into a small glass serving dish. Chill until ready to use. Let stand at room temperature before using.

FAT-FREE SPONGE LOAVES

CARAWAY SPONGE LOAF

An exquisitely flavored, light textured fat-free loaf cake.

6 eggs, separated
1 cup fine sugar, sifted
grated rind of ½ lemon
2 teaspoons lemon juice

1 cup flour, sifted
pinch salt
1 teaspoon caraway seeds
Marmalade Butter

Beat egg yolks over warm water until thick and lemon colored, about 10 minutes, adding sugar gradually, then the lemon rind and juice. Sift flour twice with salt and add to the creamed mixture, together with the caraway seeds. Beat with a wooden spoon until well blended. Fold in stiffly beaten egg whites. Grease the *bottom* of a 9" x 5" x 3" loaf pan and sprinkle lightly with a little flour or granulated sugar. Add the batter and bake in a preheated 350°F. oven for 35 to 45 minutes or until the top is gently firm to touch. Test with a toothpick; if it comes out clean the loaf is done. Invert pan on a wire cake cooler. When thoroughly cold, loosen sides with the flat side of a silver knife. Turn out onto a serving plate. Slice thinly and serve with steaming hot coffee or tea. Spread with Marmalade Butter if desired.

MARMALADE BUTTER: Soften—do not melt—1 stick (¼ pound) sweet butter and blend with 2 to 3 tablespoons Seville orange marmalade. Beat until smooth and well blended. Pack into a small serving dish. Refrigerate until ready to use. Let stand at room temperature for 10 minutes before using.

DELICATE SPONGE LOAF

4 eggs, separated	2 tablespoons cornstarch
1 cup fine sugar, sifted	⅞ cup presifted flour
¼ cup cold water	1 teaspoon baking powder
2 teaspoons grated orange rind	pinch salt

Beat egg yolks over warm water until thick; gradually add sugar. Add water and grated orange rind; beat until well blended. (Use a rotary beater or electric mixer.) Place cornstarch in a measuring cup and add enough flour to make 1 scant cup. Sift dry ingredients together. Combine with egg mixture. Fold in stiffly beaten egg whites. Bake in a 9" x 5" x 3" loaf pan, or in a 9" square baking pan. Make certain that only the *bottom* of the pan is greased. Bake in a preheated 350°F. oven for 30 to 35 minutes or until the top is gently firm to touch and delicately browned. Invert pan and cool on a wire cake rack.

HOT MILK SPONGE LOAF CAKE

2 eggs, separated	1 cup flour, sifted
1 cup fine sugar, sifted	1½ teaspoons baking powder
½ cup hot milk	pinch salt
½ teaspoon almond flavor	pinch anise seeds

Beat egg yolks over warm water until thick, about 10 minutes, adding ½ cup sugar gradually; beat well after each addition. Add milk, remaining ½ cup sugar and almond flavor. Beat well. Add sifted dry ingredients, then fold in the stiffly beaten egg whites, last the anise seeds. Grease bottom of an 8" x 4" x 2½" loaf pan and sprinkle lightly with flour or sugar. Bake in a 350°F. oven for 30 to 35 minutes or until the top is gently firm to touch. Invert pan over a wire cooling rack. When cold, loosen sides with the flat side of a silver knife.

PLAIN SPONGE CAKE

6 egg yolks
1¼ cup sifted sugar
1 tablespoon grated lemon
    rind
2 teaspoons lemon juice

6 egg whites
pinch salt
1½ cups cake flour, sifted
granulated sugar

Beat egg yolks over warm water or with an electric beater for 10 minutes until light and lemon colored. Add sugar, gradually, in a slow stream, beating constantly until the mixture is thick and smooth. Add the lemon rind and lemon juice. Beat the egg whites with salt until they hold soft peaks. Fold gently into the egg yolk batter, alternating with the flour. Turn into a 10-inch tube spring form. Bake in a preheated 325°F. oven for 45 to 50 minutes or until the top is delicately browned. Invert for 1 hour or longer until cold.

SUGGESTION: Grease bottom of spring form lightly with a little butter, top with a sprinkling of flour. Shake out excess flour. *Do not grease rest of pan.* When cold, loosen sponge with the flat side of a silver knife.

POTATO FLOUR SPONGE LOAF-CAKE

4 eggs, separated
¾ cup fine sugar, sifted
2 teaspoons grated lemon
    rind
2 teaspoons lemon juice

¾ cup sifted potato flour
pinch salt
1 teaspoon baking powder
1 teaspoon sesame seeds

Beat egg yolks until thick, adding sugar gradually, beating constantly after each addition. Add lemon rind and juice, then the stiffly beaten egg whites. Sift dry ingredients (except sesame seeds) together and fold gently into the egg mixture. Grease *bottom* of a 9" x 5" x 3" loaf pan; sprinkle lightly with a little flour or granulated sugar. Pour in the batter and if desired, sprinkle top with sesame seeds. Bake in a preheated

350°F. oven for 30 to 35 minutes or until the top is gently firm to touch. Test with a toothpick; if it comes out clean the loaf is done. Invert pan and cool on a wire cake rack. Loosen the outer edge of the loaf with the flat side of a silver knife. Shake the pan, and the loaf will fall out easily. Do not remove the sponge loaf-cakes from the pan while still warm; they are so delicate that they will not hold up on their own weight unless they are completely cold.

THINGS TO REMEMBER: Use sweet butter for greasing pans for a more delicate flavor. Butter only the bottom of the pans or spring forms for sponge loaves or cakes, for the batter cannot cling to the sides of the pans if greased, and the sponge cakes will not reach their full height. After removing the sponge loaf or sponge cakes from the oven turn the pan upside down on a wire cake rack for an hour or until completely cold.

ROLLS AND BUNS

BAGELS

The bagel, one of the most popular foods in Jewish cuisine, is fast becoming as Americanized as pizza and chow mein. It is an integral part of the Sunday morning breakfast when it is eaten spread with cream cheese and lox (smoked salmon). In the same manner, it is also served as a late night snack. Sometimes paper-thin slices of Bermuda onion are added to the "sandwich."

3¼ cups flour
1 teaspoon salt
3 tablespoons sugar
1 package dry granular yeast
⅓ cup lukewarm water
1 teaspoon sugar

⅔ cup lukewarm water
3 tablespoons salad oil
1 egg plus 1 egg yolk
4 quarts boiling water plus
2 tablespoons sugar

Sift the flour, salt and 3 tablespoons sugar into a large bowl. Dissolve yeast in ⅓ cup lukewarm water; add 1 teaspoon sugar. Stir. Cover and set aside until doubled in volume. Combine ⅔ cup lukewarm water with the oil. Add the foaming yeast to the flour mixture, then add the oil and water. Add the eggs and beat well with a wooden spoon until the mixture leaves the sides of the bowl. Turn out onto a lightly floured board and knead thoroughly until the dough is smooth and elastic. Place in a warm greased bowl. Cover and set aside in a warm place until doubled in bulk. Punch down and let rise again until doubled in bulk. Punch down; again let it rise until doubled in bulk. After the third rising turn out onto a floured board and knead until smooth. Divide dough in about 12 equal portions. Roll each into 6-inch "ropes," about ¾-inch thick, and form into circles—pinch ends together so that they will not come apart. In the meantime have ready the rapidly boiling water in a deep kettle.

Add the sugar. Drop each bagel into the boiling water, one at a time, but do not crowd the kettle. Cook until they rise to the top, then turn over and cook for a minute or two longer. Remove each with a slotted spoon and place on a greased baking sheet. Bake in a 375°F. oven for 20 to 25 minutes or until crusty and golden brown.

TOPPINGS: Before baking, for a beautiful golden gloss, brush bagels with beaten egg yolk, then sprinkle with coarse salt, or with poppy seeds, sesame seeds, or finely minced onion. The various toppings lend an appetizing taste to the bagels.

CHEDDAR CHEESE ROLLS

1 cup hot water
¼ cup sugar
½ teaspoon salt
1 package dry granular yeast
1 teaspoon sugar
½ cup lukewarm water

1 egg, well beaten
¾ cup grated cheese
3½ cups flour
melted butter
⅓ cup grated cheese

Place hot water in a large bowl; add sugar and salt. Cool to lukewarm. Sprinkle yeast and sugar over ½ cup lukewarm water. Stir. Cover and let stand until foaming and doubled in volume. Add to cooled water and sugar mixture. Add egg, ¾ cup grated Cheddar and enough flour to make a firm dough. Toss onto a lightly floured board and knead lightly until smooth and easy to handle. Form into balls. Arrange on a buttered cookie sheet. Cover and let rise until tripled in bulk. Bake in a 375°F. oven for 15 minutes. Brush with butter, sprinkle with cheese and return to oven for a few minutes until the cheese is melted. Serve at once.

QUICK CREAM CHEESE SWEET ROLLS

An ideal sweet-filled roll to serve for afternoon tea.

2 cups biscuit mix
½ cup light cream
1 teaspoon grated lemon
rind
2 3-ounce packages cream
cheese, room temperature

⅓ cup granulated sugar
½ cup chopped nuts
2 teaspoons grated lemon
rind
6 soft dates, snipped into
fourths with a scissors

Stir biscuit mix, cream and 1 teaspoon lemon rind together
with a silver knife until the dough leaves the side of the bowl.
Turn out onto a lightly floured board. Pat and roll into a
¼-inch thick rectangle. Spread with softened cream cheese,
sprinkle with sugar, nuts, lemon rind and dates. Roll up
as for a jelly roll. Cut into 1-inch slices. Bake on a lightly
buttered and floured cookie sheet in a 375°F. oven for 12 to
15 minutes. Best when served the day it is baked. To reheat
place in a slow oven for 5 to 10 minutes.

BATTER DINNER ROLLS

This is an excellent recipe for unusually light and tender rolls.
They are equally delicious with or without the sesame seed
topping.

2 tablespoons butter
1 cup scalded milk
2 teaspoons sugar
½ teaspoon salt
1 package dry granular yeast
⅓ cup lukewarm water

1 teaspoon sugar
1 egg, beaten
2 cups flour, scant
melted butter
sesame seeds

In a mixing bowl melt the 2 tablespoons butter with the hot
milk. Add 2 teaspoons sugar and salt. Cool to lukewarm.
Dissolve yeast in ⅓ cup lukewarm water; add 1 teaspoon
sugar. Stir. Cover and set aside until foaming and doubled

in volume. Add to the cooled milk mixture. Beat in the egg and 1 cup flour. Beat well with an electric or rotary beater until smooth. Add remaining cup flour and continue to beat briskly for 10 minutes, until the batter is thick but not stiff. (Add flour with a light hand.) Cover and set aside in a warm place until doubled in bulk. Cut the batter down with a wooden spoon. Cover and let rise again until doubled in bulk. Cut down and fill buttered muffin pans ⅔ full with the batter. Cover and let rise for 20 minutes. Bake in a 400°F. oven for 20 minutes or until the rolls are golden brown. Brush with melted butter and sprinkle with sesame seeds. Return to oven for a few minutes.

NOTE: Do not hurry the rising, for the rolls will keep their shape better, the dough will be lighter and much firmer. In baking rolls or biscuits a hotter oven is required than for loaves, the standard temperature being 375°F. to 400°F. depending on the individual oven.

SUGGESTION: It is a good idea to cream ingredients with a rotary or electric beater; as flour is added and the batter or dough becomes thicker, finish beating with a wooden spoon.

GERMAN GINGER BALLS

⅓ stick margarine
½ cup butter (¼ pound)
1 cup sugar
6 egg yolks
3 cups flour
3 teaspoons baking soda

1 teaspoon salt
1 teaspoon powdered ginger
2 tablespoons finely chopped candied ginger
1 cup lukewarm water
1 cup molasses

Cream margarine, butter and sugar in a large mixing bowl. Add the egg yolks one at a time, beating well after each addition. Add the sifted dry ingredients alternately with the candied ginger, lukewarm water and molasses, to the creamed butter-egg mixture. Fill well-buttered sizzling hot popover molds ⅔ full with the batter. Bake in a preheated 425°F.

141

for 15 minutes, reduce heat to 375°F. and continue to bake 20 to 25 minutes longer. Turn off heat; let gingerballs remain in oven 5 minutes longer.

QUICK LUNCHEON ROLLS

2½ cups flour
½ teaspoon salt
1 tablespoon sugar
4 teaspoons baking powder
1 teaspoon caraway seeds

⅔ stick butter or margarine
1 egg, beaten
¾ cup light cream
melted butter

In a mixing bowl, combine flour, salt, sugar, baking powder and caraway seeds. Work in the butter or margarine with a pastry blender. Add egg, then the light cream. Blend with a silver knife until the dough leaves the sides of the bowl. Toss onto a lightly floured board, pat out and roll out ¾-inch thick. Cut into rounds with a floured cookie cutter. Brush with melted butter. Arrange on a greased and lightly floured baking sheet. Bake in a 400°F. oven for 20 minutes or until nicely browned.

OATMEAL TEA SQUARES

2 cups flour
½ cup sugar
½ teaspoon allspice
1½ teaspoons baking powder
½ teaspoon baking soda

2 cups fine oatmeal
½ stick butter
1 egg, beaten
⅓ cup milk
½ cup dark molasses, scant

In a mixing bowl, sift together flour, sugar, allspice, baking powder and baking soda. Mix well, then add the oatmeal. With a pastry blender or fingers work in butter. Add the egg, milk and molasses. Beat well. Turn into a well-buttered and lightly floured 8″ square baking pan. Bake in a 325°F. oven for 30 minutes or until the top is gently firm to touch.

142

Cool, then break into squares with a wire cake cutter. Do not cut with a knife. Break the squares open and serve warm with whipped sweet butter.

ONION ROLLS

An unusually appetizing and fragrant roll, one that will be baked time and time again.

1 cup scalded milk	1 teaspoon sugar
2 tablespoons sugar	½ teaspoon baking powder
2 tablespoons butter	1 tablespoon instant mashed
½ teaspoon salt	potato mix
1 package dry granular yeast	3 to 4 cups flour
⅓ cup lukewarm water	¾ cup chopped onion

Place scalded milk in a large mixing bowl. Add 2 tablespoons sugar, butter, and salt. Cool to lukewarm. Dissolve yeast with lukewarm water, add 1 teaspoon sugar. Stir. Cover and set aside until foaming and doubled in volume. Add to the cooled milk mixture. Add baking powder, mashed potato mix and just enough flour to make a soft dough. Cover and let stand in a warm place until doubled in bulk. Turn out onto a lightly floured board and knead lightly for a few minutes. Roll out ½-inch thick. Cut in 3-inch rounds with a floured cutter. Place on a well-greased and lightly floured baking sheet. Cover and let rise until doubled in bulk. Brush lightly with melted butter; sprinkle with chopped onion and a little coarse salt if desired. Bake in a 375°F. to 400°F. oven for 20 to 25 minutes, or until golden brown.

This recipe may also be baked in a loaf, by shaping the dough and placing it in a 9″ x 5″ x 3″ loaf pan. After the last rising, brush top with melted butter or slightly beaten egg yolk and sprinkle with chopped onions. Bake as directed above for 30 to 35 minutes or until golden brown.

ORANGE ICE BOX ROLLS

1 package dry granular yeast
½ cup sugar
¾ teaspoon salt
2 cups lukewarm water
1 egg, beaten
1 tablespoon grated orange rind

4 tablespoons soft butter or margarine
7 cups flour
1 tablespoon grated orange rind mixed with 1 tablespoon crushed sugar cubes

Dissolve yeast, sugar and salt in lukewarm water. Add egg, orange rind and butter. Beat well with a wooden spoon. Add half of the flour and beat vigorously, then gradually add just enough flour to make a smooth soft dough. Turn out onto a floured board and knead into a ball. Turn into a warm, well-greased bowl. Cover, set aside and let rise until doubled in bulk. Punch down. Cover with plastic wrap and refrigerate for several hours or until needed. When ready to use, pinch off small pieces of dough to form into rolls. Brush lightly with a little melted butter. Place on a greased baking sheet. Cover and let rise again until light and doubled. Sprinkle with orange sugar. Bake in a 375°F. to 400°F. oven for 20 to 25 minutes. Refrigerate half of dough, if desired, until needed. It will keep well for at least 3 days.

ORIENTAL ROLLS

¼ cup almond paste
1 cup hot water
1 tablespoon butter
1 tablespoon sugar
½ teaspoon rose water

½ teaspoon salt
1 package dry granular yeast
⅓ cup lukewarm water
1 teaspoon sugar
3 to 4 cups flour

Dissolve the almond paste in the hot water. Stir well. Cool to lukewarm. Add butter, 1 tablespoon sugar, rose water and salt. Mix well. Dissolve yeast in lukewarm water; add 1 teaspoon sugar. Stir. Cover and set aside until foaming and doubled in volume. Add foaming yeast to the almond-water mixture. Add 2 cups flour and beat vigorously with a wooden spoon or rotary beater until the batter is smooth. Now add just enough flour to make a soft, easy-to-handle dough. The dough should be as light and as soft as can be handled. Add just a little of leftover flour to the board. Knead gently for 5 minutes then turn into a warm, greased bowl. Cover and let rise until doubled in bulk. With a floured fist punch down dough. Cover and let rise again until doubled. This will result in a lighter and very tender roll. Turn out onto a lightly floured board and shape into oval rolls. Arrange on a greased and lightly floured baking sheet, or for a softer roll — shape into balls and place close together in a greased baking pan. Cover with a clean cloth and let rise again until doubled. Brush with beaten egg yolk or milk. Bake in a 400°F. oven for 20 minutes or until golden brown.

NOTE: If the individual oval rolls are to be baked, place them about 1½-inches apart on the baking sheet. They will be crisper than the pan-baked rolls.

PARKER HOUSE ROLLS

1 teaspoon salt
1 tablespoon sugar
4 tablespoons butter or
  margarine
2 cups scalded milk

1 package dry granular yeast
⅓ cup lukewarm water
1 teaspoon sugar
6 cups flour

Place salt, 1 tablespoon sugar, butter and scalded milk in a large mixing bowl. Cool. Dissolve yeast in ⅓ cup lukewarm water and add 1 teaspoon sugar; stir. Cover and set aside until doubled in volume. Add foaming yeast to the cooled milk mixture. Beat in 3 cups flour, beating vigorously until the mixture is full of bubbles. Add remaining flour, just enough to make a soft, easy-to-handle dough. Turn out onto a lightly floured board and knead until smooth and elastic, about 8 to 10 minutes. Place in a warm greased bowl, cover and set aside in a warm place until doubled in bulk. Punch down and let rise again. Turn out onto a lightly floured board and roll into a sheet, ½-inch thick. Cut into 2½-inch rounds with a floured cookie cutter; brush with melted butter. Fold over so that the upper edge overlaps the under one, and then press edges together lightly. Arrange on a buttered baking sheet. Cover and let rise for about 1 hour. Bake in a 375°F. to 400°F. oven for 15 to 20 minutes until golden brown.

VARIATION: Divide dough in half. Use half for Parker House Rolls. Dot remaining half of dough with about ¼ pound sweet butter to make the dough "short." Fold and knead. *Knead the butter* in, do not spread it on the dough. Roll the dough out onto a lightly floured board, and cut out into small rounds with a floured biscuit cutter. Drop into boiling hot fat (360°F. to 375°F.) a few at a time. This is great fun to do, for if the dough is short enough (add more butter if desired) the rounds will puff up into delicious little golden crisp shells that will delight you. Sprinkle with a soft cloud of powdered sugar and serve at once. The shells may be filled with berries and whipped cream as a dessert treat.

QUICK PINWHEEL ROLLS

2 cups flour
4 teaspoons baking powder
½ teaspoon salt
½ stick butter or margarine

⅔ cup milk
⅓ cup melted butter
½ cup soft brown sugar
⅓ teaspoon cinnamon

Sift flour together with the baking powder and salt. Cut in ½ stick butter or margarine and then add the milk. Mix lightly with a fork, then toss the dough onto a lightly floured board. Pat and roll dough out lightly about ½-inch thick. Spread with melted butter and sprinkle with brown sugar mixed with the cinnamon. Roll up like a jelly roll. Cut into 1-inch slices and place them flat on a buttered cookie sheet. Bake in a 450°F. oven for 12 to 15 minutes. Serve warm.

SWEET ROLLS

1 package dry granular yeast
⅓ cup lukewarm water
1 teaspoon sugar
½ stick butter
5 tablespoons sugar
½ cup scalded milk

1 tablespoon grated orange rind
1 tablespoon grated lemon rind
3½ cups flour
1 egg

Dissolve yeast in lukewarm water; add 1 teaspoon sugar. Stir. Cover and set aside until foaming and doubled in volume. In a mixing bowl, combine butter, 5 tablespoons sugar, scalded milk, grated orange and lemon rind. Stir until butter melts. Cool to lukewarm and add the foaming yeast with 1½ cups flour. Beat vigorously for at least 10 minutes with a wooden spoon. Add egg and 1½ cups flour; beat until smooth, until the dough leaves the sides of the bowl. Turn out onto a lightly floured board, using the remaining ½ cup flour for the board. Knead into a soft dough (the dough should be softer than for bread). Place in a warm, greased bowl; cover and set aside in a warm place until doubled in bulk. Turn dough until thoroughly greased on all sides. Punch down with a floured fist and let rise again until doubled, about 45 to 60 minutes. Shape into round or oval rolls. Arrange on a buttered baking sheet. Cover and let rise again. Bake in a 375°F. to 400°F. oven for 20 to 25 minutes, until golden brown. Drizzle with white icing and sprinkle with chopped nuts.

VARIATION: Add 1 to 2 tablespoons raisins to the flour, or chopped dried apricots. Chopped nuts, sesame seeds, shredded citron or grated orange or lemon rind all add variety to the little sweet rolls. Brush with white icing and sprinkle with coconut, pistachio nuts or any favorite nuts. The little rolls may also be baked in buttered muffin pans or, for soft rolls, arrange closely together in buttered baking pans. For a dinner roll, omit the sugar. The basic recipe lends itself to many delicious buns or rolls, by using different shape baking pans, rolling the dough in interesting shapes.

VIENNA ROLLS

2 cups scalded milk
1 package dry granular yeast
½ cup lukewarm water
1 tablespoon sugar
5 to 6 cups flour
1 egg

¼ cup melted butter or
margarine
1 teaspoon salt
2 tablespoons sugar
1 egg white, slightly beaten
with 1 tablespoon water

Cool scalded milk to lukewarm. Dissolve yeast in lukewarm water, add 1 tablespoon sugar. Cover and set aside until foaming and doubled in volume. Add the foaming yeast to the lukewarm milk. Add 3 cups flour, one at a time, beating well for at least 10 minutes, or until the mixture is very light and smooth. Cover and set aside in a warm place until light and puffy. Add the beaten egg, melted butter, salt and 2 tablespoons sugar, then slowly add just enough flour to make a soft easy-to-handle dough. Turn out onto a lightly floured board. Knead at least 10 minutes, using as little flour as possible on the board. When the dough is satiny smooth and free from stickiness place in a warm, well-greased bowl. Cover and set aside in a warm place until doubled in bulk. Turn out onto a lightly floured board and shape into small buns, twists, and divided rolls (see below). Place on a greased baking sheet, cover and let stand until doubled. Glaze with beaten egg white. Bake in a 375°F. to 400°F. oven for 15 minutes or until golden brown.

SMALL BUNS: Shape into little balls. Glaze with beaten egg yolk or egg white.

TWISTS: Cut off three small pieces of dough. Roll each into pencil-thin ropes about 6 inches long. Braid. Pinch ends tightly. Glaze with egg white.

DIVIDED ROLLS: Make small balls, then press down the handle of a wooden spoon through the center of each ball, half way through, thus dividing it. Gently shape the ball so that it will be round, not flat.

CLOVER LEAF ROLLS: Cut off three small pieces of dough. Shape into three small balls, then place three little balls together in well-greased muffin tins. Glaze with melted butter.

148

BUNS

½ cup sugar
1 stick sweet butter or margarine (¼ pound)
1 teaspoon salt
1 mashed potato
2 cups scalded milk, cooled to lukewarm

2 packages dry granular yeast
½ cup lukewarm water
1 teaspoon sugar
6 cups flour
3 eggs

In a large mixing bowl, combine sugar, butter or margarine, salt, mashed potato and milk. Mix well. Dissolve yeast in lukewarm water, add sugar, and set aside until foaming and doubled in volume. Add yeast mixture to *cooled* milk mixture; add 4 cups flour. Beat well with a wooden spoon until the batter is light and bubbly. Add eggs and remaining flour, just enough to make a soft but stiff dough. Turn out onto a lightly floured board and knead for 10 minutes or longer until the dough is satiny smooth and elastic. Place dough in a warm, well-greased bowl, cover let rise until doubled in bulk. Punch down and let rise again. Turn out on a lightly floured board, divide dough in half. Shape into small balls and place close together in a well-greased baking pan. Cover and let rise until light and doubled in bulk. Brush with a cooled sugar-syrup mixture made with 2 tablespoons cream and 2 tablespoons sugar, dissolved over low heat. Bake in a 375°F. to 400°F. oven for 20 to 25 minutes until golden brown. Shape remaining half of dough into HOT CROSS BUNS.

HOT CROSS BUNS: Shape into small balls, then with a sharp knife cut two gashes on top, to make a cross. Cover and let rise until light and puffy. Bake as above. Glaze with a thin white icing, or brush with above sugar-syrup, 5 minutes before removing from oven, and then sprinkle the cross with granulated sugar. When golden brown remove from oven. If necessary glaze with the syrup 2 or 3 times until the glaze is glossy.

BISCUITS, MUFFINS AND SCONES

BISCUITS

Biscuits need a hot oven. Do not cut the biscuits too large because the smaller they are, the faster they will bake. Serve them piping hot; when they are split and buttered the butter should melt. The more shortening the better; a good and simple rule to follow is to use 2 tablespoons butter to each cup flour and 1 extra tablespoon for a good measure—this will add to the flakiness of the biscuits. Place the biscuits 2 inches apart on the baking sheet to give them room to expand.

For lighter and flakier biscuits fold and roll the biscuit dough several times instead of kneading. Use as little flour on the board as possible; too much will toughen the dough. The recipes are practically foolproof if directions are carefully followed. Remember, too much kneading and handling will produce tough, flat, unattractive and unappetizing biscuits. For a sweet biscuit add sugar—about 2 tablespoons or to taste—and/or grated fruit rinds, nuts, dates, raisins, etc. Add to the flour before combining with shortening and liquid.
Like to have fun? Try creating variations on your own!

BAKING POWDER BISCUITS
(Basic Recipe)

2 cups flour
4 teaspoons baking powder
½ teaspoon salt

4 tablespoons butter or other
  shortening
¾ cup sweet milk

Sift dry ingredients together into a mixing bowl, working butter into the flour with a pastry blender or fingers until crumbly. Add the milk gradually, a little at a time. Knead together for a *few seconds*. Pat out dough about 1 inch thick on a lightly floured board. Cut into rounds with a floured biscuit cutter. Arrange on a lightly greased and floured baking sheet. Bake 15 to 20 minutes in a 450°F. oven or until delicately browned.

CHEDDAR CHEESE BISCUITS

1 egg
¾ cup milk
2 cups flour
4 teaspoons baking powder
½ teaspoon salt
2 level teaspoons sugar

2 tablespoons sweet butter
4 tablespoons melted butter or margarine
½ cup coarsely grated cheddar cheese

Break egg into a small bowl and beat until well blended. Pour into a small measuring cup and add enough milk to measure ¾ cup. Sift dry ingredients together into a mixing bowl. Work in 2 tablespoons butter until crumbly. Add the milk mixture gradually, a little at a time, until the liquid is all used up. Mix. Knead on a lightly floured board for about 10 seconds. Roll out 1 inch thick, then cut into 2-inch rounds. Spread with a little soft butter and Cheddar cheese. Fold each round over, envelope fashion, brush top with melted butter and prick each with a fork. Bake in a 450°F. oven for 12 to 15 minutes. Serve as soon as they come out of the oven.

NOTE: For a tangy and different cheese biscuit, crumble blue cheese into a small bowl and combine with ⅓ chopped (fat-free) toasted cashew nuts. Mix with 1 teaspoon sour cream. Blend. Spread on little rounds, fold and bake as directed above.

GARDEN FRESH DINNER BISCUITS

2 cups flour
3 teaspoons baking powder
½ teaspoon salt
1 tablespoon freshly minced parsley
1 tablespoon minced carrot

1 sprig very finely minced watercress or the tender green part of 1 small scallion (about 1 tablespoon)
½ stick butter
¾ cup milk

Sift together dry ingredients twice, in a mixing bowl. Add minced vegetables, and toss gently with a fork until thoroughly blended with the flour. Cut in butter with a pastry blender until crumbly. Stir in just enough milk to make a soft dough. Turn out onto a lightly floured board, fold and roll dough for ½ minute, 1 inch thick. Use the flour on the board sparingly! Cut into 2-inch rounds with a floured biscuit cutter. Bake on an ungreased or very lightly greased baking sheet in a 450°F. oven for 15 to 20 minutes until golden brown. Serve hot with plenty of butter.

DROP BISCUITS

2 cups flour
4 teaspoons baking powder
½ teaspoon salt

½ teaspoon sugar
3 tablespoons butter
1 cup milk

Sift dry ingredients together into a mixing bowl. Work in butter or margarine with a pastry blender or with fingers until the mixture is crumbly. Add just enough milk to make a soft but slightly sticky dough. Drop by spoonfuls in irregular heaps on a greased and lightly floured baking sheet. Sprinkle with caraway seeds and a little coarse salt, if desired, before baking. Bake in a 425°F. oven for 12 to 15 minutes or until delicately browned. Split in half and spread with butter or, if salt and caraway seeds aren't used, favorite jam.

VERMONT MAPLE SUGAR BISCUITS

2 cups all-purpose flour
4 teaspoons baking powder
½ teaspoon salt

1 cup heavy sweet cream, whipped
⅓ cup maple sugar
⅓ cup chopped hickory nuts

Sift dry ingredients, twice, into a mixing bowl. Make a well in the center and add the whipped cream. Fold into the flour with a spatula, or with a silver knife—do not beat. Turn out onto a very lightly floured board. Fold and roll dough for ½ minute. Roll out 1-inch thick. Cut out with a 2-inch floured biscuit cutter. Sprinkle with maple sugar and chopped nuts. Pat tops lightly with fingers. Bake on an ungreased baking sheet in a preheated 425°F. oven for 12 to 15 minutes. Serve as they come out of the oven, with plenty of butter and maple syrup, if desired.

NOTE: To reheat leftover biscuits, place in a brown paper bag and run cold water gently over it until the bag is sufficiently dampened. Then secure tightly and place in a 375°F. oven for 5 to 10 minutes—the biscuits will come out hot and freshened. Serve at once.

TROPICAL RUM BISCUITS

A delicious and fragrant biscuit to serve with salads.

2 cups flour
2 teaspoons baking powder
½ teaspoon salt
3 tablespoons butter or
  margarine

¾ cup milk
12 small sugar cubes
¼ cup rum or orange juice

Sift dry ingredients together into a mixing bowl. Work in butter or margarine with a pastry blender. Add milk gradually and mix with the flat side of a silver knife until the dough leaves the sides of the bowl. Toss onto a lightly floured board; pat and roll out lightly about ¾ to 1 inch thick. Cut out with a 2-inch floured biscuit cutter. Make a dent in center of each biscuit. Place a rum-soaked sugar cube in each dent. Arrange on a lightly greased baking sheet and bake in a 450°F. oven for 12 to 15 minutes or until golden brown.

RUM SOAKED SUGAR CUBES: In a small shallow dish soak sugar cubes in rum or orange juice for a few seconds. Do not allow the sugar to soak too long as it will fall apart.

SALLY LUNN

2 cups flour
4 teaspoons baking powder
3 tablespoons sugar
½ teaspoon salt

2 beaten eggs
1 cup milk
⅓ cup melted butter
1 teaspoon grated lemon rind

Sift the dry ingredients into a mixing bowl. Add the beaten eggs, milk, butter and lemon rind. Beat with a wooden spoon until well blended. Turn into a well-greased and lightly floured baking pan. Let stand for 5 to 10 minutes, then bake in a 375°F. oven for 20 minutes or until delicately browned. Cool 10 minutes and cut into squares.

BISCUIT SHORTCAKE

2 cups flour
4 teaspoons baking powder
½ teaspoon salt
4 to 6 tablespoons butter or margarine

⅔ cup milk, or half milk and half water
1 teaspoon grated lemon rind
⅓ cup melted butter

Sift dry ingredients twice into a mixing bowl. Work in shortening with a pastry blender or the fingers until the mixture is crumbly. Add just enough milk to make a very light soft dough. Turn out onto a lightly floured board and knead lightly for less than a minute. Divide in half. Roll out ½-inch thick into two rounds. Brush each with butter, place one round on top of other. Bake on a slightly greased and lightly floured baking sheet or in a 7-inch layer cake tin, at 450°F. for 12 to 15 minutes or until done. Split, butter inside surfaces and fill with sweetened fruits or berries in season. Top with more fruit and whipped cream. Makes one large shortcake.

SHORTCAKE IN-THE-SQUARE

3 cups flour
4 teaspoons baking powder
½ teaspoon salt
⅓ cup sugar
1 stick butter (¼ pound)

1¼ cups milk
1 egg, beaten
2 teaspoons grated lemon rind

Sift dry ingredients together into a mixing bowl. Cut in butter with a pastry blender until the mixture is crumbly. Mix milk together with the egg; then add all at once to the flour. Add lemon rind. Mix lightly with a fork or the flat side of a silver knife until all the flour has been moistened. Do not beat or overmix. Turn into 9" x 9" greased baking pan. Sprinkle top with sugar. Bake in a 425°F. oven for 15 minutes or until golden brown. Cool. Split in halves, add bits of cold butter, and crushed fresh strawberries. Top with whipped cream if desired.

QUICK SOUR CREAM BISCUITS

3 cups flour
5 teaspoons baking powder
pinch salt

1 teaspoon sugar
1 teaspoon grated lemon rind
1 cup sour cream

Sift dry ingredients together into a mixing bowl. Add lemon rind and sour cream. Blend with the flat side of a silver knife until the dough leaves the sides of the bowl. Toss onto a lightly floured board and knead light for 5 seconds. Roll out 1 inch thick, then cut into 2-inch rounds with a floured biscuit cutter. Bake on a lightly greased and floured baking sheet in a 425°F. oven for 12 to 15 minutes or until delicately browned.

HINT: Instead of cutting out the biscuits in rounds and being left with scraps, pat dough into a buttered square baking pan; then, with a sharp pointed knife, cut into 2-inch squares. Brush with melted butter and sprinkle with chopped green onions (scallions), then with coarse salt. Lift them out carefully with a spatula when they come out of the oven. Split open and serve while warm with dabs of cold butter.

STANDARD MUFFIN RECIPE

2 cups flour	1 egg
4 teaspoons baking powder	⅞ cup milk (7 ounces)
½ teaspoon salt	4 tablespoons melted butter
2 tablespoons sugar	1 teaspoon grated lemon rind

Combine dry ingredients together in a mixing bowl. Add egg, milk, butter and grated rind. Beat well with a wooden spoon. Spoon ⅔ full into well-greased and lightly floured muffin pans and bake 20 minutes in a 400°F. oven until delicately browned. makes 6 large or 8 small muffins.

VARIATIONS:

WALNUT MUFFINS: Add ½ cup coarsely chopped, lightly floured walnuts to the batter.

BLUEBERRY MUFFINS: Fold ¾ cup firm, lightly floured blueberries gently into the batter with a rubber spatula.

APPLE MUFFINS: Pare, core and cut apples into small cubes. Sprinkle with a little flour and fold into batter together with 1 tablespoon plump raisins.

DATE MUFFINS: Add ½ cup quartered and lightly floured dates to batter.

ORANGE MARMALADE MUFFINS: Fill muffin tins ¾ full with batter, top with a scant teaspoon orange marmalade.

BANANA MUFFINS

1 cup quick oatmeal	1 cup flour
¼ cup buttermilk	2 teaspoons baking powder
1 small ripe banana, mashed	½ teaspoon salt
1 egg, beaten	½ teaspoon baking soda
½ cup soft brown sugar	⅓ cup butter or margarine
1 teaspoon grated orange rind	cinnamon sugar for topping

156

Combine oatmeal, milk and banana; mix well with a wooden spoon. Add egg, brown sugar and orange rind. Sift dry ingredients together and add to milk mixture. Stir cooled melted butter into the batter. Fill buttered and lightly floured muffin tins ⅔ full. Bake in a 400°F. oven for 15 to 20 minutes or until done. Sprinkle top with cinnamon sugar before baking, if desired.

HINT: When spooning a heavy batter into muffin tins, use an ice-cream scoop instead of a spoon. Each muffin will then be uniform in size, with no guess-work, and no dripping spoon!

BRAN NUT MUFFINS

1 egg
⅓ cup melted butter
¼ cup milk
4 tablespoons sugar
½ teaspoon salt
3 teaspoons baking powder

1 cup flour
1 cup crisp bran flakes
½ cup very coarsely chopped walnuts
6 to 8 soft dates, sliced
cinnamon sugar for topping

In a large bowl, beat egg until light. Add butter, milk, sugar, salt, baking powder, flour and bran flakes. Stir only enough until blended. *Do not beat.* Fold in nuts and dates, sprinkled lightly with a little flour. Spoon into well-greased muffin tins, ⅔ full. Sprinkle with cinnamon sugar. Bake in a 400°F. oven about 20 to 25 minutes or until golden brown. (Smaller muffins require less time; about 15 to 18 minutes.) Yields 6 large or 12 small muffins.

GLUTEN RAISIN MUFFINS

1 egg
½ cup water
4 ounces gluten flour

½ teaspoon baking soda
½ cup plump dark raisins (optional)

Beat egg, add water and stir. Mix flour with baking soda and raisins. Add to egg mixture. Beat until smooth. Spoon into

157

greased muffin tins. Bake in a 400°F. oven for 15 to 20 minutes or until golden brown.

NOTE: Dia'Mel gluten flour is available at most specialty and health food stores.

PAT JOHNSON'S OATMEAL MUFFINS

This marvelous recipe was a gift to us from Pat Johnson, a lovely Irish lady gently touched with a bit of "fey." The muffins are tender with a crunch to the teeth. Serve them hot from the oven, split and filled with a dab of cold sweet butter. Just right for your favorite leprechaun!

1 cup rolled oats	1 egg
1 cup buttermilk	1 cup flour
⅓ cup soft butter or margarine	1 teaspoon baking powder
	½ teaspoon baking soda
¼ cup soft brown sugar	1 scant teaspoon salt

Allow the rolled oats to soak in the buttermilk for 1 hour. Mix the shortening, brown sugar and egg together thoroughly. Sift flour, baking powder, soda and salt and stir in alternately with the rolled oats and buttermilk mixture. Fill greased muffin tins ⅔ full. Bake in a 400°F. oven until golden brown (20 to 25 minutes). Yields 12 medium-size muffins.

OLD MILL WHOLE GRAIN MUFFINS

1 beaten egg	pinch salt
½ cup milk	½ teaspoon sugar
1 cup 5-Grain Muffin Mix	1 tablespoon wheat germ
2 tablespoons melted butter	

In a mixing bowl combine egg, milk and muffin-mix. Then stir in the melted butter, salt and sugar. Bake in greased muffin pans in a 400°F. oven for 20 minutes or until golden brown. Sprinkle lightly with wheat germ, if desired, before baking. Serve hot with favorite jam or butter.

WHOLE GRAIN RYE MUFFINS

1 cup Byrd Mill Rye flour
1 cup whole wheat flour
3 teaspoons baking powder
½ teaspoon salt
pinch baking soda

2 beaten eggs
1 cup milk
4 tablespoons melted butter
or margarine
2 tablespoons dark molasses

Sift both flours together with baking powder, salt and baking soda into a mixing bowl. Add eggs, milk, butter and molasses. Mix quickly. Bake in greased muffin tins at 400°F. for 20 minutes or until done.

SCONES

RULES TO REMEMBER:

The correct amount of liquid is important for good results. Add just enough to make a soft, pliable dough. If too much is used, they will be heavy and rather doughy.

Use the flat side of a silver knife to mix, because the knife is thinner and cooler and will not force the air out of the dough.

Knead the dough very lightly for a few seconds with the fingertips until smooth. Too much handling produces leathery, tough scones.

Pat out dough, roll lightly to a thickness of ½ inch. Too thin rounds will make an uneven scone.

For drop scones mix a batter slightly thicker than pancake batter. Cook them quickly on a griddle, on a moderately hot surface. The underside should be cooked by the time bubbles appear over the top. Turn at once and cook other side. Cover with a clean tea-towel to keep them warm and soft. *Do not warm them in the oven*—this will dry and toughen the scones.

SCONES

2 cups flour
4 teaspoons baking powder
⅔ cup milk

2 eggs
2 tablespoons sugar
2 tablespoons melted butter

In a mixing bowl, combine sifted flour and baking powder. Stir in milk. Beat eggs until light and fluffy; add together with the sugar and melted butter. Drop by large tablespoonfuls onto a hot griddle. Keep turning until both sides are gently browned. Serve warm, split and toasted. Spread with warm honey or jam.

ENGLISH CREAM SCONES

Here is a scone like grandmother used to make! Not too sweet and just right to go with fresh sweet butter and favorite jams. Serve warm with piping hot coffee or tea.

2 cups flour
3 teaspoons baking powder
4 teaspoons sugar
½ teaspoon salt
4 tablespoons butter or
  margarine

2 eggs
½ cup sweet cream
1 beaten egg white
sugar for topping

Sift dry ingredients into a mixing bowl. Work in shortening with a pastry blender or fingers until crumbly. Beat eggs, add cream, and mix with the flour mixture. Toss onto a lightly floured board and roll out ½ inch thick. Cut into desired shapes. Brush with melted butter or egg white, beaten slightly. Sprinkle with a little sugar and bake in a 375°F. oven for 15 to 18 minutes.

SOUR CREAM SCONES

1 cup self-rising flour	½ cup sour cream
1 scant teaspoon salt	1 egg yolk beaten with
⅓ stick butter	2 teaspoons milk

In a mixing bowl, work butter into sifted flour and salt with a pastry blender until crumbly. Add just enough sour cream to make a soft dough. Mix, using the flat side of a silver knife, until the dough leaves the sides of the bowl. Roll out about ½ inch thick onto a lightly floured board. Cut into rounds with a 2½-inch biscuit cutter. Brush with beaten egg yolk. Bake in a 375°F. oven for 12 to 15 minutes. Serve warm wit' plenty of sweet butter and marmalade.

POPOVERS

Popovers add a luxurious touch to the plainest meal. For not only do popovers taste so good—with their crisp exterior and tender, surprise-filled inside—but they also are a delight to the eye: high-puffed, feather-light, with tops firm and golden brown. And they have to wear these tops very proudly, for limp and fallen tops signal a culinary defeat.

Fortunately, popovers are very simple to prepare if the recipes are carefully followed and these few general rules always kept in mind. The batter should be the consistency of heavy cream. The iron popover molds should always be buttered and sizzling hot when they are half-filled with the batter, and should be placed in a hot oven (*very* hot at the start) with the oven door tightly shut. If iron popover molds are not available, buttered and warm gem pans (cup cake size) may be used. For large size popovers use Pyrex custard cups. Bake popovers according to temperatures directed in the recipes, then turn off heat and let remain in oven for 5 to 10 minutes longer. Remove from oven; prick with the tines of a fork to allow steam to escape. Then return to oven for five minutes.

The versatile popover may be served in many ways: plain, with fresh sweet butter, or with honey, jam or maple syrup; as a dessert with its center filled with sugared fresh sliced peaches or berries in season, and topped with fluffy sweetened whipped cream; as a main dish, split and filled with creamed chicken, salmon or tuna fish. However, when the popovers are served as a main dish, with hot creamed fillings, always serve hot, hot, hot!

It should be noted that no baking powder is used in preparing popover batter because steam supplies the leavening action. The cold batter, poured into sizzling hot buttered molds or glass custard cups, creates the steam which causes them to "pop" (hence their name) and the correct oven temperatures will keep them "popped" until they are ready to remove from oven.

POPOVERS
(Basic Recipe)

1 cup flour
½ teaspoon salt
2 eggs

1 scant cup milk
1 tablespoon melted butter

Sift flour with salt. Beat eggs until light and mix together with the milk and butter. Combine flour with the milk mixture, beating only enough to make a smooth batter. Do not overbeat. Fill hot, buttered, iron popover molds or heavy gem pans half full with the batter. Bake in a preheated 425°F. oven for 25 minutes or until "popped" and the tops are firm; reduce heat to 350°F. and continue to bake another 15 minutes or until golden brown. Turn off oven; remove popovers and prick sides with the tines of a fork to allow steam to escape. Return to oven for 5 minutes longer.

BOSTON STYLE POPOVERS
(Without Shortening)

1 cup flour
¼ teaspoon salt

1 cup milk
1 egg, separated

Combine salt with flour. Add half of the milk, slowly, and beat until smooth. Add remainder of milk and beaten egg yolk. Fold in stiffly beaten egg white. Half fill sizzling hot iron popover molds or into pyrex custard cups. Bake in a preheated 425°F. oven for 20 minutes; reduce heat to 350°F. and continue to bake until "popped" and golden brown. The tops should be firm. Turn off heat; remove from oven, and prick sides with the tines of a fork to release steam. Return to oven for 5 to 10 minutes longer. Remove from pans at once, serve filled with dabs of cold butter, jam or maple syrup, or if desired with favorite creamed fillings.

163

CHEDDAR CHEESE POPOVERS

1 egg
1 cup milk
¼ teaspoon salt

1 cup sifted flour
½ teaspoon baking powder
½ cup grated Cheddar cheese

Beat egg with milk, using a rotary beater. Combine salt, flour and baking powder. Stir gradually into the milk. Continue to beat with a rotary beater until light. Thoroughly heat buttered iron popover molds until sizzling hot, then place a tablespoon of batter in each, top with ¾ teaspoon grated cheese, then add another tablespoon batter. Bake in a preheated 450°F. oven for 25 minutes, or until the tops begin to "pop." Reduce heat to 350°F. and continue to bake until the tops are firm and golden brown. Turn off heat and let remain in oven another 5 minutes. Prick lightly with the tines of a fork to allow steam to escape; return to oven for 5 minutes more.

GRANDMOTHER'S SPECIAL POPOVERS

3 eggs
½ cup milk
pinch salt
½ teaspoon grated lemon

rind
pinch nutmeg
½ cup flour

Beat eggs until thick and lemon-colored. Add milk, salt, lemon rind and nutmeg, then pour *very slowly* over the flour, stirring constantly. Do not add liquid mixture too rapidly. Beat vigorously. Fill sizzling hot, buttered iron popover molds or Pyrex custard cups half full with the batter. Bake in a preheated 425°F. oven for 20 to 25 minutes; reduce heat to 350°F. and continue to bake 15 minutes longer or until "popped" and the tops are firm and golden brown. Turn off heat and let remain in oven 5 minutes longer. Prick sides with the tines of a fork to allow steam to escape. Return to oven for 5 minutes more.

HIGH-RISE LEMON POPOVERS

1 cup flour, sifted
½ teaspoon salt
1 teaspoon sugar
2 eggs, beaten
1 teaspoon melted butter

1 teaspoon lemon juice
2 teaspoons grated lemon
rind
1 cup milk

Combine flour with salt and sugar. Add beaten eggs, butter, lemon juice, lemon rind and milk. Beat well together. Have ready greased and sizzling hot iron popover molds or gem pans or custard cups. Fill half full with the batter. Bake in a preheated 425°F. oven for 25 minutes, or until "popped." Reduce heat to 350°F. and continue to bake popovers 15 minutes longer or until the tops are firm and golden brown. Remove from pans, prick sides with the tines of a fork to release steam. Return to oven, turn off heat, let remain 5 to 10 minutes longer.

MILE HIGH POPOVERS

1 tablespoon melted butter
2 eggs
1 cup milk

1 cup sifted flour
½ teaspoon salt
pinch nutmeg, optional

Beat butter with eggs until thick. Add half of the milk and flour; beat hard. Add remaining milk, flour, salt and nutmeg, if used. Mix until all the flour has been moistened. Do not overmix; disregard lumps. Pour batter into well-buttered sizzling hot custard cups or iron popover molds. Place in a cold oven, set heat up to 450°F. Do not open the oven door for at least 30 minutes or until "popped" and the tops are firm. Reduce heat to 350°F. and continue to bake until golden brown, about 10 to 15 minutes longer. Turn off heat and allow to remain in oven 10 minutes longer. Puncture around neck with the tines of a fork, or make a slit on the side of the popover to allow steam to escape. Return to oven for 5 minutes more.

SOUTHERN RICE POPOVERS

Instant rice is best for this recipe because each grain is separate and dry and blends well with the flour without becoming gummy and sticky.

½ cup cold boiled rice
1 cup sifted flour
1 teaspoon baking powder
1 teaspoon grated orange rind

½ teaspoon salt
3 teaspoons sugar
1 egg, separated
2 teaspoons melted butter

Mix rice with a wooden fork to separate grains. Combine rice with flour, baking powder, orange rind, salt and sugar. Blend well. Add egg yolk, mix, then the melted butter. Mix again. Fold in beaten egg white. In the meantime preheat oven to 425°F. and heat buttered iron popover molds or Pyrex custard cups. Fill the cups half full with the batter. Bake 25 minutes until they begin to pop, and the tops are firm and golden brown. Reduce heat to 350°F. and bake another 10 minutes. Prick popovers with the tines of a fork to allow steam to escape. Turn off heat, place on a baking sheet and allow to remain in the oven 10 minutes longer.

NOTE: The original recipe calls for mashed rice. However, after experimenting with this cherished old Southern recipe we found that the whole rice grains are tastier, and result in a lighter popover.

DIERDRE'S FAVORITE WALNUT POPOVERS

3 eggs
2 cups milk
2 cups flour

1 teaspoon grated lemon rind
½ teaspoon salt
⅓ cup chopped walnuts

Beat eggs with a rotary beater or wire whisk until thick and lemon-colored. Add milk. To the flour add lemon rind, salt and nuts. Add all at once to the egg-milk mixture, beating

166

briskly until the batter is smooth. Have buttered, sizzling hot popover molds, or muffin pans or Pyrex custard cups ready. Fill the cups half full. Bake in a preheated 425°F. oven for 20 minutes; reduce heat to 350°F. and continue to bake until the popovers have "popped" and the tops are firm and golden brown. Turn off heat. Prick sides with the tines of a fork, or make a slit to let steam escape. Return to oven for 5 to 10 minutes. Insert pieces of cold butter in the slits, or favorite jam or warm maple syrup.

BREAD PUDDINGS

Countless cooks have found out that a bread pudding is a dish of many virtues. It is quick and easy to make. It is always a tasty and nourishing desert, and it is one recipe in which we can use up—advantageously—day-old or leftover bread.

We have created this original collection of bread pudding recipes solely for this book. Amazingly versatile, bread pudding can be served with a variety of toppings: meringues, whipped cream, fragrant sauces; or laced with brandy or liqueurs. And if a special occasion arises, calling for a bit of glamor, just lace it with warm brandy or rum, ignite, and serve flaming, at the table!

CHERRY BREAD PUDDING PIE

4 slices soft white bread, crusts removed
½ cup milk
2 tablespoons butter or margarine
2 tablespoons soft brown sugar
2 eggs, separated

½ teaspoon vanilla
1 teaspoon grated lemon rind
½ cup whole cherry jam thinned with
1 tablespoon Cherry Kijafa or sherry wine
4 tablespoons sugar

Break slices into small pieces. Bring milk, butter or margarine and brown sugar to a boil in a small saucepan and pour over the bread. Stir well; let stand for 10 minutes. Cool. Beat egg yolks until very light and lemon colored; add to bread-milk mixture. Add vanilla and lemon rind. Blend well with a wooden spoon. Pour into a well-buttered ovenware pie plate. Spread top with cherry jam. Bake in a 375°F. oven for 30 minutes. Beat egg whites until they hold soft peaks, add a slow stream of sugar (4 tablespoons) and continue to beat until as thick as whipped cream. Pile roughly over the baked pudding and return to oven until the meringue is a light brown. Cut into wedges and serve hot or cold.

EXOTIC FIG BREAD PUDDING

5 slices day-old white bread, cubed
⅓ cup orange juice
¼ cup sugar
4 egg yolks
2 teaspoons grated orange rind

¼ teaspoon nutmeg
4 tablespoons Cointreau or Curaçao
8 canned figs, *well drained*
6 egg whites
6 tablespoons sugar
2 tablespoons brandy

In a large mixing bowl combine the cubed bread, orange juice and sugar. Stir gently with a wooden fork, tossing the bread lightly until it has absorbed all of the juice. If dry, add another tablespoon of juice. Beat egg yolks over warm water until thick and lemon colored. Add to bread mixture, blend well; add the orange rind, nutmeg and liqueur. Cut the very well drained figs in halves. Add to mixture. Beat egg whites until they hold soft peaks; add a slow stream of sugar and continue to beat until as thick as whipped cream. Fold into the bread mixture. Pile into a well-buttered and sugared deep baking dish. Set in a pan of hot water and bake in a 325°F. oven for ¾ hour or until the pudding is puffed and golden brown. Remove the bread pudding gently from the pan of hot water; return to oven for 10 minutes. Heat the brandy for a second, ignite, and pour flaming over the pudding. This delicate and exotic pudding should be served at once. To gild the lily, if desired, top with liqueur-flavored whipped cream.

FRESH STEWED FRUIT PUDDING

2 cups fresh red sour cherries
1 tablespoon lemon juice
1 tablespoon grated lemon rind
¼ cup sherry

½ cup water
½ cup sugar
8 slices buttered white bread, crusts removed
vanilla ice cream

Combine pitted cherries with lemon juice, lemon rind, wine, water and sugar. Bring to a boil, reduce heat at once, then cook gently until the fruit is soft and the liquid is slightly thickened. Arrange 4 slices of the buttered bread in a well-buttered square Pyrex baking dish, making alternate layers of the hot stewed fruit, juice and all, leaving a thick layer of the stewed fruit for the top. Cover with plastic wrap, place a heavy weight on top. Refrigerate for several hours or overnight. When ready to serve cut into squares and top with vanilla ice cream, if desired.

GERMAN BREAD PUDDING

2 cups soft pumpernickel crumbs
2 cups soft rye bread crumbs
½ cup water
⅓ cup plump raisins
3 eggs, beaten
1 tablespoon grated orange rind

¼ cup orange juice
¼ cup lemon juice
½ cup sugar
1 egg white stiffly beaten with
1 tablespoon brown sugar
1 teaspoon cinnamon sugar

Soften bread crumbs in water. Squeeze dry. In a mixing bowl combine softened crumbs, raisins, eggs, orange rind, juice and sugar. Beat well until thoroughly blended. Fold in the beaten egg white. Pour into a well-buttered baking dish. Sprinkle with cinnamon sugar. Bake in 350°F. oven for 30 minutes or until the top is crisp and golden.

PLUMP RAISINS: Soften raisins in warm water 5 to 10 minutes. Dry with soft paper towels.

DELICATE SPICED MERINGUE-TOPPED BREAD PUDDING

3 cups soft bread crumbs
2 cups hot milk
3 tablespoons sugar
1 tablespoon grated orange rind
¼ teaspoon salt
3 egg yolks, beaten
½ cup pitted lichee nuts, cut in halves

3 egg whites
pinch salt
6 tablespoons sugar
pinch nutmeg
¼ teaspoon powdered cloves
¼ teaspoon ginger
⅓ cup chopped toasted almonds

Put the bread crumbs in a large mixing bowl; add the hot milk. Stir together and add sugar, grated rind, salt. Cool to lukewarm. Beat the egg yolks over warm water until thick and fluffy. Add to bread-crumb mixture. Fold in the lichee nuts. Mix thoroughly and bake in a 350°F. oven in a deep, well-buttered baking dish for 30 minutes or until the pudding is firm to touch. Beat egg whites until they hold soft peaks; add sugar gradually, then the nutmeg, cloves and ginger. Pile roughly on top of baked pudding, sprinkle with almonds, and return to oven for a few minutes to brown lightly.

SUGAR PLUM BREAD PUDDING

1 tablespoon flour
½ stick melted sweet butter
1½ cups soft bread crumbs
½ cup fruit juice, saved from canned fruits or ½ cup orange juice
2 tablespoons sherry

2 eggs, beaten
8 fresh, ripe, small purple plums
½ cup sugar
cold butter
¾ cup cold sour cream

Combine flour with butter, bread crumbs, fruit juice, sherry and eggs. Roll plum halves in sugar until thickly coated. Chill until the sugar is slightly hardened. Pour the bread-crumb mixture into a buttered and lightly sugared Pyrex baking dish. Top with the sugared plums. Dot with bits of cold butter. Bake in a 350°F. oven for 30 minutes or until the plums are soft. Serve warm topped with cold sour cream for an unusual taste-treat.

RASPBERRY BREAD PUDDING

¾ cup milk
3 egg yolks
pinch salt
8 slices day old white bread
   or leftover plain coffee cake
½ cup raspberry jam

2 tablespoons raspberry
   liqueur or port wine
3 egg whites
pinch salt
⅓ cup sugar
½ cup coarsely chopped nuts

Combine milk with egg yolks, beat well; add salt. Remove crusts from bread, or thinly slice leftover coffee cake. Dip bread or cake slices in the milk-egg mixture. Let stand until the liquid has been absorbed. Arrange 4 slices in a well-buttered shallow baking dish. Blend jam well with liqueur or wine. Spread over all. Top with 4 more slices, sandwich fashion. Beat egg whites with salt until they hold soft peaks; add a slow stream of sugar and continue to beat until thick and glossy. Fold in chopped nuts. Spread over top of pudding. Bake in a 350°F. oven until delicately browned, about 25 to 30 minutes.

BREAD PUDDING SOUFFLE

½ cup hot milk
2 cups soft bread crumbs
1 tablespoon butter or margarine
⅓ cup sugar
1 tablespoon grated lemon
   rind
3 tablespoons sherry or rosé
   wine

3 egg yolks
⅓ cup firm currant jelly, cut
   into small cubes
3 egg whites
pinch salt
3 tablespoons sugar
⅓ cup finely chopped
   toasted almonds

Pour hot milk over bread crumbs; add butter or margarine and sugar. Let stand for 5 minutes. Add lemon rind and sherry or rosé. Beat egg yolks over warm water until thick and lemon colored. Fold into the bread mixture; add cubed currant jelly. Beat egg whites with salt until they hold soft peaks; add sugar in a slow stream and continue to beat until as thick as whipped cream. Fold in chopped nuts. Add the meringue to the bread mixture, about a third at a time, folding it in gently with a rubber spatula. Turn the mixture into a well-buttered and sugared baking dish. Bake in a 350°F. oven for 30 to 35 minutes or until the pudding is puffed but firm and golden brown. Serve at once with Apricot Wine Sauce.

APRICOT WINE SAUCE: In a medium-size sauce pan, combine ¾ cup apricot jam, ¼ cup sherry and 1 teaspoon grated lemon rind. Heat gently over *low heat* until the mixture is quite warm. Remove from heat and beat vigorously until smooth and well-blended. Serve either hot or cold over pudding.

TOASTED BREAD PUDDING
With
Chocolate Rum Sauce

8 slices of buttered day-old bread
pinch salt
½ cup sugar
2 eggs, beaten
¾ cup hot milk, cooled
1 tablespoon grated orange rind

4 squares of dark sweet chocolate
1 tablespoon hot coffee
1 tablespoon butter
1 tablespoon rum
1 egg yolk, beaten
½ cup chopped walnuts
2 tablespoons rum

Toast bread *very lightly* and spread with butter while still hot. Arrange 4 slices of toast in a square well-buttered baking dish. Combine salt, sugar, eggs, hot milk and grated rind. Beat until well blended. Pour half of the milk-egg mixture over the toast. Let stand until absorbed. Heat the chocolate over warm water together with the coffee and butter until the chocolate is melted. Beat until smooth. Cool 5 minutes, then beat in the rum and egg yolk. Add walnuts. Spread over toast mixture. Cover with remaining slices of toast. Add remaining milk-egg mixture. Bake in a 350°F. oven for 30 to 35 minutes or until a cake tester or toothpick inserted in the center comes out clean. Cool slightly and cut into squares. Heat rum, ignite, and pour flaming over the baked pudding. Serve topped with vanilla ice cream or slightly sweetened whipped cream if desired.

NOTE: The toast should absorb practically all of the liquid. If the top slices of the toast are too dry, soak for a few minutes in the remaining half of the egg-yolk mixture, then arrange on top of chocolate filling, and pour any leftover liquid over all. This will brown the top nicely.

TROPICAL BREAD PUDDING

6 slices lightly toasted white bread

3 tablespoons softened sweet butter

½ cup Seville orange marmalade, thinned with

1 tablespoon sherry

3 eggs, slightly beaten

1½ cups milk

2 tablespoons candied orange peel, chopped

2 tablespoons candied ginger, chopped

2 tablespoons candied citron, shredded

2 tablespoons dark rum

⅓ cup moist coconut

Lemon sauce

Spread the warm toast with butter and marmalade, then cube the bread. Turn the cubes into a well-buttered and lightly sugared Pyrex baking dish or casserole. Add beaten eggs to the milk; add candied orange, ginger and citron. Blend well. Fold in the rum and coconut. Pour over the bread cubes. Bake in a 300°F. oven for 45 minutes or until the custard tests done (a cake tester or toothpick inserted in the center comes out clean). Top with Lemon Sauce.

LEMON SAUCE: Follow directions on 1 package of lemon pie filling. Cook until thickened. Cool. Beat until smooth, then thin down with 2 to 3 tablespoons white wine. Fold in a generous ½ cup whipped cream.

BREAD STUFFINGS

Onion Bread Stuffing for Veal:

> 4 cups day-old bread crumbs
> 3 onions, chopped and sautéed in 2 tablespoons fat
> 4 tablespoons butter or margarine, melted
> ½ cup water or soup stock
> 1 teaspoon salt
> pinch white pepper
> pinch sage
> 1 egg yolk, beaten
> 1 egg white, stiffly beaten

Combine all ingredients except egg white. Toss with a wooden spoon. Fold in stiffly beaten egg white. Use as a stuffing for veal.

Bread Stuffing for Chicken or Turkey:

> 4 cups day old bread crumbs
> salt and pepper to taste
> ⅓ teaspoon thyme
> pinch poultry seasoning
> 2 tablespoons fresh minced parsley
> ⅓ cup chopped celery, with a few leaves
> ½ cup chicken stock or water
> 1 egg, beaten
> ⅓ cup melted butter or margarine
> 2 tablespoons sherry

In a large mixing bowl combine all ingredients and toss with a wooden spoon until well-blended. Use as a stuffing for poultry or small turkey.

Chestnut Bread Stuffing for Turkey or Veal:

>   4 cups day-old bread crumbs
>   ½ cup chicken stock or water
>   2 cups shelled and boiled chestnuts
>   (brown skins removed),
>   coarsely chopped
>   salt and pepper to taste
>   pinch sage
>   2 tablespoons fresh chopped parsley
>   ½ cup chopped celery with a few leaves
>   2 tablespoons sherry
>   ⅓ cup chopped scallions, sautéed in
>   1 tablespoon butter or margarine
>   1 cup sautéed sliced mushrooms

In a mixing bowl combine all ingredients and toss together with a wooden spoon. If desired, for a more moist stuffing add 1 beaten egg. Use as a stuffing for poultry or a small turkey.

Stuffing for Ducks:

>   3 cups day old bread crumbs
>   1 cup mashed potatoes
>   1 egg
>   salt and pepper to taste
>   ⅓ cup chicken stock or water
>   pinch sage
>   ½ cup chopped celery with a few tender leaves,
>   finely minced
>   1 tablespoon grated orange rind

Combine all ingredients, mix well with a wooden spoon. Use as a stuffing for duck.

Bread and Fruit Stuffing for Duck or Poultry:

> 4 cups day-old bread crumbs
> ⅓ cup sherry
> ⅓ cup melted butter or margarine
> salt and pepper to taste
> 1 cup pared and stewed apples
> 1 cup soft prunes, parboiled in ½ cup sherry, with
>   1 tablespoon sugar and 1 slice lemon
> ½ cup coarsely chopped walnuts
> pinch cinnamon or ginger
> 1 teaspoon sugar

Stew sliced apples until nearly done, in a little water, with sugar to taste and 2 tablespoons sherry. Stew prunes until nearly done. Cut into thirds. Combine all ingredients. Mix well. Toss with a wooden spoon until well-blended. Excellent also for stuffed veal breast.

BRIOCHES & BABAS

BRIOCHE

The versatile brioche is a light, cake-like yeast bread or roll, rich with butter and many eggs. In France, where it shares national popularity with the croissant for breakfast or tea, the brioche roll is traditionally round-shaped with a little round ball or "hat" perched on its top.

The brioche may also be hollowed out and its shell filled with creamed chicken or fish for a delightful luncheon dish, or as a dessert, with its shell filled with fresh berries or fruits in season, and topped with cold custard sauce perfumed with an aromatic liqueur or with rum-flavored whipped cream.

BRIOCHE ROLLS

⅓ cup lukewarm water
1½ packages dry granular yeast
1 tablespoon sugar
¼ pound sweet butter or margarine
⅓ cup sugar
½ teaspoon salt

½ cup scalded milk, cooled to lukewarm
4 eggs, slightly beaten
4½ cups flour, plus 1 to 2 tablespoons for board
1 egg yolk beaten with 1 tablespoon water

Place lukewarm water in a small bowl or cup. Sprinkle with yeast and 1 tablespoon sugar. Stir. Cover and set aside until foaming and doubled in volume, about 5 minutes. Cream butter with sugar and salt in a large mixing bowl. Add lukewarm milk and eggs. Beat well until thoroughly blended. Add foaming yeast mixture and 1 cup flour. Beat well, then add enough of the remaining flour to make a soft dough. Beat well. Knead on a lightly floured board for 5 to 10 minutes. Turn into a warm, buttered bowl; set aside in a warm place,

178

covered, until doubled in bulk. Stir down with a wooden spoon. Cover with a sheet of greased plastic wrap. Refrigerate overnight. Turn soft dough out onto a lightly floured board. Knead lightly until smooth. Cut off ⅓ of dough to make small balls. Cut remaining dough into 12 even pieces. Shape into 2½-inch balls. Place in greased muffin pans. Make a deep indentation in the center of each ball. Shape remaining ⅓ dough into 12 small balls. Dampen each indentation *slightly* with a little cold water, then press each little ball gently into the larger ones. Cover and set aside in a warm place until a little more than doubled in bulk. Brush with beaten egg yolk. Bake in a preheated 375°F. oven for 20 minutes or until a nice golden brown. If desired, bake in individual fluted brioche tins for a real French touch!

BRIOCHE IN THE FRENCH MANNER

2½ packages dry granular yeast

½ cup lukewarm water, scant

2 teaspoons sugar

½ cup scalded milk, cooled to lukewarm

1½ teaspoons salt

1 tablespoon grated orange rind

4½ cups presifted flour

½ pound soft sweet butter (1 cup)

5 eggs

1 egg yolk beaten with 1 tablespoon water or milk

In a large mixing bowl combine dry yeast, lukewarm water and sugar. Stir. Cover. Set aside until foaming and doubled in volume. Add milk, salt, orange rind and 2 cups flour. Beat vigorously with a large wooden spoon, then add the soft butter. Continue to beat until the butter is well-blended. Add remaining flour and eggs, beating well after each addition. Continue beating the dough until smooth and shiny. From time to time, in the French manner, lift the dough out of the bowl as if you were stretching it, then slap it hard on a very lightly floured board, until the dough is satiny smooth and no longer sticky. Place the dough in a warm, well-greased bowl, cover and set aside in a warm place, free from drafts, until doubled in bulk—about 1½ to 2 hours. Do not rush the rising; if necessary let rise a little longer until the dough is light and springy. Punch down with a floured fist. Cover and refrigerate overnight. Next day turn dough out on a lightly floured board. Knead for a few minutes. Divide dough into two portions. Cover and let stand for 10 to 15 minutes at room temperature. Shape into two loaves. Turn into 2 well-buttered and lightly floured 9″ x 5″ x 3″ loaf pans. Cover and let rise in a warm place until doubled in bulk. Brush with beaten egg yolk. Bake in a 375°F. oven for 45 minutes or until the loaves are a nice golden brown. Let cool in pans for 15 minutes, then turn out onto wire cooling racks.

NOTE: Brioche dough may be baked in well-buttered and lightly floured 1-quart Pyrex mixing bowls, or braided into two twists. If desired.

ALMOND BRIOCHE

3 packages dry granular yeast
½ cup lukewarm water
2 teaspoons sugar
½ cup scalded milk, cooled to lukewarm
1 teaspoon salt
1 scant teaspoon almond flavor

½ cup toasted almonds, coarsely chopped
4½ cups presifted flour
1 cup soft sweet butter
5 eggs, slightly beaten
⅓ cup pulverized brown or clear rock candy

In a large mixing bowl, stir together yeast, lukewarm water and sugar. Cover. Set aside until foaming and doubled in volume. Add milk, salt, and almond flavor. Stir. Combine almonds with 2 cups flour and beat into the yeast mixture with a wooden spoon for about 10 minutes. Add soft butter, eggs, one at a time, and remaining flour. Continue to beat vigorously, after each addition, until the dough is smooth and shiny. In the French manner. pull the dough out of the bowl, and slap it hard, several times, onto a very *lightly floured* board until it is satin smooth and no longer sticky. Place in a warm, well-greased bowl, turning dough several times until greased on all sides. Cover and let rise in a warm place until doubled in bulk, about 1 to 1½ hours. Punch down with a floured fist and turn out onto a lightly floured board. Pat into a rectangle. Sprinkle with ¼ cup pulverized rock candy.

Knead into a ball. Divide in half. Shape into two balls. Place in two well-buttered and lightly floured 1-quart Pyrex mixing bowls or fluted brioche baking pans. Cover with wax paper, then with a clean cloth. Let rise until doubled in bulk. (If desired, refrigerate the dough for several hours, or overnight.) Brush tops lightly with melted butter or lightly beaten egg white. Sprinkle with remaining rock candy. Bake in a 375°F. oven for 30 to 35 minutes or until done. Let cool in pans for 10 to 15 minutes, then turn out onto wire cooling racks.

BASQUE BRIOCHE

½ cup scalded milk
½ cup sweet butter
  (¼ pound)
½ cup sifted sugar
½ teaspoon salt
¼ cup lukewarm water
1½ packages dry granular
  yeast
1 teaspoon sugar

4 eggs
3¼ to 3½ cups flour
½ cup roasted chestnuts,
  chopped
1 tablespoon grated lemon
  rind
1 slightly beaten egg white
  mixed with 2 teaspoons
  water and 1 teaspoon sugar

Scald milk. Cool to lukewarm. Cream butter with sugar until light and fluffy. Add salt. In a large mixing bowl stir yeast and sugar into ¼ cup lukewarm water until dissolved. Cover and let stand until foaming and doubled in volume. Add milk and creamed mixture. Add eggs, 1 at a time, beating well after each addition. Add flour gradually, then the chopped roasted chestnuts and lemon rind. Beat vigorously for 10 minutes. Cover. Let rise in a warm place until doubled in bulk. Punch down. Beat thoroughly. Cover tightly with buttered wax paper. Refrigerate overnight. Punch down. Turn out soft dough onto a lightly floured board. Pinch off a small piece of dough; shape into 2 small balls. Divide rest of dough in half. Shape into 2 balls. Place in well-greased and lightly floured brioche pans. Make a deep indentation in the center of each ball. Brush lightly with a little water. Press the smaller balls into the indentations. Cover and let rise again until doubled in bulk. Brush with the egg white-sugar mixture. Bake in a preheated 375°F. oven for 35 minutes or until done.

FRAGRANT CITRUS PEEL BRIOCHE

Brioche batter may be baked in any well-buttered and lightly floured favorite shape baking dish or pan. This rich, light and fragrant classic French bread, bright with citrus peel and long a breakfast favorite, is served with cold sweet butter and jams.

2 packages dry granular
  yeast
⅓ cup hot water
2 teaspoons sugar
⅓ cup sweet butter
½ cup scalded milk, cooled
  to lukewarm
⅓ cup sugar

pinch salt
1 whole egg, plus 2 egg yolks
1 tablespoons grated orange
  rind
1 tablespoon grated lemon
  rind
1 tablespoon shredded citron
2½ cups presifted flour

Dissolve yeast in the lukewarm water. Add sugar. Stir. Cover. Set aside until foaming and doubled in volume. In a large mixing bowl stir together the butter, lukewarm milk, sugar and salt until the butter is melted. Beat in the eggs, grated orange, lemon and citron rinds and 1 cup flour. Beat vigorously with a wooden spoon, then add the remaining 1½ cups flour and continue beating the batter for 10 minutes. Cover with wax paper, then with a clean cloth. Set aside in a warm place until doubled in bulk. Beat down with a wooden spoon. Cover with wax paper and refrigerate for several hours or overnight. When ready to use, beat down again, then spoon the batter into two 1-pound well-buttered and lightly floured coffee tins, or into two well-buttered fluted brioche baking pans. Cover and let rise again until the dough reaches the top of the pans. Bake in a 375°F. oven for 35 minutes or until done. Brush top with melted butter; return to oven for a few minutes until the top is glossy. Let cool 10 minutes before removing from pans. Cool on wire cake racks.

QUICK GOLDEN RICH BRIOCHE
(From Hot Roll Mix)

This makes an unusually tender, rich brioche, with the delicate aroma of orange rind. Its keeping qualities are excellent.

1 package hot roll mix
   (13¾ ounce)
½ cup lukewarm water
4 teaspoons sugar
5 egg yolks
1 tablespoon grated orange
   rind

2 tablespoons soft butter
1 egg white, slightly beaten
   with 1 tablespoon cold
   water
orange-flavored white icing
⅓ cup toasted almonds,
   coarsely chopped

Place the yeast from the package of hot roll mix in a large mixing bowl. Add lukewarm water and sugar. Stir. Cover with a paper towel for 5 minutes. The yeast mixture will begin to foam. Beat in the egg yolks, then add the orange rind and half the package of roll mix. Beat well; add the remaining flour mixture. Beat or mix with a silver knife until the dough leaves the sides of the bowl. If too sticky to handle, add 1 tablespoon of flour. Turn out onto a lightly floured board and knead for 5 minutes. Shape into a ball. Grease a warm mixing bowl with the 2 tablespoons butter. Turn the dough until completely greased on all sides. Cover with wax paper and then with a clean cloth. Set aside in a warm place until doubled in bulk, about 1 hour. Punch down. Cover with buttered wax paper and refrigerate for several hours or overnight. Turn out onto a lightly floured board. Cover and let rest for 10 to 15 minutes at room temperature. Knead for 5 minutes. Divide in half. Shape into two loaves or braids. Turn into 2 well-buttered and lightly floured 8″ x 4″ x 2½″ loaf pans. Cover with a clean cloth and let rise again until doubled in bulk. Brush with beaten egg white. Bake in a 375°F. oven for 35 to 40 minutes or until done. Dribble with orange-flavored white icing (1 cup confectioners sugar beaten with 1 tablespoon orange juice) and sprinkle with chopped nuts.

RICH BRIOCHE WITH CHOPPED LICHEE NUTS

2 packages dry granular
   yeast
⅓ cup lukewarm water
2 teaspoons sugar
4 cups presifted flour
½ teaspoon salt
2 tablespoons sugar
7 eggs
2 sticks (½ pound) sweet
   butter

½ cup plump dark raisins
½ cup chopped lichee nuts
1 to 2 teaspoons flour
1 tablespoon grated orange
   rind
powdered sugar
2 tablespoons grated chocolate

Dissolve yeast in lukewarm water, add sugar. Stir. Cover. Set aside until foaming and doubled in volume. Add enough flour to make a soft ball, about 1 cup. Knead the little ball of dough; then with a sharp knife, slash the top with a criss-cross. Drop it into a small bowl of lukewarm water until doubled in bulk. In the meantime, in a large mixing bowl, beat the remaining flour, salt, sugar and 4 eggs until thoroughly blended. Add softened butter in small bits; beat until smooth. Then add the rest of the eggs, one at a time, beating until smooth. When the little ball of dough is doubled and light and spongy, remove with a slotted spoon, and add to the egg mixture. Dust the raisins and lichee nuts with 1 to 2 teaspoons flour; mix with the orange rind. Work them into the dough until well distributed. Turn the dough into a warm, well-greased bowl. Turn dough several times until greased on all sides. Cover with buttered wax paper, then with a clean cloth. Set in a warm place until doubled in bulk. Punch down. Cover with wax paper. Refrigerate overnight. Turn the dough out onto a lightly floured board; knead for 5 minutes, then shape into a long roll. Fit into a well-buttered and lightly floured 10-inch tube spring form. Cover. Set in a warm place until doubled in bulk. Bake in a 375°F. oven for 40 to 45 minutes or until done. Remove from oven. Let cool 10 minutes. Remove outside rim from spring form. When cool, sprinkle with a soft cloud of powdered sugar, then with grated chocolate, and lastly, again with powdered sugar.

LICHEE NUTS: Remove shell and pits, chop the fruit or snip into small pieces with sharp scissors. The lichee nut is the fruit of a Chinese tree, cultivated in India. It is oval in shape with a sweetish fruity flavor. The pulp is dark and firm, similar to a date. It is available in Chinese markets and most fine gourmet stores.

BABA AU RHUM

The baba au rhum or babka is a cake-like sweet bread made of leavened dough rich with butter and eggs, mixed with currants, and steeped in rum, brandy or kirsch. Introduced in France in the early 19th century, the baba quickly became a national French favorite, although its popularity has since spread far beyond the borders of its birth. But it was in France that famous pastry cooks originated unusual shapes for the baba, changing the syrups constantly, and basting it with hot fruit sauces such as thick apricot and orange glazes perfumed with fruit liqueurs. Recipes for the aromatic flavorings were closely guarded secrets as the pastry chefs' stock-in-trade.

The babas of Polish origin are similar to our coffee kuchen or kugelhopf. They are frequently laced with a thick rum-flavored syrup and served flaming, with a good dark rum.

BABA AU RHUM, FLAMBEED

2 packages dry granular yeast
½ cup lukewarm water
2 teaspoons sugar
4 eggs
4 tablespoons sugar
1 stick sweet butter, melted (¼ pound)
2¼ cups presifted flour
½ teaspoon baking powder
1 tablespoon lemon rind

½ cup currants, sprinkled lightly with a little flour

SAUCE:
1 cup apricot nectar
1 cup sugar
2 tablespoons apricot jam
2 tablespoons apricot brandy
2 tablespoons brandy for flaming
French vanilla ice cream

Dissolve yeast in lukewarm water. Add 2 teaspoons sugar; stir. Cover and set aside until foaming and doubled in volume. In the meantime, beat eggs in a large mixing bowl over warm

185

water until thick and lemon colored. Add sugar and butter gradually, and continue to beat until well blended. Add foaming yeast, mix with a wooden spoon, then add 1 cup flour and the baking powder. Beat vigorously, add rest of flour, lemon rind and currants. Continue to beat the batter for at least 10 minutes. Cover. Set aside in a warm place until doubled in bulk. Beat down with a wooden spoon. Have ready a well-buttered and lightly floured 9-inch tube spring form or a fluted tube baking pan. Cover, let rise again until doubled. Bake in a 375°F. oven for 30 minutes, reduce heat to 350°F. and continue to bake 10 to 15 minutes longer or until the baba tests done. (If it sounds hollow when tapped, it is done.) Cool 10 to 15 minutes in pan. Unmold on a deep serving dish. Heat brandy, ignite and pour flaming over the top of the baba. Baste with the hot sauce until completely glazed. Top with French vanilla ice cream.

SAUCE: Combine apricot nectar with the sugar and jam in a medium saucepan. Bring to a rolling boil; reduce heat to medium and cook until the sauce thickens, about 20 minutes. Stir frequently. Remove from heat. Beat in 2 tablespoons apricot brandy or liqueur.

ORANGE GLAZED BABA AU RHUM

1 cup milk, scalded, cooled to lukewarm
1½ packages dry granular yeast
2 teaspoons sugar
½ cup flour
3½ to 4 cups presifted flour
½ teaspoon salt
1 tablespoon grated orange rind

⅔ cup melted sweet butter
6 fresh eggs
⅓ cup currants
½ cup chopped walnuts

SAUCE:
½ cup orange marmalade
2 tablespoons sherry
1 cup sweetened rum-flavored whipped cream

Cool scalded milk in a large mixing bowl to lukewarm. Add yeast and sugar. Stir. Cover for 5 minutes until the yeast begins to foam. Beat in ½ cup flour. Place over a bowl of hot water for 20 to 30 minutes or until the mixture is very spongy. Beat in remaining flour, salt and orange rind, alternating with the butter and eggs, adding the eggs one at a time. Beat well after each addition, until the mixture is smooth and well blended. Sprinkle a little flour over the currants and nuts and work them into the batter. Beat well with a large wooden spoon. Cover; set in a warm place to rise until doubled in bulk. Beat again. Spoon batter into a well-buttered and lightly floured 9" or 10" tube spring form. Cover with a clean cloth. Let rise again until doubled in bulk. Bake in a 375°F. oven for 30 to 40 minutes or until done. Glaze with Orange Sauce.

ORANGE SAUCE: Heat orange marmalade in a small skillet together with the wine. Beat well until smooth and syrupy. Cool baba 15 minutes. Remove from pan, cool on a wire rack. Place on a serving plate, pour hot sauce over all. Keep basting until the baba is well glazed. Top with sweetened rum-flavored whipped cream.

RUM FLAVORED WHIPPED CREAM: Beat 1 cup heavy sweet cream until thick, add 2 tablespoons confectioners sugar and 1 to 2 tablespoons rum. Blend. Chill until ready to serve.

POLISH RUM BABA
(Without Yeast)

Created for royalty, this fragrant baba was often served with a sweetened wine sauce, the center filled with luscious glazed fruits topped with rich cream. However, any favorite sauce or topping may be used.

4 eggs
1¼ cups sugar
½ teaspoon salt
1½ cups milk
3 cups flour
2½ teaspoons baking powder
2 teaspoons chopped candied orange peel
4 tablespoons grated candied ginger

½ teaspoon mace
½ cup melted sweet butter

SAUCE:
1 cup sugar
1 tablespoon orange marmalade
½ cup orange juice
⅓ cup rum
1 cup sweetened rum-flavored whipped cream

Beat eggs over warm water until thick and lemon colored. Beat in sugar gradually, then add salt and milk. Gradually add flour, baking powder, orange peel, ginger and mace. Beat well. Beat in melted butter until thoroughly blended with the batter. Spoon into a well-buttered and lightly floured 9" or 10" Turk's Head or fancy ring mold. Bake in a 375°F. oven for 35 to 45 minutes or until the baba tests done. Cool 10 minutes, then turn out onto a wire cooling rack. Baste baba while still warm with the hot sauce.

SAUCE: Combine sugar, marmalade and orange juice. Bring to a rolling boil, until the syrup spins a thread. Add half of the rum (use remaining rum for whipped cream). Cool slightly. Spoon sauce over the baba, keep basting until the baba is glazed. Serve topped with the rum-flavored whipped cream.

TOASTS AND DUNKERS

BREAKFAST TOAST

Good toast is simple to make; often it is too dry or too brown. The ideal toast to greet us at breakfast time should be a light golden brown, crisp on the outside and with a tender crumb inside, and *hot* when served.

For perfect toast, the bread should be quite fresh. Never slice bread for toast more than ¼-inch thick, unless otherwise specified. Turn the toaster dial to "light." Toast once; when ready to serve, return to toaster and toast lightly once more. For large quantities of toast, spread bread on a large baking sheet, toast in oven until a delicate brown on one side; then turn and toast ½ minute longer. Have butter at room temperature, so it will be soft enough to spread evenly. Butter the toast at once and serve.

CINNAMON TOAST

6 slices white bread
⅓ stick softened sweet butter

⅓ cup cinnamon sugar

Spread lightly toasted bread with butter and sprinkle generously with cinnamon sugar. Serve piping hot. If desired, place under broiler for a few seconds until the sugar begins to bubble. Serve at once.

ORANGE MINTED CINNAMON TOAST

6 slices soft white bread, ¼-inch thick
soft butter
½ teaspoon cinnamon

½ cup soft brown sugar
fresh or dried mint, minced
grated rind of ½ orange
powdered sugar

Spread bread with soft butter. Mix cinnamon with brown sugar and sprinkle over each slice, then sprinkle with mint and orange rind. Add a good dash of powdered sugar. Place under a hot broiler, several inches away from heating element, and glaze quickly for just a minute. Garnish with orange slices and sprigs of fresh mint. Serve at once with hot orange pekoe with a twist of orange peel.

HOME MADE WHIPPED BUTTER: In a medium-size mixing bowl, place ½ pound sweet butter. Let stand at room temperature, then whip with a rotary beater until it becomes quite creamy. Beat in 1 tablespoon heavy sweet cream. Wonderful texture and easy to spread on golden crisp toast.

COCONUT TOAST

8 slices white bread, crusts removed
½ stick softened sweet butter
½ cup soft brown sugar
1 teaspoon grated lemon rind
1 cup moist coconut
1 teaspoon powdered sugar

Cut slices in halves. Spread with butter creamed with brown sugar and lemon rind. Place under broiler, several inches away from heating element. Toast quickly until the topping begins to bubble. Remove at once. Combine coconut with the powdered sugar and sprinkle over toast generously. Return to oven for ½ minute, until a delicate light golden color.

FRENCH-FRIED ENGLISH MUFFINS

A shortage of sliced white bread dictated this delicious recipe!

4 fresh English muffins
3 eggs
¾ cup hot milk
pinch salt
butter for frying

190

Split muffins in half with the tines of a fork. Do not cut with a knife. In a shallow dish, beat eggs and gradually add the milk, beating well after each addition. Soak muffin halves in the egg-milk mixture for ½ hour. Fry in bubbling hot butter until golden brown on both sides. Serve at once with favorite jam or marmalade.

ALTERNATE METHOD: Instead of frying the muffins, arrange them in a well-buttered Pyrex baking dish. Pour any leftover egg-milk mixture over all. Place in a hot oven (400°F.) and bake about 15 to 20 minutes until golden brown. Do not turn. Remove with a spatula and spread with favorite jam or marmalade. For a delightful change, pour warm maple syrup over the golden muffins and top with a dab of sour cream.

FRENCH TOAST

According to legend, a French woman, at a loss what to serve a poor beggar who came to her door, took some hard bread out of her cupboard and quickly dipped it into some warm milk and beaten egg. This she grilled until golden brown, and served it topped with warm honey.

Whatever its origin, "French toast" is centuries old, and enjoys popularity in most European countries, where it is served in many different ways: baked, broiled or toasted and topped with fresh fruits, hot syrups, jams and a choice of tasty grated or melted cheese. The French call it *pain perdu* or "lost bread"; the Belgians, *pain trove,* or "found bread," but whatever the name it is a gastronomic delight.

6 slices white bread, untrimmed	½ cup milk or light cream
3 eggs	pinch salt
	butter for frying

Place bread in a large shallow dish. Beat eggs, milk and salt. Pour over bread. Let stand in mixture for 10 minutes. Heat a large skillet; add 2 tablespoons butter or margarine. Lift bread slices with a spatula and place in the hot bubbling butter. Do not crowd skillet. Fry over medium heat until brown. Turn and brown other side. Serve at once with the hot maple syrup or strawberry jam.

VARIATION: Slice French bread 2 inches thick. Soak in the egg-mixture until the bread has absorbed the liquid. Melt 3 to 4 tablespoons butter or margarine in a large shallow baking dish. Arrange bread slices in the hot bubbling butter. Bake in a 350°F. oven until golden brown. Serve very hot with favorite jam, marmalade or warm honey.

BAKED FLUFFY FRENCH TOAST

1 cup milk
2 eggs, beaten
½ cup flour
½ teaspoon baking powder
½ teaspoon salt
½ stick butter
6 to 8 slices white bread

Pour milk in a shallow dish. In another shallow dish combine eggs, flour, baking powder and salt. Melt butter in a large skillet. Dip bread in the milk, one slice at a time, then in the egg mixture, turning several times to coat the bread thoroughly. Cover skillet and fry gently for a few minutes. Then place in a preheated 375°F. oven until puffed and delicately browned. Do not turn. Serve at once with hot syrup.

SYRUP: Heat 1 cup honey or maple syrup in a small saucepan. Add 1 tablespoon butter and a pinch each of cinnamon and nutmeg. Simmer gently over low heat for 5 minutes. Serve hot from a pitcher with the baked French toast.

BLUSHING FRENCH TOAST

½ cup condensed tomato soup
½ cup water
2 eggs, beaten
4 thick slices white bread
½ to ¾ cup grated Cheddar cheese

Combine tomato soup and water in a shallow bowl. Beat until well blended. Add the eggs, one at a time, until thoroughly mixed. Dip bread slices into the mixture, turning to coat both sides. Let rest in the tomato-egg mixture for 10 minutes. Place in a well-buttered baking pan. Sprinkle generously with coarsely grated Cheddar cheese. Bake in a 375°F. oven for 10 minutes or until puffed and the cheese is melted into a soft luscious golden topping.

HARRY SCHAFFER'S FRENCH TOAST
A LA PÊCHE

An epicurean contribution from a busy lawyer who occasionally sets aside his legal duties and dishes up some notable gourmet creations. This recipe varies slightly from the usual French toast; its fresh peach flavor adds a surprise touch to an otherwise simple dish.

2 eggs
2 tablespoons light cream or milk
2 tablespoons water
pinch pepper
pinch cinnamon
2 to 3 tablespoons orange juice

1 ripe peach, pared
4 slices white bread, ¾-inch thick
butter or margarine for frying

Whiz for 1 second in a blender the eggs, cream or milk, water, pepper, cinnamon and orange juice. Cut pared peach into small pieces and add to the egg mixture. Whiz again until the peach is thoroughly mixed with the egg batter. Pour into a large shallow dish. Add bread slices. Let stand until the egg mixture has been completely absorbed. Heat a skillet; add butter or margarine. Keep flame low until butter is bubbling hot, but not browned. Add the bread. Brown gently on both sides. Serve hot topped with jam or warm maple syrup, if desired.

TOASTED GARLIC BREAD

1 loaf French or Italian bread	2 cloves garlic, crushed
1 stick sweet butter or margarine	dash paprika
	½ cup grated Parmesan cheese

Cut bread in diagonal slices, about 1½ to 2 inches thick, but not all the way through the bottom. Spread each slice with softened butter mixed with the finely crushed garlic. Reshape loaf. Spread top crust with softened butter, sprinkle with a dash of paprika, and then generously with grated cheese. Wrap loaf in aluminum foil. Place on a baking sheet in a 375°F. oven and bake for 15 to 20 minutes. Remove foil carefully, since the bread will be very hot. Break off chunks and serve at once. To reheat, place in a damp brown paper bag in a hot oven for 5 to 10 minutes.

TOASTED MANDELBROT
(Almond Bread)

These dry, crisp, almond toasts keep very well when stored in a dry tightly covered glass jar or metal container. They are great favorites with the "dunker" set!

3 cups flour	2 teaspoons lemon juice
3 teaspoons baking powder	1 cup sugar
pinch salt	6 tablespoons melted butter or margarine
3 eggs, beaten	½ cup sliced almonds
2 teaspoons grated lemon rind	⅓ cup finely chopped almonds

In a mixing bowl, sift flour, baking powder and salt together. Beat eggs until thick and lemon colored. Add to flour, then add the lemon rind, juice, and gradually the sugar, beating constantly until all the sugar has been used up. Add the melted butter, sliced and chopped almonds. Mix well. Turn

194

out onto a lightly floured board. Knead for a minute, divide dough into 2 parts, and shape into long narrow loaves. Place on a buttered baking sheet and bake in a 350°F. oven for 35 to 45 minutes or until firm and delicately browned. Cool, but slice while still warm, place on a cookie sheet, return to oven, (275°F.) and toast slices until crisp and golden brown.

MELBA TOAST

Remove crusts from 1 loaf unsliced stale white bread. Then slice very thinly with a sharp knife. Cut each slice in half. Arrange on a large cookie sheet. Bake in a very slow oven (250°F.) until the pieces are evenly browned on both sides. Store in a cool place in an airtight container. Serve with salads, spread with butter or margarine, cream cheese or whatever.

VARIATION: Toast thinly sliced whole wheat bread, rye bread or pumpernickel as directed above.

COUNTRY TEA-TOAST

½ stick sweet butter, softened

3 to 4 tablespoons maple sugar

6 slices thin white or whole wheat bread

⅓ cup heavy sweet cream

Combine soft butter with maple sugar. Beat until very smooth and well blended. Spread evenly on bread. Top each with a spoonful of sweet cream. Arrange the bread on a lightly buttered baking sheet. Bake in a moderate oven (350°F.) until the bread is lightly toasted and the cream-sugar topping begins to bubble. Serve at once.

VARIATION: Combine softened butter with maple sugar, cream and 1 heaping tablespoon sesame seeds. Mix well until thoroughly blended. Spread over bread. Place on a lightly buttered baking sheet and bake in a 350°F. oven until the top begins to bubble. Serve at once.

TROPICAL TOAST

4 thick slices white bread,
  crusts removed
sweet butter
¼ cup soft brown sugar
¼ cup granulated sugar

pinch ginger
⅓ cup frozen pineapple
  juice concentrate
2 tablespoons moist coconut

Toast the bread slices lightly. Spread with softened butter. Combine brown sugar, white sugar, ginger, and the pineapple concentrates. Spread over toast. Sprinkle with coconut. Place under broiler, 5 to 6 inches away from heating element, to brown top. Watch carefully! When bubbly, remove at once. Serve hot.

VIRGIN ISLAND TOAST

1 loaf white bread
½ stick sweet butter
3 tablespoons cinnamon
  sugar

3 firm ripe bananas
⅓ cup rum
powdered sugar

Cut six ¾-inch thick slices of bread. Remove crusts. Spread with butter and sprinkle with cinnamon sugar. Cut bananas in half, then lengthwise to cover each bread slice. Place on a baking sheet, and toast in a 325°F. oven until the bananas are soft and the bread lightly toasted. Heat rum, ignite, and pour flaming over the banana-topped toast. Sprinkle generously with powdered sugar, place under the broiler for 1 second and serve at once with hot demitasse. Add a twist of orange rind to each cup.

WALNUT TOAST

6 slices stale brioche or coffee kuchen
2 cups milk
3 to 4 eggs, beaten
½ cup coarsely chopped walnuts

3 tablespoons crystalized sugar (pulverized rock candy)
pinch cinnamon
powdered sugar

Use stale brioche, plain coffee cake, kuchen or white bread. Slice 1 inch thick. Mix milk with eggs; beat until well blended. Dip each slice into the milk-egg mixture. Sprinkle with walnuts. Combine pulverized sugar with cinnamon. Sprinkle over walnuts. Arrange slices on a well-buttered baking sheet. Bake in a 350°F. oven until golden brown. Serve at once with a dash of soft, sifted powdered sugar. *Do not turn!*

THE POOR KNIGHTS OF WINDSOR
FRIED BREAD

This unusual recipe is 150 years old, and is as good today as it was long ago.

6 slices white bread, crusts removed (½ inch thick)
½ cup white wine
1 tablespoon sugar

3 egg yolks
3 tablespoons white wine
sweet butter for frying
cinnamon sugar

Soften bread in ½ cup wine for 2 to 3 minutes. (Do not soak too long, as the bread will fall apart.) Beat sugar, egg yolks and the 3 tablespoons wine until well blended. Lift each slice of bread out of the wine with a slotted spatula. Dip the wine-soaked bread in the beaten egg-yolk mixture. Heat a skillet large enough to hold all the bread, or use 2 skillets. Add butter; when it begins to bubble, add the bread slices. Fry gently on both sides until golden brown. Sprinkle with cinnamon sugar and serve at once with small glasses of favorite white wine. Serves 3.

ZWIEBACK

2 packages dry granular
    yeast
½ cup lukewarm water
2 teaspoons sugar
⅓ cup sugar
4 tablespoons melted butter
    or margarine

½ cup lukewarm milk
pinch salt
pinch nutmeg
¼ teaspoon anise seeds
3 eggs
2¾ cups flour (about)

Soften yeast in lukewarm water; add sugar. Stir. Cover. Set aside in a warm place until the yeast foams and doubles in volume. In a large mixing bowl, combine ⅓ cup sugar, butter, milk, salt, nutmeg, anise and eggs. Beat with a wooden spoon. Add yeast mixture, then just enough flour to make a soft, pliable dough. Turn into a warm, well-greased bowl. Cover; set aside and let rise until double in bulk. Turn out onto a lightly floured board and form into long narrow loaves, each about 2½-inches thick. Place on a buttered baking sheet. Cover and let rise again until doubled in bulk, about 1 hour. Bake in a 400°F. oven for 20 minutes or until golden brown. Cool. Cut into slices, about ½ to ¾ inch thick. Spread on a cookie sheet and return to a very slow oven (250°F.) until crisp.

COFFEE DUNKERS

A plain, sweet dunker.

4 cups flour
3 teaspoons baking powder
pinch salt
1 cup sugar
½ stick butter or margarine
½ cup lukewarm water

2 eggs, beaten
2 teaspoons grated orange
    rind
1 tablespoon orange juice
granulated sugar

Mix dry ingredients together in a large mixing bowl. Work in the butter with fingers or a pastry blender until the mixture is crumbly. Add lukewarm water, beaten eggs, orange rind and juice. Mix with a silver knife until the dough leaves the sides of the bowl. Turn out onto a lightly floured board and roll out about ½ inch thick. Sprinkle with a little sugar. Cut out into desired shapes with a floured cookie cutter, or cut into squares with a sharp knife. Bake on a buttered and lightly floured baking sheet in a 350°F. oven for 10 to 15 minutes or until crisp and golden brown. Place on a wire rack to cook.

CRISP LITTLE DUNKERS

These little dunkers are light and crisp and easy to make. Made in a hurry and eaten just as fast! Nice for holiday time, when they can be placed on a Christmas tree. String on gaily colored ribbons, tie with a bow and hang on branches.

½ stick sweet butter
½ cup sugar
1 beaten egg yolk
1 teaspoon shredded citron
1 teaspoon anise seed
⅓ cup corn meal

½ cup flour
pinch cinnamon or ginger
pinch salt
powdered sugar with a pinch of cinnamon (optional)

Cream sugar and butter. Add egg yolk; cream until light and fluffy. Add citron, anise seeds, corn meal, flour, cinnamon and salt. Mix well. Pinch off small pieces of dough and roll into 3-inch strips, shape into rings. Arrange on a lightly buttered and floured baking sheet. Bake in a 350°F. oven for about 8 to 10 minutes. Cool. Sprinkle with powdered sugar, if desired. String on ribbons, and hang in a convenient spot to dry. Delicious served warm as they come out of the oven.

GINGER ROCKS

1 cup molasses
½ cup soft butter
½ cup granulated sugar
1 teaspoon baking soda, dissolved in ½ cup boiling water

1 level teaspoon ginger
1 tablespoon chopped candied ginger
1½ cups presifted flour

Combine all ingredients, adding just enough flour to make a soft dough. If too sticky add a little more flour. Turn out onto a lightly floured board. Roll ½ inch thick. Cut out with a floured 2-inch cookie cutter. Bake on a greased baking sheet in a 350°F. oven for 15 to 20 minutes. Let cool in pan for 10 minutes, then place on a wire cake rack. The rocks will harden into ideal dunkers.

CRISP HONEY DUNKERS
(Fat Free)

Another crisp dunker containing no shortening, ideal with hot fragrant coffee or tea. Let stand for a few hours to harden.

1 cup sugar, plus 1 tablespoon
3 eggs
¾ cup honey
pinch cloves and ginger

1 teaspoon orange marmalade
4 cups sifted flour
⅓ teaspoon baking soda

Sift sugar into a large bowl. Beat eggs until light and the consistency of whipped cream, about 8 to 10 minutes. Add gradually to the sugar, beating well after each addition. (Use electric mixer or rotary beater for a well-blended batter.) Beat in the honey, spices and orange marmalade. Add the flour and baking soda, mix well. Drop from teaspoon onto a well-buttered and lightly floured cookie sheet. Bake in a 300°F. oven for 12 to 15 minutes or until firm. Do not overbake—remove at once to cooling racks.

TOASTED PINE NUT DUNKERS
(Fat Free)

3 eggs
½ cup sugar
2 teaspoons grated lemon
   rind
1½ cups flour
2½ teaspoons baking
   powder

pinch salt
½ cup toasted pine nuts,
   coarsely chopped
⅓ cup toasted pine nuts,
   whole

Beat eggs for 5 minutes over warm water until thick and lemon colored. Add lemon rind. Add sugar gradually and continue beating until well blended. Sift flour, baking powder and salt together; add chopped and whole pine nuts and mix well. Add to the beaten eggs. Mix well with a wooden spoon. Pour into a well-buttered and lightly floured 8" x 4" x 2½" loaf pan, and bake in a 350°F. oven for 30 to 40 minutes or until the loaf is firm and tests done. Cool. Slice about ½ inch thick with a very sharp knife while still warm. Place on a cookie sheet, return to a slow oven (250°F.) and toast until crisp and golden brown. Makes an excellent crunchy dunker.

NOTE: If a richer dunker is desired, add ½ stick melted butter or margarine.

TOASTED PINE OR PIGNOLI NUTS: Available in all supermarkets or Italian stores. Spread in a small baking pan and toast lightly in a slow oven. Cool.

PUGATCHELS
(Hungarian Butter Dunkers)

The size of the pugatchels varies according to personal taste. A dunker with a personality, it may be baked plain, without sugar, or if a slightly sweeter pugatchel is desired add a little more sugar. Cut out thinner than the dunker, if desired, and bake as a cookie.

½ pound sweet butter
2½ cups flour
1 teaspoon baking powder
3 tablespoons sugar
2 egg yolks

1 tablespoon lemon juice
1 teaspoon grated lemon rind
⅓ cup sour cream

Cut cold butter into the flour and baking powder with a pastry blender or fingers until the mixture is crumbly. Add sugar, egg yolks, lemon juice and rind. Mix well. Work in the sour cream until a soft ball is formed. If necessary, add another tablespoon of sour cream. Refrigerate for several hours or overnight, or until the dough is quite firm and easy to handle. Roll the dough out on a slightly floured board, about ½ inch thick. Cut out with a 2-inch cookie cutter. Make a criss-cross mark on the top of each cookie with a pointed sharp knife. Brush with melted butter and sprinkle with a little sugar if desired. Bake on a buttered and lightly floured baking sheet in a 350°F. oven 20 minutes or until a light golden brown. Cool on wire racks. Let dry for a few hours. Use as *dunkers* with hot fragrant coffee.

TOASTED RUSK DUNKERS

2 cups flour
pinch salt
2 teaspoons baking powder
1 teaspoon sugar

1 stick sweet butter (¼ pound)
1 egg, beaten
4 tablespoons milk

Combine dry ingredients. Cut in butter with a pastry blender. Add egg and milk and stir with a fork into a stiff dough. Toss onto a lightly floured board, roll out and cut out rounds with a 3-inch floured biscuit cutter. Bake on a greased baking sheet in a 350°F. oven for 15 minutes or until golden brown. Break apart, place on a baking sheet and return to oven, rough side up until lightly toasted. Serve hot and dunk, dunk, dunk.

SHORT'NIN' BREAD DUNKERS

1 cup light brown sugar   1 pound butter
4 cups flour

In a large mixing bowl, mix together the sugar and flour. Work in butter until the mixture holds together. Form into a ball. Place on a floured board and pat out ½ inch thick. Cut into round, diamond or small square shapes. Bake in a 325°F. oven for 20 minutes or until delicately browned. Cool on wire cake racks.

REGIONAL COFFEE BREADS

BOSTON BROWN BREAD

¾ cup dark molasses
2 cups buttermilk
1 cup unbleached or all-purpose flour
1 cup whole wheat flour
1 cup yellow corn meal

2 teaspoons baking soda
½ teaspoon salt
½ cup dark plump raisins
¼ cup currants
½ cup coarsely chopped pecans

In a large mixing bowl, beat molasses and buttermilk together until well blended. Combine dry ingredients; add to the molasses mixture, gradually, beating with a wooden spoon after each addition. Sprinkle a little flour over the raisins, currants and pecans. Fold into the batter. Turn into well-greased and lightly floured medium-size loaf pans and bake at 350°F. for 35 to 40 minutes or until the bread shrinks away slightly from the sides of the pans. Insert a toothpick; if it comes out clean, the bread is done. Cool in pans for 15 minutes. Cool on wire cake racks and let stand for a few hours before slicing.

THREE-GRAIN BOSTON BROWN BREAD

1 cup white corn meal
½ cup sifted graham flour
1 cup sifted rye flour
½ cup unbleached white flour
1 cup molasses
1½ cups buttermilk

1 teaspoon baking soda
1 scant teaspoon salt
1 egg, beaten
2 tablespoons melted butter or margarine
½ cup dark raisins

Combine corn meal, graham flour, rye and unbleached flour together. Stir in molasses, buttermilk, baking soda, salt, egg and melted butter or margarine. Beat well. Sprinkle a little flour over raisins and fold into the batter. Fill two well-greased and lightly floured 8-inch loaf pans. Bake in a 350°F. oven for 40 minutes or until the top is gently firm to touch and shrinks away *slightly* from the sides of the pan. Test with a toothpick—when it comes out clean, the bread is done. Cool. Turn out onto wire cake racks until thoroughly cold.

CALIFORNIA SUNSHINE LOAF CAKE

½ cup butter or margarine
1 cup sifted sugar
2 eggs, beaten
1 cup milk
¼ teaspoon salt
pinch pumpkin pie spice
2 tablespoons grated orange
  rind

4 teaspoons baking powder
¾ cup chopped pecans
1¾ cups flour
¼ cup whole wheat flour
Orange Frosting

Cream butter or margarine with sugar; add eggs, then the milk. Beat until well blended. Add salt, spice, orange rind, baking powder, nuts and 1 cup flour. Beat well, add remaining flour and continue to beat until the batter is smooth. Fill two well-greased and lightly floured 8-inch loaf pans slightly more than half full. Cover with wax paper and let stand for 20 minutes. Bake in a preheated 350°F. oven for 40 to 45 minutes until golden brown, and the loaves test done.

ORANGE FROSTING: Combine 1 cup confectioners sugar with 1 tablespoon orange juice; beat until smooth. Add 1 teaspoon coarsely grated carrot. Blend. Spread over top of loaves.

EATONTOWN HUCKLEBERRY LOAF

4 tablespoons sugar
½ stick butter
1 egg
3 cups flour, loosely packed
4 teaspoons baking powder
½ teaspoon salt
⅞ cup milk
2 teaspoons grated lemon
rind

¾ cup perfect huckleberries
1 teaspoon flour
1 cup cold sour cream,
chilled
1 package (3-ounce) cream
cheese at room temperature
2 teaspoons cinnamon sugar

Cream sugar with butter, add the egg, and beat until smooth.
Combine flour, loosely packed, with baking powder and salt.
Add to the creamed mixture, alternating with the milk. Mix
well. Add lemon rind. Place the berries in a larger strainer,
sprinkle with 1 teaspoon flour, shake until they are completely
coated with the flour. Fold very gently into the batter. Turn
into greased and lightly floured medium-size loaf pans; bake
in a 375°F. oven for 25 to 30 minutes or until golden brown
and the top is gently firm to touch. Cool on a wire cake rack.
Whip sour cream with the softened cream cheese until light
and fluffy. Top each portion with the whipped-cream mixture. Sprinkle lightly with cinnamon sugar.

FLORIDA CITRUS BREAD

4 tablespoons softened butter
(not melted)
¾ cup sifted sugar
1 egg
¾ cup orange juice
1 tablespoon grated orange
rind
1 tablespoon grated lemon
rind

2¼ cups flour
3 teaspoons baking powder
⅓ teaspoon baking soda
½ teaspoon salt
3 teaspoons coarse sugar
mixed with
2 teaspoons grated lemon
rind

Cream butter with sifted sugar until fluffy. Add egg and continue to beat until the mixture is creamy; then add the orange juice, orange and lemon rind. Alternate with the mixed dry ingredients, except the coarse sugar mixture. Blend well. Turn the batter into a buttered and lightly floured 9″ x 5″ x 3″ loaf pan. Crush a piece of rock candy into coarse particles, mix with grated orange rind and sprinkle over top of batter. Bake in a 350°F. oven for 30 minutes or until the top is gently firm to touch and tests done. Cool 10 minutes. Turn out onto a wire cake rack until cold.

GEORGIA PECAN LOAF

⅓ cup sugar
2 cups flour
4 teaspoons baking powder
½ teaspoon salt
¼ teaspoon nutmeg
3 tablespoons butter, softened

¾ cup milk
1 egg plus 1 egg yolk
⅓ cup chopped pecans
2 teaspoons cinnamon sugar
½ cup very coarsely chopped pecans, mixed with 2 teaspoons cinnamon sugar

Combine sugar, flour, baking powder, salt and nutmeg. Mix well. Blend in the butter, beat well. Add the milk and eggs, beating thoroughly with a wooden spoon. Spoon half of the batter into a well-buttered and lightly floured 9″ x 5″ x 3″ loaf pan. Sprinkle with the chopped pecans and cinnamon sugar. Add remaining batter. Top with the coarsely chopped pecans and cinnamon mixture. Bake in a 350°F. oven for 30 to 35 minutes, or until the loaf tests done. Cool 10 minutes, then turn out onto a wire cake rack until cold.

JERSEY CRANBERRY BOG NUT BREAD

2 cups flour
½ teaspoon salt
1 teaspoon baking powder
1 teaspoon baking soda
¾ cup sugar
1 tablespoon grated orange rind
¾ cup coarsely chopped walnuts

1 egg plus 1 egg yolk
¾ cup milk
4 tablespoons melted butter
1 stiffly beated egg white
½ cup whole cranberry sauce
2 teaspoons cinnamon sugar

Combine flour, salt, baking powder, baking soda, sugar, orange rind and walnuts. Mix until the nuts are completely coated with the dry mixture. Gradually add eggs, milk and melted butter. Beat until blended. Fold in the stiffly beaten egg white, then the whole cranberry sauce. (Break up the cranberry sauce, very carefully, so as not to crush the berries, before folding into the batter.) Spoon into an 8″ x 4″ x 2½″ loaf pan or into an 8″ x 8″ square buttered and lightly floured baking pan. Bake in a 350°F. oven for 35 to 40 minutes or until the loaf tests done. Sprinkle top of baked loaf while still warm with cinnamon sugar.

KENTUCKY MINT JULEP LOAF

2 cups flour
3½ teaspoons baking powder
½ teaspoon salt
2 to 3 tablespoons butter
3 tablespoons sugar
½ cup milk

2 eggs
⅓ cup plump raisins marinated in
1 tablespoon Kentucky bourbon or brandy
Mint Julep Frosting

In a medium-size mixing bowl combine flour, baking powder, and salt. With a pastry blender work in the butter, then the sugar. Mix. Add milk gradually and then the eggs. Beat vigorously with a wooden spoon or rotary beater. Fold in the raisins and brandy. Bake in a greased and lightly floured loaf pan in a 350°F. oven for 30 minutes or until the loaf tests done. Do not overbake. Cool. Spread with frosting.

MINT JULEP FROSTING: In a small mixing bowl blend 1 cup sifted confectioners sugar with ⅓ cup melted mint jelly. Beat until smooth and a lovely pale green color. If too thin add a little more sifted confectioners suger. Spread over top of loaf.

LANCASTER BREAKFAST BREAD

½ stick butter
1 cup sugar, scant
2 eggs
1 cup milk
½ teaspoon vanilla
2 teaspoons baking powder
½ teaspoon salt
2 cups flour, presifted

1 tablespoon oatmeal

TOPPING:
4 tablespoons soft brown sugar
2 tablespoons flour
2 tablespoons soft butter
1 tablespoon oatmeal
½ cup chopped Brazil nuts

Cream butter with sugar, add eggs and beat until the mixture is smooth. Add the milk gradually with the vanilla. Combine dry ingredients; add to the creamed mixture. Beat with a wooden spoon until thoroughly blended, or use your electric beater. Spoon batter into a greased and lightly floured 9" x 9" x 2½" baking pan.

TOPPING: Blend brown sugar, flour, butter, oatmeal and chopped nuts with the fingers until the mixture is crumbly. Spread over top of batter. Pat down gently with fingers. Bake in a 350°F. oven for 30 minutes or until the loaf tests done. Cool before slicing.

LOUISIANA YAM BREAD

¼ cup butter
½ cup soft brown sugar,
  firmly packed
2 eggs, beaten
1 cup mashed cooked
  Louisiana yams, fresh or
  canned
2 tablespoons milk
1 teaspoon grated orange
  rind
2 cups flour
4 teaspoons baking powder

¼ teaspoon salt
½ cup chopped cashew nuts
3 tablespoons orange
  marmalade
1 thinly sliced orange,
  unpeeled

TOPPING:
1 3-ounce package cream
  cheese
2 tablespoons orange
  marmalade

Cream butter; add brown sugar and beat until light and fluffy.
Add eggs, mashed yams, milk and orange rind. Beat with a
rotary beater or electric mixer. Sift flour, baking powder and
salt together; add with nuts to the yam mixture. Mix thoroughly until smooth. Spread 3 tablespoons orange marmalade in
a 9″ x 5″ x 3″ buttered loaf pan. Arrange orange slices on
top af marmalade. Turn batter very carefully into the loaf
pan and bake in a preheated 350°F. oven for 35 to 45 minutes
or until a toothpick inserted in the center of the loaf comes out
clean. Do not open oven door first 25 to 30 minutes. Let cool
in pan 10 minutes. Remove to cake rack. Cool before slicing.

TOPPING: If desired pass a small bowl or orange marmalade
beaten with softened cream cheese. Whip the cream cheese
until the consistency of whipped cream. Add the marmalade
and beat with a fork until well blended. Keep cool until ready
to use, then let stand at room temperature for easy spreading.

MAINE CHOCOLATE LOAF CAKE
(With Mocha Topping)

½ cup milk
3 ounces semisweet chocolate
1 cup hot mashed State of
  Maine potatoes
¾ cup sweet butter
1 cup sugar
4 egg yolks, beaten
2 cups sifted cake flour

3 teaspoons baking powder
¼ teaspoon salt
2 teaspoons grated orange
  rind
4 egg whites, stiffly beaten
¼ cup sugar
Mocha Topping

Heat milk and chocolate together. Stir until melted. Combine with mashed potatoes in a large mixing bowl. Cream butter and sugar until very light and fluffy. Add to chocolate mixture. Beat egg yolks over warm water for 5 to 8 minutes until thick and lemon colored. Add to chocolate mixture. Mix flour with baking powder, salt and orange rind. Stir gradually into the chocolate mixture. Beat egg whites until they hold soft peaks; gradually add the sugar and continue beating until thick and glossy. Fold gently into the batter. Spoon batter into two greased and lightly floured 8" x 4" x 2½" loaf pans. Bake in a 350°F. oven for 30 minutes or until the loaves test done. Cool in pans 10 minutes. Remove to wire cake racks. When cold, serve with Mocha Topping.

MOCHA TOPPING: Beat 1 cup heavy sweet cream until thick; add 2 tablespoons confectioners sugar. Beat for 1 second, just enough to blend in the sugar. Melt 1 ounce chocolate over warm water, add 2 teaspoons strong hot coffee. Beat until smooth. Cool. Fold into the whipped cream. Blend well. Keep chilled until ready to use.

NEW ENGLAND BLACK WALNUT BREAD

3 tablespoons butter
2 eggs
½ cup sugar
1½ cups milk
3 cups flour
4 teaspoons baking powder
½ teaspoon salt

¾ cup chopped black
walnuts
1 tablespoon finely shredded
citron
1 teaspoon cinnamon sugar
powdered sugar

Cream butter, beat well with a wooden spoon, then add the eggs and sugar, beating until the mixture is smooth and creamy. Add the milk and the mixed dry ingredients, alternately, beating after each addition. Fold in ½ cup of chopped walnuts and the shredded citron. Turn into two 8″ x 4″ x 2½″ greased and lightly floured loaf pans. Sprinkle top of batter with remaining ¼ cup walnuts and cinnamon sugar. Cover. Let stand for 10 to 15 minutes. Bake in a 350°F. oven for 30 to 35 minutes or until the top is gently firm to touch. Test for doneness with a toothpick. Cool in pan for 10 minutes. Turn out onto a cooling rack. Sprinkle with soft powdered sugar; cool thoroughly before slicing.

NEW YORK SOUR CREAM COFFEE LOAF

1 stick butter or margarine
(¼ pound)
1¼ cups sugar
3 eggs
1 cup dairy sour cream
1 teaspoon lemon rind
¼ teaspoon salt

2 cups flour
2 teaspoons baking powder
½ cup chopped almonds
2 tablespoons brown sugar
1 teaspoon instant cocoa mix
1 teaspoon cinnamon sugar

Cream butter and sugar until light and fluffy. Add eggs, one at a time, beating until well blended. Fold in sour cream and lemon rind. Combine salt, flour and baking powder; fold gradually into the creamed mixture, but do not beat. Spoon half of the batter into a greased and lightly floured 9" x 5" x 3" loaf pan. Blend the nuts, brown sugar, cocoa and cinnamon sugar. Sprinkle half over the batter. Spoon on remaining batter, and top with the remaining nut mixture. Pat down gently. Bake in a 350°F. oven for 35 to 45 minutes or until golden brown and the loaf tests done.

OATMEAL BREAD
(Maine)

This excellent oatmeal recipe is a gift from Johnie Crossman from the great State of Maine. A good basic recipe, its nutritional value may be increased by adding 1 tablespoon instant non-fat dry milk to the 2 cups boiling water, and 2 teaspoons wheat germ.

2 cups boiling water
1 cup oatmeal
1 cake compressed yeast or
　1 package dry granular
　yeast
½ cup warm water

½ cup sugar
5 to 5½ cups sifted flour
1 tablespoon salt, level
2 tablespoons butter or
　margarine

Pour the boiling water over oatmeal. Stir and allow to cool. Crumble yeast or sprinkle dry yeast into a bowl, add the lukewarm water, ¼ cup of sugar and ½ cup flour. Beat until smooth. Cover and set aside in a warm place until light and bubbly. Stir in oatmeal mixture. Add remaining ¼ cup sugar, salt and butter or margarine. Add remaining flour. Brush dough with shortening. Cover and let stand in a warm place until doubled in bulk. Punch down and shape into 2 loaves. Place in greased and lightly floured 8-inch pans. Brush top with butter. Cover and let rise again until doubled in bulk. Bake in a 375°F. oven for 50 to 60 minutes.

PENNSYLVANIA DUTCH APPLE LOAF

½ stick butter
¾ cup sifted sugar
1 egg
3 teaspoons baking powder
2½ cups flour
½ teaspoon salt

pinch mace or nutmeg
1 cup milk
2 apples, pared, cored and chopped
2 teaspoons cinnamon sugar
Meringue Topping

Cream butter with sugar, add egg and continue to beat until the mixture is light and fluffy. Add the dry ingredients, sifted together, alternately with the milk. Beat the batter with a wooden spoon until smooth. Spoon into a greased and lightly floured baking pan. (A shallow 9-inch square or oblong baking dish is just right for this recipe, since the loaf can easily be cut into uniform squares.) Top the batter with chopped apples and sprinkle with cinnamon sugar. Spread with Meringue Topping. Bake in a 350°F. oven for 30 minutes or until the loaf tests done. Cool.

MERINGUE TOPPING: Beat 2 egg whites until stiff but not dry. Fold in 4 tablespoons sifted fine sugar. Beat for 1 second. Add 1 tablespoon chopped nuts. Spread over top of chopped apples, making small peaks with the tines of a fork. Sprinkle lightly with a dash of cinnamon sugar.

ST. AUGUSTINE LEMON BREAD

2½ cups plus 1 tablespoon flour
½ teaspoon salt
½ teaspoon baking soda
3 teaspoons baking powder
2 tablespoons wheat germ
⅞ cup fine sugar

½ stick sweet butter
grated rind of 1 large lemon
2 eggs
⅓ cup lemon juice mixed with
⅓ cup water
Lemon Icing

In a large mixing bowl, combine flour, salt, baking soda, baking powder and wheat germ. Cream sugar with the butter until smooth, add the lemon rind, and beat until well blended. Add eggs, beating well after each addition. Add the dry ingredients to the creamed mixture alternately with the lemon-water mixture. Stir into a smooth batter. Grease and lightly flour a 9" x 5" x 3" loaf pan; spoon in the batter and bake in a 350°F. oven for 45 to 50 minutes or until the top is gently firm to touch and the bread shrinks slightly away from the sides of the pan. Test with a toothpick inserted in the center of the loaf—if it comes out clean, the loaf is done. Cool 10 minutes. Turn out onto a wire cake rack until cold. Frost with Lemon Icing if desired.

LEMON ICING: Beat 1 cup confectioners sugar with 1 tablespoon lemon juice until smooth, drizzle over top of lemon bread. If too thick, add a few more drops of lemon juice.

VERMONT MAPLE SUGAR BREAD

2 cups unbleached or all-purpose flour
4 teaspoons baking powder
½ teaspoon salt
1 teaspoon shredded citron
2 eggs, separated
1 cup milk

¾ cup maple sugar
¼ cup soft brown sugar or granulated brown sugar
2 tablespoons melted sweet butter
Maple Butter

In a large mixing bowl, combine flour, baking powder, salt and citron. Blend. Beat the yolks and milk together, then add gradually to the dry ingredients, beating after each addition. Add maple and brown sugar in small amounts until thoroughly blended. Add butter, stir into the batter. Fold in the stiffly beaten egg whites. Turn into a greased and lightly floured 9" x 9" x 2½" square baking pan or into a 9" x 5" x 3" greased loaf pan. Cover. Let stand for 5 minutes. Bake in a 350°F. oven for 30 minutes or until golden brown. Test with a toothpick or cake tester. Cool. Serve warm with whipped Maple Butter.

MAPLE BUTTER: Soften ¼ pound sweet butter. Do not melt. Blend with 2 to 3 tablespoons soft maple sugar or maple syrup. Whip until light and fluffy. Refrigerate until needed. Let stand at room temperature for a few minutes before using.

WAYNESBORO MENNONITE CHERRY LOAF

If fresh cherries are not available, use *well-drained* canned sour cherries. (Let drain in a strainer until completely free from cherry juice.) This unusually delicious loaf cake, with the taste of tart cherries, is at its best served slightly warm with a cold topping of whipped cream.

1½ sticks sweet butter	pinch nutmeg
¾ cup sugar	2 teaspoons baking powder
⅓ cup boiling water	¾ cup fresh sour cherries,
⅓ cup milk	pitted and sponged dry
3 cups presifted flour	1 teaspoon flour
3 eggs, beaten	powdered sugar

Cream butter until soft, gradually add sugar. Beat until light and fluffy. Add boiling water, stir well. Add milk, then, all at once, 1½ cups flour. Mix well. Beat eggs with a rotary beater until very light, add to mixture. Add remaining 1½ cups flour, mixed with nutmeg and baking powder. Stir quickly until just blended. Do not overmix. Dry the pitted cherries with soft paper towels, sprinkle with 1 teaspoon flour and shake until they are completely coated. Fold into the batter. Spread into 2 greased and lightly floured medium-size loaf pans. Bake in a 350°F. oven for 30 minutes or until golden brown and tests done. Cool in pans for 15 minutes, then turn out onto wire cake racks until cold. Serve plain or sprinkle with a thick cloud of powdered sugar, or pass a bowl of cold sweetened whipped cream combined with ¾ cup sweetened cherries.

WILLIAMSBURG OLD FASHIONED NUT LOAF

4 eggs, separated
¾ cup sifted sugar
⅞ cup flour
pinch salt
1½ teaspoons baking powder
¼ cup strong sweet coffee

½ cup coarsely chopped pecans or filberts
½ teaspoon instant coffee
⅓ cup powdered sugar
1 tablespoon powdered sugar

Beat egg yolks over warm water until thick and lemon colored, about 10 minutes. Add sugar gradually and continue beating until the consistency of thick cream. Combine flour, salt, and baking powder. Add to the creamed mixture. Blend well. Mix in the sweetened coffee and chopped nuts. Beat the egg whites until they hold soft peaks and gently fold into the batter. Bake in a greased and lightly floured 9" x 5" x 3" loaf pan, or in a tube spring form, at 350°F. for 30 to 35 minutes or until the top is gently firm to touch and the loaf tests done. Cool in pan for 10 minutes, then turn out onto a wire cooling rack until cold. Mix instant coffee with ⅓ cup powdered sugar. Sprinkle over top of loaf, then sprinkle again with 1 tablespoon sifted powdered sugar.

BREADS FROM OTHER LANDS

In assembling this unusual collection of foreign bread recipes we first dug deep into old family archives—from our own and those of friends, their mothers and grandmothers. We also owe our thanks, to the friendly and recipe-generous ethnic bakers who, with old-country pride, still supply the breads of their native lands, and to the enthusiastic and cooperative staffs of historical libraries and museums. As a consequence of their help we found ourselves with enough material to fill a book of its own.

The selection here includes those which best fill the needs of the housewife, and which could be adapted with locally procurable ingredients to our modern ovens. Many of the loaves originating in age-old country kitchens were baked in brick ovens heated only by burning logs until the "desired" temperature was reached. Each housewife must have had a built-in intuitive-timer to know when to remove the bread! And to make matters more complex often the wheat and corn would be ground with hand-operated millstones and the flour would be aged or gently toasted a light delicate golden brown before using.

Among the many fascinating recipes in this chapter are those for Russian Easter Bread with Pashka, the Slovak Babovka; the beautiful, delicate, braided Brazilian Sweet Tea Bread, golden glazed and topped with crushed rock candy; the traditional Italian Panetone, filled with a variety of rum-soaked dried fruits, and the Israeli Raisin Bread, baked in the round and so light it practically puffs up out of the bowl during its rising!

Truly, all of the foreign breads included in this chapter are a delight to the eye and appetite. And perhaps many of our readers will recall, through the bread of their forebears some of the traditions practiced in their own homes.

218

AUSTRIAN STOLLEN

Wrapped in clear plastic and tied with colorful ribbons, this rich aromatic fruit bread makes an eye-appealing package for holiday gift giving. Stollen recipes vary in the use of liquids and flavorings. Fruit juices, spices, even a dash of wine, nuts, dried and candied fruits are added to the luscious fillings. Candied and dried fruits are usually marinated in rum or brandy. Honey or half honey, half sugar adds to the flavor. Sometimes a fleck or saffron or a dash of mace or nutmeg is thrown in to lend a mysterious flavor to this most popular of all holiday coffee cakes.

1 cup scalded milk, cooled	½ teaspoon almond flavor
½ cup sugar	4 cups flour
1 teaspoon salt	2 to 3 tablespoons cinnamon
2 packages dry granular yeast	sugar
	½ cup chopped walnuts or
2 eggs plus 1 egg yolk	pecans
½ cup sweet butter, melted	½ cup chopped candied
1 tablespoon grated lemon rind	fruits
	½ cup plump white raisins
1 tablespoon grated orange rind	½ cup candied red cherries

In a large mixing bowl, combine milk, sugar, salt and yeast. Cover. Let stand until foaming and doubled in volume. Add eggs and egg yolk, butter, lemon and orange rind and flavor. Beat until well blended. Add 2 cups flour; beat vigorously, then add remaining flour until a soft dough is formed. If the dough is sticky add one tablespoon of flour. Turn out onto a lightly floured board and knead for 10 minutes. Place dough in a warm and well greased bowl. Turn dough to grease top. Cover. Set aside in a warm place until doubled in bulk. Punch down and knead again. Cover and let rise until doubled. Roll out on a lightly floured board into one large or two medium-size rectangles. Sprinkle with cinnamon sugar; then spread with nuts, top with candied fruits, raisins and ¼ cup candied cherries. Fold the dough over and press the folded dough down gently with a rolling pin. Brush top with a little melted butter and fold over again, in half. Brush top with soft butter. Cover and let rise again. Bake on a well-greased and lightly floured baking sheet in a 375°F. oven for 35 to 45 minutes or until a nice golden brown. Cool. Glaze with White Icing and decorate with candied cherries.

WHITE ICING: Combine 1 cup sifted confectioners sugar with 1 tablespoon orange juice or white wine; mix well until free from lumps.

BRAZILIAN SWEET TEA BREAD

½ cup sugar
½ teaspoon salt
½ stick sweet butter
½ cup scalded milk
½ cup lukewarm water
2 packages dry granular
  yeast
2 teaspoons sugar
4 egg yolks

1 tablespoon grated orange
  rind
⅓ cup chopped Brazil nuts
4½ cups flour
1 egg yolk beaten with 2 teaspoons cold water
2 tablespoons crushed brown
  or clear rock candy

Add sugar, salt, and butter to milk. Stir. Cool to lukewarm. Add yeast and sugar to lukewarm water. Stir until dissolved. Cover and set aside until foaming and doubled in volume. Add to the lukewarm milk mixture. Beat egg yolks until thick and lemon colored; stir into yeast mixture, together with the orange rind and Brazil nuts. Mix well with a wooden spoon, then beat in 2 cups sifted flour until the batter is very smooth. Add enough additional flour to make a soft, easy-to-handle dough. Turn out onto a lightly floured board and knead until smooth and elastic, about 10 minutes. Place in a warm buttered bowl. Let rise in a warm place until doubled in bulk (about 1 hour). Punch down. Turn out onto a lightly floured board and divide in half. Divide each half into 3 equal parts. Roll each into a smooth ball, then into "ropes" about 12 inches long. Place 3 ropes on a well-greased and lightly floured baking sheet; pinch top ends together and braid. Secure ends tightly. Repeat with three remaining ropes. Place second braid on top

of first braid. Tuck ends tightly together. Cover. Set aside in
a warm place until doubled in bulk. Let braids rise just a
little bit longer than loaf bread. Brush with beaten egg yolk
and sprinkle with crushed rock candy. Bake in a preheated
375°F. oven for 20 minutes, then reduce heat to 350°F. and
continue to bake 30 minutes longer or until a nice golden
brown. Test by tapping top and bottom of braid: when it
sounds hollow it is done.

CHALLAH
(Jewish Sabbath Bread)

Throughout the centuries, the making of challahs for the
Sabbath has been both a legendary and symbolic custom of the
Jewish people. As the lighting of stoves was not permitted on
the Sabbath it was—and still remains—customary to bake
the challahs early on a Friday so that it would be in readiness
before sundown, which marks the beginning of the holy day.

At the table the loaf is set on a breadboard covered with
a snowy white tea towel or embroidered cloth. Before the
meal begins, the head of the household first uncovers the
bread, pronounces the ancient Hebrew grace and then pro-
ceeds to slice the challah.

The practice of open house on the Sabbath makes the
occasion a happy one. In Israel flowers were placed in front
of the house door to announce to guests—and to strangers—
that the Sabbath meal was ready and that all were welcome to
enter.

The challah is an unusually fine-tasting bread, rich with
eggs and butter or margarine, and it bakes to a fragrant,
golden, attractively textured braid, or it may be formed into a
myriad of fanciful shapes.

CHALLAH

2 packages dry granular yeast
½ cup lukewarm water
1 tablespoon sugar
½ cup softened sweet butter or margarine
3 eggs
1 tablespoon honey
1 cup hot potato water (saved from cooking the potato)
1 boiled potato, mashed until smooth
1 teaspoon salt
4 cups flour plus 2 tablespoons
1 beaten egg yolk mixed with 2 teaspoons water
poppy seeds or sesame seeds

Sprinkle yeast over warm water; add sugar. Stir. Cover and set aside until foaming and doubled in volume. In a large mixing bowl, beat together the softened butter or margarine, eggs, honey, hot potato water and mashed potato. Cool to lukewarm. Add foaming yeast. Beat in 2 cups of the flour and salt. Beat vigorously until the batter is smooth. Add remaining flour, just enough to make a soft pliable dough. Turn out onto a lightly floured board and knead for 10 minutes until the dough is satiny smooth and elastic. Place in a warm greased bowl, turning until the dough is greased on all sides. Cover and set aside in a warm place, free from drafts, until doubled in bulk (about 1 hour). Turn out onto a lightly floured board, and knead again for 5 minutes. Divide dough in half. Divide each half in three parts. Let rest for 10 minutes. Roll each part into ropes about 14 inches long, with the center of the rope thicker than the ends. Braid three ropes together and pinch ends securely. Place on a greased and lightly floured baking sheet. Repeat with remaining three ropes and place on top of first braid. Make sure ends of the braids overlap each other. Secure tightly. Brush with beaten egg yolk, sprinkle with poppy seeds. Cover and let rise until a little more than doubled in bulk. Bake in a preheated 375°F. oven for 40 to 45 minutes or until a beautiful golden brown. Tap bottom and top of braid. If it sounds hollow, it is done. Cool on wire rack.

CHINESE ALMOND LOAF

½ cup butter (¼ pound)
½ cup sugar
2 eggs, beaten
2 teaspoons baking powder

½ teaspoon almond flavor
½ cup coarsely chopped
  toasted almonds
2 cups rice flour

Cream butter and sugar together until light and fluffy. Add eggs and continue to beat until the mixture is creamy. Add baking powder, almond flavor and nuts. Work in flour and form into a soft dough. Turn into a well-greased and lightly floured 8″ x 4″ x 2½″ loaf pan. Decorate top with split almonds, if desired. Bake at 350°F. until a delicate golden brown, and the loaf tests done. Cool well before slicing.

NOTE: Rice flour is available in specialty and health food stores.

EGYPTIAN ONION BREAD

The Egyptians have always been extremely fond of onions as a food; the ancients respecting it to such a degree that they were known to take a sacred vow by placing their right hand on an onion! The onion was also regarded as a protector from the evil eye, and its strong odor was believed to help fight off illness. It was also used as a poultice to heal wounds. Flat onion bread or rolls are available in most ethnic bakeries with the toppings of chopped onions sprinkled with coarse salt, sesame seeds or grated cheese.

1 large onion, coarsely
  chopped
3 eggs
1 cup water
5 cups sifted flour
5 teaspoons baking powder

1 scant teaspoon salt
½ cup sesame seeds
1 beaten egg mixed with 2
  teaspoons water
1 teaspoon dry onion soup
  mix

Place coarsely chopped onion in a large mixing bowl. (Save 2 teaspoons for later use.) Add eggs and water and beat with a wire whisk or rotary beater until well blended. Combine flour with baking powder, salt and sesame seeds. Gradually add to egg mixture, beating well after each addition, until a soft ball is formed. Turn out onto a lightly floured board; knead lightly for 3 minutes and then roll out about ¾ inch thick. Cut out into large flat rounds, each about 8 inches in diameter. Brush lightly with beaten egg, sprinkle with remaining onion and onion soup mix. Place on a well-greased baking sheet. Bake in a 350°F. oven for about 25 minutes or until the onion bread is delicately browned. Wonderful served slightly warm with cold fresh whipped sweet butter. The rounds may be baked in 8 or 9-inch layer cake tins if desired.

ENGLISH BATTER BREAKFAST BREAD

½ cup soft sweet butter
1 cup sugar
3 eggs
4 cups milk
½ cup currants
5½ cups flour

½ cup corn meal
5 teaspoons cream of tartar baking powder
1 tablespoon finely shredded citron
½ teaspoon vanilla

Cream butter with sugar until light and fluffy. Add eggs, one at a time, beating constantly until the mixture is creamy. Add milk; beat well with an electric or rotary beater. Mix currants with flour, corn meal, baking powder and citron. Add gradually to the milk mixture. Lastly add the vanilla. After each addition beat well until the batter is thoroughly mixed. Grease and lightly flour one large Turk's head (fancy mold), or a 9- or 10-inch tube springform, or two loaf pans (8″ x 4″ x ½″). Bake in a 350°F. oven for 40 minutes or until the top is gently firm to touch and tests done.

ENGLISH BROWN BREAD WITH CLOTTED CREAM

A favorite English holiday bread. It is aged for 24 hours, then flamed with hot rum. Serve thinly sliced, topped with clotted cream.

1 small package mincemeat	1 teaspoon baking powder
½ cup cold water	¼ teaspoon salt
2 tablespoons sherry	⅓ cup dark molasses
1 cup corn meal	1½ cups milk
1½ cups all-purpose flour	2 tablespoons dark rum for
½ cup graham flour	flaming
1½ teaspoons baking soda	Clotted Cream

In a small saucepan, combine mincemeat, water and sherry. Break mincemeat up with a fork and cook gently over medium heat until the mixture is free from lumps. Continue to simmer gently for 5 minutes or until all the liquid has been absorbed. Stir. Shake saucepan over heat until the mixture is dry. Cool. Mix together corn meal, white flour and graham flour, and add the soda, baking powder and salt. Stir into the cooled mincemeat. Beat molasses and milk together until well blended. Add gradually to the mincemeat mixture. Beat well with a wooden spoon. Spoon batter into a well greased and lightly floured 9" x 5" x 3" loaf pan or into two 8" x 4" x 2½" loaf pans. Set aside for 20 minutes. Bake in a 350°F. oven for 45 to 55 minutes or until the top is gently firm to touch and the loaf leaves the sides of the pan slightly. Cool in pan for 10 minutes, then cool thoroughly on a wire cake rack.

CLOTTED CREAM: Beat two 3-ounce packages of cream cheese until very light and fluffy. Beat 1 cup heavy sweet cream until thick; combine with fluffy cream cheese. Beat for 1 second with a rotary beater. The original recipe calls for long and tedious preparations while this recipe is easy and requires only minutes to prepare. Keep cool until ready to serve.

ENGLISH ROLLED SWEET BREAD
(Yorkshire)

1 package dry granular yeast
⅓ cup lukewarm water
2 teaspoons sugar
1 cup hot water, cooled to lukewarm
2 eggs plus 1 egg yolk
½ stick soft butter or margarine
1 tablespoon grated orange rind
2 teaspoons salt
5½ cups flour

½ stick soft sweet butter
½ cup finely crushed rock candy or sugar cubes
½ cup currants
⅓ cup raisins
¼ teaspoon nutmeg mixed with 2 teaspoons sugar
1 egg white slightly beaten with 1 tablespoon water
2 tablespoons crushed rock candy

Sprinkle yeast over ⅓ cup lukewarm water; add sugar. Stir. Cover and set aside until foaming and doubled in volume. In a large mixing bowl, combine the cup of lukewarm water, eggs, egg yolk, ½ stick butter or margarine, and grated orange rind. Beat well. Add salt and 2 cups flour and continue to beat briskly until the batter is smooth. Add 2 more cups of flour, beat well, then just enough of the remaining flour to make a soft but easy-to-handle dough. Turn out onto a lightly floured board. Roll out into a large square or oval. Brush with half of the ½ stick soft or melted butter; fold in half and roll out again. Cover with a layer of crushed rock candy and currants, fold dough in half, and roll out again. Spread with remaining butter, raisins and the sugared nutmeg, and roll up as a jelly roll. Fit into a 9" x 5" x 3" well-buttered loaf pan. Secure ends, placing the loaf seam side down. If there is a leftover piece, place in a small greased pan or ovenproof bowl. Cover. Let rise in a warm place until doubled in bulk. Brush lightly with beaten egg white. Sprinkle with crushed rock candy. (If rock candy is not available, coarsely crush sugar cubes.) Bake in a 425°F. oven for 10 minutes, reduce heat to 350°F. and continue to bake 35 to 40 minutes longer or until done. Cool.

226

FRENCH HONEY SPICE BREAD
(Pain d'Epice)

This honey bread tastes better the day following the baking. Keep wrapped in plastic or wax paper. Slice thin, and spread with tart orange marmalade blended with softened cream cheese. Serve with hot spiced tea.

3½ cups flour
¼ teaspoon salt
1½ teaspoons baking powder
1 teaspoon baking soda
½ teaspoon allspice
½ teaspoon cinnamon
¼ teaspoon nutmeg
1 tablespoon grated orange rind
1 tablespoon candied cherries, chopped
½ cup plump raisins

2 tablespoons shredded candied citron
¾ cup assorted nuts, chopped (walnuts, almonds, Brazil nuts)
4 eggs
¾ cup brown sugar
3 tablespoons soft butter
½ cup dark coffee
¾ cup honey
1 heaping tablespoon orange marmalade
2 tablespoons brandy

Sift flour together with the salt, baking powder, baking soda and spices. Add orange rind, cherries, raisins, citron and nuts. Mix well, so that the fruit and nuts are coated with the flour mixture. Beat eggs until light and fluffy; add brown sugar and continue to beat until thick and smooth. Continue beating, adding the butter, coffee, honey, and tart orange marmalade. Then stir in the flour mixture, a little at a time, until well blended. Turn into two 8" x 4" x 2½" well-buttered and lightly floured loaf pans. Bake in a preheated 325°F. oven for 45 to 55 minutes or until the top is gently firm to touch and tests done. Cool on wire cake rack. Heat brandy, ignite and pour flaming over the honey loaf. When ready to serve flambe again, with 2 tablespoons brandy or rum.

SPICED GERMAN GINGERBREAD

4 eggs
½ cup sugar
2 tablespoons soft butter or margarine
¼ teaspoon mace
¼ teaspoon cinnamon
¼ teaspoon powdered cloves
¼ cup chopped candied orange peel
¼ cup chopped candied ginger
2 cups flour
2 teaspoons baking powder
¼ teaspoon salt
½ cup blanched almonds split in halves
Topping

Beat the eggs over warm water until thick and fluffy. Add sugar and butter and continue to beat until the mixture is well blended. Combine spices, chopped orange peel and candied ginger with the flour, baking powder and salt. Add to creamed egg mixture, about ⅓ at a time, beating well after each addition. Fold in almonds. Spoon batter into a shallow, well-greased and lightly floured 9-inch square baking pan. Bake in a 350°F. oven for 25 minutes or until the top is gently firm to touch and tests done. Cool. Sprinkle with Topping.

TOPPING: Combine 2 tablespoons sweet cocoa with ½ teaspoon ginger. Sprinkle over top of gingerbread. Then sprinkle with a soft cloud of powdered sugar. Serve slightly warm.

GREEK HOLIDAY BREAD

2 packages dry granular yeast
½ cup lukewarm water
2 teaspoons sugar
½ teaspoon salt
½ cup hot scalded milk
½ teaspoon rose water
½ cup sweet butter
3 tablespoons light honey (orange blossom)
2 eggs plus 1 egg yolk
2½ cups flour
⅓ cup chopped nuts
½ teaspoon anise seeds
⅓ cup shredded citron
⅓ cup thinly sliced dried apricots
1 egg white beaten with 2 teaspoons water

Sprinkle dry yeast over lukewarm water; add sugar. Stir. Cover and set aside until foaming and doubled in volume. In a large mixing bowl combine salt, milk, rose water (available from gourmet stores and most drugstores), butter and honey. Beat well; cool to lukewarm. Add beaten eggs and foaming yeast. Mix. Add 1 cup flour; beat well. Sift remaining flour over nuts, seeds, citron and apricots. Add to batter. Beat well until the dough leaves the sides of the bowl. Turn out onto a lightly floured board and knead until satiny and elastic. If the dough is slightly sticky, add a little more flour to the board or dip the heel of the hand in flour. Turn into a warm, well-greased bowl. Cover and let rise until doubled in bulk. Punch down and let rise again. Turn out onto a lightly floured board; knead a few minutes then divide the dough in half. Turn into two small well-buttered Pyrex bowls, or into one large (1½- to 2-quart Pyrex bowl) or, if desired, shape into a loaf and place in a buttered 9" x 5" x 3" loaf pan. (Shape the dough into a round ball for the round Pyrex bowl.) Cover and let rise again, until doubled in bulk. Brush with egg white. Bake in a 375°F. oven for 40 minutes or until golden brown. The small round loaves require less baking time. Dribble anisette-flavored white icing over top of holiday bread. (Blend 1 cup confectioners sugar with 1 tablespoon anisette liqueur; beat until smooth. If too thick, add a few drops of water.)

DOUGH FLOWERS: For a decorative holiday bread, reserve a small ball of dough. Cut into small pieces, shape into petals, flatten slightly, and form into little flowers on top of bread. Brush with slightly beaten egg white. Let dry for a few minutes. Brush again. Sprinkle lightly with sugar and bake as directed.

GREEK HYMETTUS HONEY BREAD

4½ cups flour
½ teaspoon salt
2 packages dry granular yeast
⅓ cup lukewarm water
1 tablespoon sugar
¾ cup soft butter
½ cup sugar
6 egg yolks

½ cup light cream or
evaporated milk
3 tablespoons Greek
Hymettus honey
½ teaspoon rose water or
rose essence
4 crushed sugar cubes
½ teaspoon anise seeds

Sift flour with salt. Dissolve yeast in lukewarm water, add sugar. Set aside until foaming and doubled in volume. Turn into a mixing bowl and add ½ cup of the flour; beat well. Cover and let rise until bubbly for 15 to 20 minutes. Cream together soft butter with ½ cup sugar. Beat in egg yolks, one at a time until thoroughly blended. Add light cream or evaporated milk, honey and rose water (available in gourmet stores and most drugstores), alternating with the remaining flour mixture. Add yeast sponge. Beat briskly with a wooden spoon until smooth. Turn into a warm, greased bowl. Cover. Let rise in a warm place until doubled in bulk, about 1½ to 2 hours. Turn out onto a lightly floured board. Knead for 8 to 10 minutes. Divide dough in half, shape into 2 balls. Let rest for 10 minutes. Knead and shape into two loaves. Place in two greased and lightly floured 8″ x 4″ x 2½″ loaf pans. Brush tops with melted butter or beaten egg yolk. Blend crushed sugar with anise seeds. Sprinkle over top. Cover with soft paper towels and let rise until doubled in bulk. Bake in a 375°F. oven for 35 to 40 minutes or until done.

NOTE: If desired, roll out dough to fit a 13″ x 9¼″ x 2″ well-buttered and lightly floured baking pan. Cover and let rise until doubled. Brush with melted butter or beaten egg yolk and sprinkle with crushed sugar cubes and anise seeds. Bake in a 350°F. oven for 30 minutes or until done. Cut into strips and serve warm.

HAWAIIAN COCONUT AND MACADAMIA LOAF

½ stick softened butter
1 cup sugar
1 egg
1 cup milk
2 teaspoons baking powder

2 cups flour
½ cup coconut
½ cup macadamia nuts,
   coarsely chopped

Cream butter with sugar. Add egg and continue to beat until the mixture is light and fluffy. Add the milk, gradually, together with the baking powder and flour. Beat together vigorously until well blended. Fold in coconut and macadamia nuts. Spoon batter into a 8" x 4" x 2½" well-greased and lightly floured loaf pan. Bake in a 375°F. oven for 30 minutes or until the top is gently firm to touch and tests done. Cool on a wire cake rack. Sprinkle thickly with powdered sugar, or top with rum-flavored whipped cream and coconut flakes, if desired.

HUNGARIAN POPPY SEED SWEET BREAD

The ground poppy seed filling adds a delightful nutty flavor to this typical Hungarian sweet bread, which is further enhanced with nuts, honey, raisins, fruit rinds and sour cream. This recipe, long a family favorite, is served at the coffee hour or late supper.

2 packages dry granular yeast
½ cup lukewarm water
2 teaspoons sugar
½ cup scalded milk
½ cup sugar
2 tablespoons honey
⅔ stick butter or margarine
3 eggs, beaten
½ teaspoon salt
4½ cups flour
1 slightly beaten egg white

1 tablespoon coarsely
  crushed sugar cubes or
  rock candy

POPPY SEED FILLING
1 cup ground poppy seeds
½ cup hot milk
2 tablespoons honey
½ cup coarsely chopped nuts
½ cup white raisins
1 tablespoon grated lemon
  rind
2 tablespoons sour cream

Sprinkle yeast over lukewarm water; add 2 teaspoons sugar. Stir. Cover and let stand until foaming and doubled in volume. In a large mixing bowl beat hot milk, ½ cup sugar, the honey, butter or margarine and eggs with a rotary beater or with a wooden spoon until completely blended. Cool. Add foaming yeast mixture, salt and 2 cups flour. Beat briskly until smooth, then add remaining flour until a soft dough is formed. Turn out onto a lightly floured board and knead for 10 minutes, until the dough is satiny smooth and elastic. Place dough in a warm greased bowl, turning until the top is greased. Cover and let stand in a warm place until doubled in bulk. Turn out onto a lightly floured board and knead for 5 minutes, then roll out into a 10″ x 15″ rectangle. Spread with poppy seed filling (see below). Roll up, as for a jelly roll. Fit into a well-greased and lightly floured 9- or 10-inch tube springform. Cover and let rise again until doubled. Brush lightly with beaten egg white; sprinkle with crushed sugar. Bake in a 350°F. oven for 40 to 45 minutes or until the bread is golden brown and shrinks just slightly away from sides of pan.

POPPY SEED FILLING: Combine poppy seeds with hot milk. Let stand for 15 minutes. Drain through a very *fine strainer.* Mix with honey, nuts, raisins, lemon rind and sour cream. Spread on rolled dough.

NOTE: Freshly ground poppy seeds are available in small tins in most markets or in Hungarian and ethnic food stores.

VARIATION: If desired, bake Hungarian Poppy Seed Sweet Bread on a well-greased baking sheet or in any type baking pan preferred. We think the round tube springform is best— the bread rises high, tender and golden.

PAT'S IRISH SODA BREAD

3 cups biscuit mix	1 tablespoon currants
¼ cup sugar	¾ teaspoon caraway seeds
¼ teaspoon salt	1 cup buttermilk
1 teaspoon baking soda	1 tablespoon brandy
1 teaspoon baking powder	flour
¾ cup raisins	

Combine biscuit mix with sugar, salt, baking soda and baking powder. Blend, then add raisins, currants and caraway seeds. Mix until the raisins, currants and caraway seeds are coated with the flour. Stir in buttermilk to make a soft dough. Toss onto a lightly floured board, shape, and pat into a well-greased and lightly floured deep round baking pan. The dough will be slightly sticky. Cut a gash on top of bread with a sharp knife. Bake in a 400°F. oven for 15 minutes. Reduce heat to 375°F. and continue to bake until golden brown. Cool a few minutes, then brush top of warm loaf with brandy or Irish whiskey (give it two coats). Return to oven for 5 minutes. Cool on a wire cake rack. Dust lightly with a little flour. When cold, slice thinly and serve with freshly whipped sweet butter. This bread is at its best the day it's baked. Serve slightly warm, if desired.

ISRAELI HOLIDAY RAISIN BREAD

During the High Holy Days this bread is baked in cylindrical loaves; the round shape signifies a wish for a good year "all year round." The breads are decorated with little flowers made out of dough or, more often, with ladders made of dough to signify the prayers of the devout ascending more easily to heaven.

The loaf is placed on a breadboard, covered with a beautiful embroidered cloth and so served at the table. When the time arrives to "break bread" this special time-immemorial prayer of thanks is said: "Blessed be Thou, King of the Universe, who brought forth the bread of the Earth!"

4 packages dry granular yeast
¾ cup lukewarm water
2 tablespoons sugar
½ cup butter or margarine
½ cup scalded milk or hot water

2 eggs, beaten
6 cups flour
1½ teaspoons salt
½ cup white Sultana raisins
1 egg yolk, beaten with
1 tablespoon water

Sprinkle yeast over lukewarm water in a large 2 cup measuring cup. Add sugar. Stir. Cover and set aside until foaming and doubled in volume. In a large mixing bowl stir butter or margarine into milk and cool to lukewarm. Add foaming yeast mixture. Mix in eggs and 2 cups flour. Beat vigorously

233

until the batter is very smooth. Sift 2 more cups of flour with salt over the raisins and add to the yeast mixture. Beat well. Add just enough of remaining flour to make a soft, easy-to-handle dough. Turn out onto a lightly floured board and knead for 10 minutes until satiny smooth. Place in a warm greased bowl, turning dough until the top is greased. Cover and let rise in a warm place until doubled in volume. Punch down. Turn out on a lightly floured board. Divide dough into three parts. Knead and shape into three balls. Form into round loaves and place in three well-greased and lightly floured 1-quart Pyrex bowls, or into two 1½-quart bowls. Cover and let rise again until doubled. Brush with beaten egg yolk. Bake in a 400°F. oven for 10 minutes; reduce heat to 350°F. and continue to bake 30 to 35 minutes longer or until the loaves are golden brown and test done (tap with fingers; if they sound hollow they are done). Cool. Place on wire cake racks. Cut with a large, serrated bread knife for crumb-free even slices.

ITALIAN COFFEE BREAD

7 eggs, separated
1 cup sugar
2 ounces melted semisweet
 chocolate
½ cup chopped walnuts
½ cup shredded citron
pinch powdered cloves

pinch ginger
pinch anise seeds
pinch salt
½ cup plus 2 tablespoons
 flour
1 teaspoon baking powder
2 tablespoons rum

In a large mixing bowl beat egg yolks over warm water for 10 minutes until very light and as thick as whipped cream. Add sugar gradually. Add melted chocolate, nuts, citron, spices, salt, flour, and baking powder. Beat well until thoroughly blended; fold in beaten egg whites. Pour batter into a well-greased and lightly floured 8- or 9-inch baking pan. Bake in a 350°F. oven for 35 minutes or until top is gently firm to touch, or until loaf tests done. Cool. Heat rum, ignite and pour flaming over bread. Sprinkle thickly with a soft cloud of powdered sugar or top with rum-flavored whipped cream.

ROMAN SWIRLED NUT BREAD

2½ cups flour
3 teaspoons baking powder
½ teaspoon salt
⅓ cup sugar
⅓ cup soft brown sugar
¾ cup shelled pistachio nuts
   coarsely chopped

1 egg plus 1 egg yolk
1 cup milk
3 tablespoons sweet butter
¼ teaspoon anise seeds
2 tablespoons semisweet
   cocoa

In a mixing bowl, combine flour, baking powder, salt, white and brown sugar and ½ cup very coarsely chopped pistachio nuts. Mix well. Beat egg, egg yolk, milk and melted butter in a small bowl: add to dry ingredients. Mix thoroughly. Spoon batter into a well-buttered and lightly floured loaf pan. Mix anise seeds with cocoa and sprinkle over top of batter. Swirl top gently with a fork two or three times to give a marbled effect. Sprinkle top with remaining ¼ cup pistachio nuts. Bake in a 350°F. oven for 30 to 35 minutes or until the top is gently firm to touch and tests done. Cool.

NOTE: Use the natural pistachio nuts, which come in a natural cream-colored shell, not those dyed red. Shell; rub off brown skins. Chop coarsely. The delicate flavor of the pistachio nuts and its pale green color lends an exotic touch to this well-flavored sweet bread.

RUSSIAN EASTER BREAD WITH PASHKA

2 packages dry granular yeast
⅓ cup lukewarm water
2 teaspoons sugar
6 egg yolks
¾ cup sugar
1 tablespoon hot water
¼ teaspoon dry or 3 threads
   saffron
1 stick plus 2 tablespoons
   soft butter
1 cup scalded milk

¼ teaspoon salt
1 tablespoon grated orange
   rind
4 cups flour, sifted
½ cup candied fruits, cut
   into small bits, marinated
   for half an hour in
3 tablespoons rum
⅓ cup plump white raisins
Russian Pashka (see recipe
   below)

Sprinkle yeast over lukewarm water. Add 2 teaspoons sugar. Stir. Cover and set aside until foaming and doubled in volume. In a mixing bowl, beat egg yolks over warm water until thick; gradually add the ¾ cup sugar, beating well after each addition. Pour the tablespoon of hot water into a small cup; add the saffron and let steep for a few minutes. Strain. Then add the saffron to the egg mixture, together with butter, hot milk, salt and grated orange rind. Stir. Cool to lukewarm. Add foaming yeast and 2 cups flour. Beat vigorously until the batter is smooth. Drain the candied fruits and dry with paper towels. Mix with remaining flour and add to the smooth mixture, with just enough of the flour to make a soft, easy-to-handle dough. Turn out onto a lightly floured board, knead lightly into a ball. Place the dough in a warm buttered bowl, turning the dough until completely greased. Cover. Set aside in a warm place free from drafts until doubled in bulk. Punch down. Let rise again for 30 minutes. Turn out onto a lightly floured board and knead for 2 or 3 minutes. Shape into a ball. Place the ball of dough into a well-buttered and lightly floured tall coffee tin (3 pound size) or divide in half, shape into two balls, place in two 2-pound well-buttered coffee tins or into two well-buttered and lightly floured 1½-quart Pyrex bowls. Cover and let rise again until the dough almost reaches the top of the tins or bowls. Bake in a 375°F. oven for 20 to 25 minutes. Reduce heat to 350°F. and continue to bake 20 minutes longer or until golden brown and tests done. (Tap top and bottom of bread with fingers—if it gives off a hollow sound it is done.) Cool in tins on wire cake racks. Remove bread carefully. If necessary, loosen sides *gently* with the flat side of a silver knife. They should slide out very easily. Lay on side until cold. Cut into rounds, serve with Russian Pashka, a delectable, spectacular cheese creation.

RUSSIAN PASHKA

Pashka means "Easter" in Russian, but refers here to a traditional cheese "cake" prepared in flower pots and served mainly during the Easter holidays together with fragrant, rich coffee cakes, kuchens, or kulichs.

1 pound cream cheese
½ pound dry cottage cheese
3 tablespoons sour cream
½ stick soft sweet butter
¾ cup fine sifted sugar
½ teaspoon vanilla
1 teaspoon grated lemon rind

1 teaspoon grated orange rind
½ cup assorted candied fruits, cut into small bits
⅓ cup shelled chopped pistachio nuts
candied violets or rose petals

Put cream cheese and cottage cheese through a strainer, rubbing through, a little at a time, into a large mixing bowl. Beat until smooth with a wooden spoon. Add sour cream and butter; beat well until the mixture is thoroughly blended. Add sugar, vanilla, grated lemon and orange rind. Beat well. Fold in the candied fruits and nuts. If desired, add ½ cup white Sultana raisins. Mix well. The mixture should be quite firm—if not, add more cream cheese and 1 tablespoon confectioners sugar. Line a clean flower pot (with a hole in the bottom) with a *large* square of (double thickness) cheesecloth. Allow ends to hang over sides of pot. Fill the lined flower pot with the cheese mixture. Fold the cheesecloth ends over the top, covering the cheese mixture. Place a weight on top, and a deep pan or bowl underneath to collect the liquid as it seeps out. Refrigerate overnight. Turn out onto a serving plate, lifting the Pashka gently by the ends of the cheesecloth. Stand upright on a serving plate and peel off the cloth. Decorate top and sides with candied violets or rose petals (if not available, use candied red and green cherries). Surround with gaily colored glazed fruits and grapes.

NOTE: Candied flowers and rose petals are available in most fancy food and gourmet stores. They are packed in handsome glass jars or in tins. Keep tightly covered when not in use.

SCOTCH SHORTBREAD

4 cups flour   ½ cup sugar
½ pound butter   pinch salt

Place the flour, butter, sugar and salt in separate mounds on a
pastry board. Break up butter in small pieces; blend in the
flour, sugar and salt, rubbing it well with the hands, almost
kneading it, until it forms a ball. Pat and roll out into a sheet,
¾ inch thick. Cut into four large squares. Prick all over with
the sharp tines of a fork. Arrange on a baking sheet. Bake in a
425°F. oven for 10 minutes; reduce heat to 350°F. and continue to bake the shortbread 25 minutes longer or until a pale
golden tint.

RICH SLOVAK BABOVKA
(Rum Coffee Cake)

The Slovaks and also the Czechs are well known for their
skill in baking rich tea loaves, yeast cakes, kolaches and
kuchens filled with a tantalizing mixture of candied or dried
fruits saturated in fruit-flavored brandies or liqueurs. A soft
delicate yeast dough is used for most of the coffee cakes and
sweet loaves but the babovka, a rich type of coffee cake, is
always baked in special molds. It is customary to serve these
beautiful cakes on special occasions, such as holidays and
"name days" (birthdays).

⅔ cup sugar   2 tablespoons rum
1 stick softened sweet butter   1 tablespoon grated lemon
4 eggs, separated   rind
4 cups flour   4 teaspoons vanilla sugar
2 teaspoons baking powder   2 tablespoons rum
1 cup milk   Apricot Glaze

Cream sugar with butter, add egg yolks, one at a time, beating
until the mixture is smooth and creamy. Then add the flour
mixed with the baking powder alternately with the milk to the
creamed butter mixture. Beat well. Add 2 tablespoons rum, a

238

few drops at a time; blend. Add lemon rind. Fold in stiffly beaten egg whites beaten with 4 teaspoons of vanilla sugar. Butter and lightly flour a kugelhopf or Turk's head baking pan or, if desired, a 9- or 10-inch tube springform. Spoon in the batter. Bake in a 350°F. oven for 35 to 45 minutes or until the cake tests done. Cool. Turn out onto a wire cake rack. While still slightly warm, place the babovka on a shallow serving plate. Warm 2 tablespoons rum, ignite, and pour flaming over all. Baste with hot Apricot Glaze.

APRICOT GLAZE: Combine ½ cup plus 1 tablespoon apricot jam with ¼ cup white wine. Beat with a wire whisk or rotary beater until well blended. Cook over medium heat until slightly thickened. Add 1 tablespoon rum, stir into glaze, and spread over top of babovka while still warm.

VANILLA SUGAR: Place 1 cup sifted granulated sugar in a 1 pint jar, add a 1-inch piece of vanilla bean. Cover tightly, shake well and let stand for a few days until fragrant with the aroma of vanilla. Shake from time to time to distribute the vanilla flavor. Vanilla sugar, already prepared, may be procured in specialty food stores.

QUICK SPANISH SWEET BREAD

A wonderfully different tasting quick coffee loaf—the top crusty, the bread filled with the nuts-and-currants topping which sinks into the batter during baking. Cool thoroughly before slicing.

1 cup cold sweet butter or margarine
2 cups sugar, sifted
4 eggs, separated
1 cup milk
3½ cups flour
6 teaspoons baking powder
⅛ teaspoon powdered saffron (see below)

1 tablespoon soft brown sugar
½ cup currants
½ cup chopped roasted peanuts
pinch powdered cloves rubbed with 1 level teaspoon sugar

Cream butter or margarine with sugar until light and fluffy. Add egg yolks one at a time, beating briskly until the mixture is very creamy. Add milk gradually, alternating with the flour sifted with the baking powder and saffron. Beat well with a wooden spoon. Beat egg whites until they hold soft peaks and fold into the batter. Turn into two greased and lightly floured 8" x 4" x 2½" loaf pans, or into a large square shallow pan. Sprinkle top of batter with soft brown sugar, currants and roasted peanuts. Combine cloves with sugar, rub with the back of a spoon until completely blended. Sprinkle over the topping. (This method will distribute the powdered cloves evenly.) Let stand for 10 minutes. Bake in a 350°F. oven for 35 minutes or until the loaf tests done.

SAFFRON: Use either the dry powdered saffron, or dissolve 3 to 4 threads of saffron in 1 tablespoon boiling water. Let stand for several minutes until the water turns a dark orange. Cool and add to the creamed mixture. Use saffron with a light hand, too much will result in a strong flavor.

SWEDISH KAFFE KAKA

½ pound sweet butter
½ cup sugar
2 eggs, separated
¼ teaspoon baking soda
½ teaspoon baking powder
1½ cups flour
¼ teaspoon salt
2 teaspoons grated lemon rind

1 to 1½ cups dried apricots, cooked and pureed
½ cup soft brown sugar
⅔ cup chopped walnuts
2 teaspoons grated lemon rind
1 tablespoon cinnamon sugar

Cream butter with sugar, add egg yolks, and beat until very creamy. Mix and sift together baking soda, baking powder, flour and salt. Add to creamed butter mixture together with 2 teaspoons grated lemon rind. Beat batter until stiff and smooth. Spread into a 13" x 9¼" x 2" well-greased and lightly floured baking pan. Spread with pureed apricots. Beat egg whites until they hold soft peaks, then add sugar, beating until the sugar is completely blended. Fold in chopped nuts and

240

2 teaspoons lemon rind. Spread over apricot topping. Sprinkle lightly with cinnamon sugar. Bake in a 350°F. oven for 40 minutes. Cool. Cut into squares.

APRICOT PUREE: Cook 1 pound dried apricots in ½ cup water together with ½ cup sugar and 3 tablespoons sherry until soft. Press through a sieve. Beat until smooth. (*Note:* Apricot Lekvar (pureed apricots) is available in pint jars in most Hungarian food stories, or in tins in local markets. Use right from the jar, flavored with a little wine, if desired. A time-saving, excellent spread.)

SWEDISH LIMPA BREAD

1 package dry granular yeast
1 cup lukewarm water
1 tablespoon sugar
1 cup hot water
½ cup plus 2 tablespoons soft brown sugar
1½ teaspoons salt

3 tablespoons soft sweet butter
2 teaspoons caraway seeds
½ teaspoon fennel seeds
grated rind of 1 small orange
2 cups rye flour
4½ to 5 cups all purpose flour

Soften yeast in lukewarm water; add 1 tablespoon sugar. Stir. Cover and set aside until foaming and doubled in volume. In a large mixing bowl combine the hot water, brown sugar, salt, butter, seeds and orange rind. Stir and cool to lukewarm. Add foaming yeast and 1 cup rye flour; beat vigorously until the batter is smooth. Add another cup of rye flour and 2 cups white flour, unbleached if possible. Beat until smooth and well-blended. Now add just enough flour to make a soft dough, but stiff enough to handle. Turn out onto a lightly floured board and knead for 10 minutes. Place the dough in a warm, well-greased bowl; cover and let rise until doubled in bulk. Knead and shape into two round loaves. Place in a two 1½ quart Pyrex bowls, well-buttered and lightly floured. Bake in a 350°F. oven for 45 minutes or until done. Tap bread with fingers—if it sounds hollow, the bread is done.

QUICK SYRIAN COFFEE LOAF

¼ cup butter
1 cup sugar
2 eggs
1 teaspoon rose water

½ cup milk
1½ cups flour
2 teaspoons baking powder
½ teaspoon anise seeds

Cream butter and sugar, add eggs an continue to beat until the mixture is very creamy. Add rose water (available in gourmet stores and most drugstores) and milk alternating with the flour, baking powder and anise seeds. Beat until well blended. Spoon into a greased and lightly floured loaf pan (8″ x 4″ x 2½″). Bake in a 350°F. oven for 35 to 40 minutes or until the top is gently firm to touch and the loaf tests done.

VALENCIA SPONGE LOAF WITH A VEIL

3 eggs
3 egg yolks
1 cup sugar
2 teaspoons grated lemon
  rind
½ teaspoon anise flavor
3 egg whites

pinch salt
1 cup almonds, finely ground
1 cup cake flour
1 tablespoon semisweet cocoa
⅓ teaspoon crushed anise
  seeds
½ cup soft powdered sugar

Beat the three eggs plus the three egg yolks over warm water until very light and the consistency of whipped cream. Gradually add the cup of sugar in a slow stream, beating constantly after each addition. Add lemon rind and anise flavor. Beat egg whites with a pinch of salt until they hold soft peaks. Do not overbeat. Fold into egg mixture. Blend almonds into flour. Gradually add to the egg mixture, a little at a time, folding it in with a rubber spatula. Turn into an ungreased 9″ x 5″ x 3″ loaf pan or into a medium-size tube springform. Bake in a 375°F. oven for 30 to 35 minutes or until the top is gently firm to touch and tests done. Invert loaf over a wire cake rack until cool. Place on a serving plate. Crush anise seeds in a mortar if possible, or with the back of a heavy spoon. This will release the oils. Blend with the cocoa. Sprinkle top with cocoa mixed with anise seed, then with a soft cloud of powdered sugar, completely covering the sides and top of loaf. (If desired, instead of the powdered sugar, spread anisette-flavored whipped cream over top and sides of loaf. Very special.)

RICH VIENNA KUCHEN

2 packages dry granular yeast
⅓ cup lukewarm water
2 teaspoons sugar
1 cup sweet butter
    (½ pound)
1 cup sugar
1 cup scalded milk, cooled
    to lukewarm
4 eggs, beaten
½ teaspoon pure almond
    flavor

1 tablespoon grated orange
    rind
2 tablespoons orange juice
4 cups flour
1 teaspoon baking powder
½ cup toasted almonds,
    coarsely chopped
½ cup raisins, marinated in
    2 tablespoons rum

Dissolve yeast in lukewarm water: add 2 teaspoons sugar. Cover and set aside until foaming and doubled in volume. In a large mixing bowl, cream butter with the cup of sugar; add milk and beat thoroughly. Add eggs, almond flavor, orange rind and juice. Mix well. Add foaming yeast. Dry raisins carefully with soft paper towels. They must be *completely* dry and free from moisture. Sift flour with baking powder over the almonds and raisins; add to creamed yeast mixture. Add flour, 1 cup at a time, beating well after each addition until the batter is thick and smooth. Cover and let rise until doubled in bulk. Grease a large kuchen (or bundt) mold. Sprinkle with a little sugar and bread crumbs. Fill the mold a little less than ⅔ full. Cover; let rise in a warm place until doubled. Bake in a 350°F. oven for 45 to 50 minutes or until golden brown and the kuchen tests done. Cool in pan for 10 to 15 minutes; then turn out onto a wire cake rack. When cold drizzle with white icing flavored with a little of the rum left from the marinated raisins.

In every country where bread is baked there exists a hundred varieties of local breads differing, according to the locality, in size, shape and content. The following list is merely illustrative of a few of such "local loaves"—these from ovens throughout the United Kingdom.

FRUIT BREADS: Very popular throughout the United Kingdom, they range from a slightly enriched dough to which fruits have been added (usually currants, peel and white raisins), to a more enriched dough with added sugar, eggs and shortening, and then to more heavily fruited varieties such as:

Cornish Saffron Cakes—Rich loaves, heavily fruited with currants and flavored with saffron tea. Cut peel is sometimes added.

Edinburgh Loaf—A very heavily fruited loaf especially popular for holiday celebrations. The outside crust is made from an enriched yeast dough which is rolled out thin and used as a lining for the pans. The fruit mixture is placed inside, pressed down, and then lidded with the bread dough.

Irish Brack—This fruited loaf is popular in all the Irish counties. The dough is enriched with eggs, milk, sugar and shortening; each pound of dough embraces an equivalent weight of currants, white raisins and peel which vary in proportion according to the recipe of the county. The loaves are usually baked in tins, in low-temperature ovens.

LARDY CAKES: Popular in the Midlands and north of England where they appear in various forms. The cakes are made from fruited dough rolled out into a sheet, spread with butter as for puff pastry, then folded up and rolled out quite thin, and then rolled up as for a jelly roll. Some areas prefer all raisins in the cakes, others all currants.

WILTSHIRE SHALLEYS: Made from plain dough and shortening. The shortening is sprinkled with white raisins, currants, granulated sugar and mixed spices before being rolled into the dough.

BAPS: The Scottish bap is immensely popular as traditional breakfast fare in Scotland. Oval-shaped and weighing from

1½ to 2 ounces each, the baps are made of flour, water, salt, yeast, lard and a little sugar.

The Irish bap, made in the same way, is usually dusted lightly with flour before baking. The Dublin bap is made from a sweeter rolled dough to which white raisins have been added.

CORNISH TURNOVER: This is a round of dough, rolled flat, then folded in two. It is allowed to rise, then dusted with flour and baked.

WELSH PLANC BREAD: In Wales this bread is usually made at home or on the farm and gets its name from the planc, which is the baking-iron of Wales. The planc is placed over a fire and the risen dough, a circle about 1½ inches thick, is baked on the iron for about 20 minutes on one side, then turned and baked for the same length of time on the other side.

INDEX

252